MW00334888

TEACHING COMPUTATIONAL THINKING

An Integrative Approach for Middle and High School Learning

Maureen D. Neumann and Lisa Dion
with Robert Snapp

The MIT Press
Cambridge, Massachusetts
London, England

The MIT Press would like to thank the anonymous peer reviewers who provided comments on drafts of this book. The generous work of academic experts is essential for establishing the authority and quality of our publications. We acknowledge with gratitude the contributions of these otherwise uncredited readers.

This book was set in Stone Serif and Stone Sans by Westchester Publishing Services. Printed and bound in the United States of America.

Library of Congress Cataloging-in-Publication Data

Names: Neumann, Maureen D., author. | Dion, Lisa (Computer scientist), author.
Title: Teaching computational thinking : an integrative approach for middle and high
    school learning / Maureen D. Neumann and Lisa Dion with Robert Snapp.
Description: Cambridge, Massachusetts : The MIT Press, 2021. | Includes bibliographical
    references.
Identifiers: LCCN 2021000766 | ISBN 9780262045056 (paperback)
Subjects: LCSH: Computer science—Study and teaching (Secondary) | Critical thinking—
    Study and teaching (Secondary)
Classification: LCC QA76.27 .N474 2021 | DDC 004.071—dc23
LC record available at https://lccn.loc.gov/2021000766

10   9   8   7   6   5   4   3   2   1

Contents

Preface

This book provides teachers with a dynamic learning experience using computational thinking, computer programming, and unplugged activities that are grounded in different learning theories and pedagogical strategies to help students gain twenty-first-century skills.

It is generally accepted that there is an urgent need to introduce computer science concepts and skills into the K–12 curriculum of the United States (Barr and Stephenson 2011; Cuny 2011; Grover and Pea 2013; Kafai and Burke 2014; Nager and Atkinson 2016; Walser 2008; Wilson et al. 2010; Wing 2006, 2008, 2016). As digital technology becomes more ubiquitous around the world, the need for professionals with computing skills is expected to increase. Even those employed in other fields will need to learn about the capabilities and limitations of computers, data networks, and mobile devices. One might also argue that all citizens need to be able to respond to the political and ethical issues that advances in digital technology bring to the forefront (e.g., trade-offs between personal privacy and convenient data access, copyright protection vs. fair use, and the security of the nation's data infrastructure, including the integrity of electronic voting). We believe that the solutions to these problems encompass policy, cultural, and educational change. Our book focuses on the latter. As more schools add computer science to their curricula, more teachers will need to learn about computational thinking to provide a solid foundation for incorporating computer science principles and applying programming skills. Our book offers a way to present these concepts to all middle and high school teachers and students.

In brief, we integrate a variety of pedagogical practices, across content and curricula, to demonstrate how computational thinking is a fundamental skill that we all (not just computer scientists) use. We believe that computational thinking enhances every student's learning of the core content subjects as well as every child's repertoire of reading, writing, and arithmetic. We concur with Jeanette Wing's (2006) views that computational thinking teaches students critical thinking skills: how to think algorithmically (i.e., how to solve problems using a progression of logical steps) and how to create useful and artistic artifacts with digital technology. Just as the printing press facilitated the spread of the "three Rs" (reading, writing, and arithmetic) during the Renaissance, computing and computers facilitate the spread of computational thinking and complex problem-solving abilities.

Since computational thinking is derived from human thought processes, it is vital to demonstrate its relevance to every student and every teacher. Children naturally learn algorithms (e.g., the sequence of steps required to tie their shoes) as well as logical systems (e.g., the rules of a game). Likewise, computational thinking can be integrated into many different contexts. Our book demonstrates ways for middle and high school teachers to incorporate computational thinking through the incorporation of computer science principles and programming skills into a broad range of subjects. For example, we show how art teachers can develop lessons on algorithmic art (also called generative art). By writing programs in Scratch or Codesters, students learn how to apply algorithms and geometric properties to create interesting and artistic computer images. Likewise, our book shows how English language arts students can use topological graphs to analyze the social networks that explicitly connect fictional characters in a given literary work. Social studies teachers see how to include algorithms in their lessons to help students generate Cretan, Roman, and medieval labyrinths using a simple algorithm.

With our combined 60 years of teaching mathematics, coding, and educational topics across the K–20 spectrum, we have found that a variety of open-ended problem-solving tasks, project-based inquiries, and paper-and-pencil activities enable students to develop a concrete understanding of the abstract principles needed for creating code and other digital artifacts. We employ a low-threshold, high-ceiling pedagogical practice for the activities and rich tasks we include for computational thinking. The activities and rich tasks we present in this book grew out of our experience teaching students in grades 5–12 during after-school programs (e.g., Girls Who Code) and summer camps (e.g., Governor's Institutes and Code Camp). We present our activities and rich tasks in broad strokes because it is our intent to give teachers flexibility and choice in how to present the material to their students rather than being too prescriptive with timing, organization, and procedural steps. We believe all teachers are smart, industrious, and continuous learners, but some may not currently have an understanding of computational thinking and are seeking ways to transform their teaching practice. We understand that not everyone will be able to use these activities as they are provided, but we are confident in teachers' professional ability to choose and adapt activities that work for them in their context.

In creating this book, we are motivated by our belief that computational thinking, like written and oral communication and basic numeracy, is too important to relegate to a single subject. By inserting computational thinking into many different contexts, students will learn well before high school that computer science and programming has broad relevance. Distributing these "seeds" early and widely should generate greater interest in the need for studying computer science in high school and college. Broad coverage of computer science across K–12 education enables students from underrepresented groups to access information and experiences they may not have had at home or after school. Moreover, by recruiting teachers to add computational thinking strategies (and possibly coding) to their curricula, we may be able to gradually increase the number of students interested in computer science as a career or their ability to use these strategies and skills in other careers of interest.

We also wish to emphasize that this book is designed to help all teachers see how to include computational thinking and computer programming in a wide range of subjects, including literature, history, physical sciences, social sciences, and the visual arts. Though our primary focus is on middle and high school grades, some ideas can be used in the elementary grades. As awareness of the importance of computer science in education increases, we hope that this curriculum-integration model will be replicated across a variety of learning spaces.

Maureen D. Neumann
Lisa Dion
Robert Snapp

Acknowledgments

This book would not have been completed without the support and patience of our editor, Susan Buckley, and the anonymous reviewers who gave us thoughtful, thorough, and helpful feedback. We would also like to thank our family and friends who championed our cause and didn't balk at the lost weekends and summer days we spent writing rather than with them. We would like to give a shout out to all the teachers who worked with us for the teacher's voice in the book: Drew Blanchard, Sara Fergus, Leah Hammond, and Sue McKegney. We would like to thank William R. Doyle for his ideas and teacher's perspective on chapter 5, and Radhakrishna Dasari, Bernice Garnett, and Curtis Wilcox, who helped us with chapter 6. We would also like to thank David Miller for his thoughtful review and ideas for an encore edition. We appreciate the time Roman Vogel and John Miller took to read too many versions of this book over the years. Finally, we want to thank the people at Westchester Publishing, Planet Cat Books, and Insightful Indexing who helped get the book through its final stages.

1 Introduction

In this chapter, we advocate for introducing computational thinking into traditional content areas taught across a spectrum of middle and high school classes, including art, English language arts, social studies, and the physical and social sciences.

Our society has been reshaped by technological innovations that were unforeseen a decade ago. These breakthroughs have altered our patterns of living, working, and learning. While today's adolescents are highly dependent on the use of technology for their entertainment (video streaming and gaming), social lives (social media), and learning (Google and Apple apps for learning), these digital natives are only using technology that has already been planned, tested, and marketed by others (Simpson and Clem 2008). Though technology may be ever-present in our lives, only a narrow and select band of our population has the skills and knowledge needed to program the devices that are enmeshed in our society (Hill, Corbett, and St. Rose 2010; Rideout, Foehr, and Roberts 2010), knowledge and skills that are sorely needed for the twenty-first century.

Successful workers in the twenty-first century will need to demonstrate creativity, flexibility, perseverance, and information fluency in a technology-rich society (Dede 2010; Saavedra and Opfer 2012). Consequently, schools and educators are being pressed to redesign traditional learning environments as ones that inspire innovation, accept complexity, and foster students' development of dynamic, creative, and critical thinking skills that are essential for thriving in the complex life and work environments of today (Barrios et al. 2004; Jacobs 2010; Jacobs and Alcock 2017). Students who acquire these skills—such as an ability to solve problems, communicate, persevere, work as a team, and learn from mistakes—are applying some of the fundamental components of computational thinking.

Computational thinking has been defined in many ways in the educational lexicon. We see computational thinking as a set of mental and cognitive skills that are applied to the problem-solving process to help individuals discover and apply different strategies and algorithmic solutions to challenging and complex problems. We echo Jeannette Wing's view that "the essence of computational thinking is abstraction" (the mental tools of computing), that computational thinking is everywhere and for everyone, and that computational thinking is a human endeavor that represents a cross-disciplinary skill set that should be taught before college (Wing 2008, 3717). Computational thinking involves defining and understanding the core components of a complex problem (Grover and Pea 2013; Lu and Fletcher 2009) and uses a reflection process to analyze the appropriateness of the strategies used to solve the problem (Lee et al. 2011).

Computer programming, computer science principles, and computational thinking are often intertwined in the literature, but they are not equivalent concepts. Programming provides a context that enables us to practice and incorporate computational thinking and computer science principles. Computer science principles entail creativity with computing, abstraction to reduce information to its relevant concepts, processing data and information, algorithm applications to solve problems, developing computer programs for new knowledge and creative expression, and appreciating the power of the internet and the global impact computing has had on our world (College Board 2017). Computational thinking includes the general principles of computer science in its repertoire; however, it also applies a thought process that enables students to unpack and solve challenging complex problems by leveraging the use of abstraction with the capabilities of computers to develop and test solutions (Aho 2012; ISTE 2016).

Many disciplines require, promote, and teach problem-solving skills, logical thinking, or algorithmic thinking without computers (Bell et al. 2009; Denning 2017b). Computational thinking shares many elements with scientific, mathematical, and engineering thinking strategies and draws on a rich legacy of related complex thinking and problem-solving frameworks (Boulden et al. 2018; Bundy 2007; Henderson et al. 2007; Nardelli 2019; Weintrop et al. 2016). However, in addition to scientific thinking and scientific modes of inquiry, researchers can employ computational thinking to process and analyze large amounts of data to find answers to questions or to model or simulate situations that in the past, without computing power, were unattainable (Denning 2017a; Nardelli 2019; NRC 2012).

Computational thinking is integrally linked to critical investigations in medicine, environmental science and sustainability, manufacturing, automation, commerce, and communication. It is central to the creativity involved in the arts, such as movie special effects, music, and visual art, and facilitates communication and information gathering through social media and web searches (Kafai and Burke 2014; Margolis et al. 2008; Margolis and Fisher 2002; Wing 2008). As a result, several different entities across education, industry, government, and professional organizations are aligning toward making computational thinking part of the everyday school curriculum (ISTE 2016; NCSS 2017; NCTM 2014; NGSS Lead States 2013; Wing 2016), but knowing how to help students think computationally in the K–12 classroom has not been clearly laid out for teachers (Angeli et al. 2016).

The ability to use technology does not necessarily lead to a literate technology user, just as the ability to read a word does not lead to its comprehension. Within the context of technology, technological literacy is often seen and taught in unsophisticated ways (e.g., using apps or downloadable programs that have been created by someone else) that are divorced from a social or historical context rather than seen as creative, interactive, or reflective work (Vee 2013). We believe that employing computational thinking and computer science principles, along with creating computer programs, can lead to more fully literate technology users.

We discuss how to integrate computational thinking into instructional practice, and why, through integrated classroom activities and rich tasks that cross a variety of content areas using computer programming (e.g., Scratch, Codesters, and Python) and follow a low-threshold, high-ceiling, wide-wall learning format. Along with coding experiences, each chapter in this book includes activities that do not rely on the use of digital technology. We integrate computational thinking into a broad range of content areas in the middle and high school curricula (e.g., art, social studies, physical and environmental sciences, English language arts, and mathematics), and the activities and tasks described connect directly to national standards. In the middle and high school grades, computational thinking can be applied either by using computers or with pencil-and-paper activities. We include each of these types of activities incorporating problem solving, abstraction, and teamwork, and we differentiate the learning experiences for students by including embodied learning activities, group work experiences, and varying student products or processes of learning. We also show how students can code solutions to different questions by using open-source programming environments.

1.1 Learning for the Twenty-First Century

During the early 1900s, public schools were designed to transfer skills (in reading, writing, and basic mathematics) to a burgeoning population of immigrant children. Public education became a means to assimilate and acculturate a diverse population of young people to work in American factories and industries (Jacobs and Alcock 2017; Labaree 1997; Tyack and Cuban 1995). In this earlier environment, recall and memorization were valued skills. A hundred years later, schools are being summoned to prepare people for a very different world, one that focuses on the process of knowing rather than the recall of facts.

The goal of education in the twenty-first century is for students to experience an active learning environment and to metacognitively understand how, as students, they acquire and process new knowledge in addition to learning new information and facts. Twenty-first-century learning therefore has students engaging in solving and discussing rich tasks that are situated in real-life contexts and interacts with students' prior understanding (Bransford, Brown, and Cocking 2000; Delpit 2006; Tomlinson 2017). Twenty-first-century skills represent the ability to think, learn, reason, and solve complex problems; to overcome struggles, work through barriers, and learn from mistakes; to communicate, collaborate, and contribute effectively in a team setting; and to adapt and apply knowledge in new situations (Boaler 2015, 2016; Dweck 2006; Hattie 2009; Johnson and Johnson 2010). These twenty-first century skills enables people to continually learn, adjust, and respond to an ever-changing world and environment (Kay 2010). With this form of knowledge, more students will be empowered to ask questions or complete complex tasks that they could not have done without using technology (Muir 2006; Puentedura 2014). The attributes for twenty-first-century learning span many disciplines, but in this book we are going to focus on how these skills intersect with computational thinking.

To Situate Learning in Real-Life Contexts and Rich Tasks
Learning is based on the presupposition that knowledge is actively constructed by the individual through experiences and is not the result of knowledge passively received from an outside source (Brooks and Brooks 1999; Cathart et al. 2016; Fosnot and Perry 1996; von Glasersfeld 1990). When creating rich tasks, teachers draw from the contexts, culture, conditions, and language of their students' lived experiences, or they can provide a common experience from which their students' work originates (Gutstein and Peterson 2013; NCTM 2014; NRC 2012), thus ensuring that *all* students have the opportunity to engage in high-level thinking. Diverse, rich tasks engage students in meaningful learning through individual and collaborative experiences that promote the students' ability to make sense of the content they are learning. Students feel empowered to ask questions and solve problems with technology and to modify

and adapt technology to meet their interests and needs (Brennan and Resnick 2012). A rich task

- is accessible for a wide range of learning abilities and has multiple entry points (low threshold);
- provides opportunities for extended learning and challenges advanced learners (high ceiling);
- incorporates a variety of approaches and representations (wide walls);
- is grounded in real-life experiences;
- encourages collaboration and discussion;
- engenders interest and engagement with the topic;
- sparks students' curiosity and promotes decision-making; and
- fosters creativity, individuality, and variety in the application of that knowledge

(Ahmed 1987; Boaler 2015; Grover and Pea 2013; NCTM 2014; Papert 1980; Piggott 2011; Repenning, Webb, and Ioannidou 2010; Resnick 2016; Tomlinson 2017; Turchi and Malizia 2016; Wolf 2015).

Authentic activities allow students to view the skills they are learning as tools that they can then apply and adapt in future settings, and the understandings and perceptions that result from these experiences lead to increased competence for transferring learning to new situations (Boaler 2015). When rich tasks are more closely connected to students' personal interests and real-life contexts, students are more likely to engage in and become curious about completing the task, thereby increasing their motivation and knowledge of the content (Aguirre, Mayfield-Ingram, and Martin 2013; Gutstein and Peterson 2013; Hogan 2008; ISTE 2016; Jansen and Middleton 2011; NCTM 2014; NRC 2012). Rich tasks that focus on having students develop the processes and skills of problem solving and reasoning result in learning strategies that apply and transfer to a myriad of other contexts and disciplines (Boaler 2000, 2016).

To Think, Learn, and Reason through Problem Solving
Thinking, learning, reasoning, and growth are the fundamental aspects of an education. Twenty-first-century learning engages students in solving and discussing rich tasks that promote adaptive reasoning (i.e., the capacity to think logically and to justify one's thinking) and strategic competence (i.e., the ability to formulate, represent, and solve problems) (Kay 2010; NCTM 2014). Applying computational thinking is an active process, in which each student builds their knowledge from personal experiences, coupled with feedback from peers and teachers through engaging and real-life problems (Angeli et al. 2016; Bransford, Brown, and Cocking 2000; Cuny 2011; Mayer 2004; Wing 2016).

Brains are not fixed or static; our ability to think and learn expands over time and from experience (Boaler 2016; Sousa 2016). Being computer literate or being able to code is "not a binary state of there or not there at a single point in time" (Brennan and Resnick 2012, 23). Any approach to teaching computational thinking that includes computer science principles and coding needs to encourage a growth mindset (that ability and proficiency are developed through experience) rather than a fixed mindset (some people have the "genes" for using computers and programming code and others do not). A growth mindset values all students' thinking; it uses pedagogical practices such as differentiated tasks, mixed-ability groupings, and public praise for contributions and perseverance when working through complex problems (Boaler 2011, 2016).

By providing multiple approaches to learning the content, either by varying the process through which a student learns or varying the product in which a student demonstrates that knowledge, students are better able to learn the content and demonstrate their knowledge (Tomlinson 2017). Not all students in the same grade learn in the same way, nor are they alike in their interests, personalities, or hobbies. When using computational thinking to solve complex problems, a variety of strategies or solutions may be possible. The key is how the students explain and justify the choices they made.

All students can learn, and develop knowledge, from experiences (Boaler 2011, 2015, 2016; Tomlinson 2017). The greatest amount of learning takes place in classrooms where tasks and activities consistently encourage high-level student thinking and reasoning (Boaler and Staples 2008; Hattie 2009, 2017). A modern take on the work of leading learning theorists of the twentieth century (e.g., Dewey 1916, 1938, 1964 [1899]; Piaget 1954, 1973, 1977; Vygotsky 1997 [1978]) reflects a constructed, hands-on, real-life approach to learning that is articulated and shared. These learning theorists argued that learning and understanding take place when learners are actively engaged in constructing meaning about their lives and the world around them through hands-on experiences and social interactions that challenge their preconceived notions, resulting in an extension and/or refinement of their initial thinking.

Vygotsky (1997 [1978]) argued that knowledge is socially constructed through social interaction with peers and teachers. As students explain their ideas for solving a problem and evaluate each other's strategies, they develop a deeper understanding of their thinking and thereby engender learning (Boaler 2015; Sherin, Mendez, and Louis 2000). When students share their thinking with their peers and justify their reasoning and strategies for how and why they coded a certain way, they develop the cognitive skills needed to verbalize how they constructed their understanding of the problem. Sharing programs and coding strategies also enables other students in the classroom to become flexible thinkers because the students become aware of other strategies that may be more efficient, easier to perform, or more understandable for them (Lee et al. 2011; Jacobs and Ambrose 2008). Furthermore, when students have a misconception that may be highlighted by explaining their reasoning, they experience a disequilibrium that challenges their initial beliefs or perceptions about a topic in order to change their initial perceptions, and sharing and justifying thinking can provide that equilibrium (Piaget 1954, 1973, 1977).

To Struggle Productively and Learn from Mistakes
In the twenty-first century, students need to learn how to persist when answers do not come easily, to experience productive struggle, and to see mistakes not as a point of failure but as an experience from which to learn and grow (Bray 2013). Having students experience productive struggle helps them gain a deeper understanding of a topic, making learning engaging and therefore a worthwhile effort. After a student productively overcomes a struggle point, they feel empowered and proud of what they accomplished (Boaler 2015; NCTM 2014; Warshauer 2015). When students make a mistake, understand how and why they made that mistake, and learn from it, connections are made within their brains that enhance the memory of that learning (Boaler 2015; Sousa 2016). However, too much complexity in a problem or task without the requisite knowledge or problem-solving skills leads to frustration and feelings of inadequacy, whereas too easy a problem or task leads to boredom and disengagement (Boaler 2016; Dweck 2006; Lemke 2010). Sousa (2016) underscored how the learner's emotions can impact learning either positively or negatively and how the learning context affects the

ability to retain and transfer new learning. Struggle that creates frustration and leads to a mental shutdown is not an effective learning experience. Teachers can create opportunities for students to experience productive struggle by balancing the complexity of a task with the students' current repertoire of knowledge and strategies (ISTE 2016; NCTM 2014; NRC 2012).

Some forms of computer programming can enable students to learn persistence in problem solving and turn mistakes into a successful learning experience. During the process of testing and debugging their code, students are applying higher-order thinking skills and persevering through a struggle point (Lee et al. 2011). The systematic steps to find the mistake in a nonworking coded program, understand why the code is not working, and then fix it demonstrate perseverance, problem solving, content knowledge application, and productive struggle, and exemplify applying computational thinking.

To Contribute, Communicate, and Collaborate in a Team Setting

Twenty-first-century skills and computational thinking are grounded in the realization that in real life most problems are too complex to be solved by a single person but are solvable when many minds work on the problem together. The ability to collaborate, communicate, and work together as a team has been fundamental for successful learning and achievement in any century (ABET 2018; Lingard 2010). Collaboration or working together as a group in order to achieve a shared goal or a specific task (by members contributing, communicating, and adding their ideas to the group) enhances learning for all students (Cohen 1994; Johnson and Johnson 2010). Discussion, cooperation, and collaboration within groups promote more frequent summarizing, explaining, and elaborating of what we know. They enhance our ability to listen, question, process, discern, and learn the perspectives of other people in the group. Collaboration also has the added benefit of getting input from peers as well as getting their critical feedback (Johnson and Johnson 1992).

Effective group work skills are not an innate ability but rather are taught. Two common problems that inhibit effective group work are the status ordering within a group and the group dynamics that are created by status ordering. Elizabeth Cohen describes status ordering as "an agreed upon social ranking where everyone feels it is better to have a higher rank within the status order rather than a lower rank" (Cohen 1994, 27). Status characteristics are general expectations for competence that are perceived by other people. A person's status is often determined by their race, social class, gender, education, attractiveness, and athleticism (Cohen and Lotan 1995, 1997). In the K–12 classroom, a student's status is often determined by their reading ability, mathematical knowledge, and artistic ability. The status of the students has a direct impact on the effectiveness of a group and their ability to work together (Lotan 2006). Understanding status ordering and how it plays out is important when using group work with technology.

The person with the strongest technology skills is often working the keyboard and mouse, deciding which technology is used, and dominating the learning experience. The other members of the group or pairing are passive learners—leaving decisions to be made by the person with stronger technology skills (higher status). Effective group work strategies can address some of these status issues that occur in the classroom and reduce status ordering in the group. One way to mediate status domination is to assign students roles and responsibilities in their group and have those roles and responsibilities change or rotate as the lesson or unit proceeds. Another teaching strategy is to notice the contributions and skills of students who are not high on the social status ladder and highlight areas of contribution they made. By providing opportunities for classroom discourse and social interaction that leverage students' strengths, they learn about the contributions that everyone brings to the classroom (Cohen 1994; Cohen and Lotan 1995; Lotan 2006; Tomlinson 2017).

To Adapt and Apply Previous Learning in New Situations

A twenty-first-century learner must possess not only basic skills but also the capability of acquiring and adapting new ones (Tyson 2012; Jacobs and Alcock 2017). A Twitter tweet by Neil deGrasse Tyson characterizes learning in the twenty-first century: "Knowing how to think empowers you far beyond those who know only what to think" (@neiltyson, May 19, 2012). A fluid intelligence reflects a person's ability to use their knowledge and skills to analyze complex relationships, to infer and deduce commonalities, and to transfer previous knowledge and skills to solve novel problems (Bransford, Brown, and Cocking 2000; Sousa 2016).

Interdisciplinary approaches to learning require that students and teachers connect, transfer, and apply concepts flexibly across the curriculum in various contexts (Drake and Burns 2004). Knowledge that is taught in multiple contexts and across disciplines is more likely to support flexible transfer than is knowledge taught in a single context (Bransford, Brown, and Cocking 2000). According to Fuchs et al., "The broader the schema, the greater the probability that individuals will recognize connections between familiar and novel problems and will know how to apply the solution methods they have learned" (Fuchs et al. 2004, 419). Computational thinking represents a problem-solving skill set that engages students in learning and extends beyond computer science classes into a broad range of content areas (Voogt et al. 2015; Yadav, Hong, and Stephenson 2016).

To Empower More Students to Be Proficient in Technologically Prolific Environments

A growing body of research (e.g., Hattie 2009; Manchester, Muir, and Moulton 2004; Muir 2006; Solomon and Shrum 2007) asserts that technology can produce positive academic outcomes when properly integrated into school content. Its influence depends heavily on the purpose and context of the integration (Barrios et al. 2004; Florida Center for Instructional Technology 2017; Puentedura 2009). Some of the biggest educational technology initiatives in the United States are based in the middle grades, largely because adolescents are among the most avid computer users and find technology particularly engaging (Rideout, Foehr, and Roberts 2010; Simpson and Clem 2008). Most adolescent students acquire a sense of themselves as being strong or weak in certain areas, such as math, science, humanities, or computers, and develop a fixed mindset about their abilities during middle school (Boaler 2016; Margolis and Fisher 2002). One reason why so few students study computer science (CS) and information computing and technology (ICT) is the disconnection between students' understanding of these fields and the opportunities available to them in intermediate and secondary schools (Barr and Stephenson 2011; Wilson et al. 2010).

In addition to using different computer applications, today's digital natives should know how to write and modify computer programs. People who are technologically illiterate in the twenty-first century will increasingly find themselves marginalized socially and economically. Currently, few students, especially women and minorities, pursue CS majors or ICT careers (Hill, Corbett, and St. Rose 2010; Logan and Crump 2007; Margolis and Fisher 2002; Margolis et al. 2008; National Center for Education

Statistics 2016; Whitney and Taylor 2018). This is clearly a problem, since women and people of color provide diverse perspectives, voices, and knowledge in the STEM (science, technology, engineering, and mathematics) workplace (Belenky et al. 1996; Fox, Sonnert, and Nikiforova 2009). These diverse voices and perspectives must be part of the computer hardware and software design teams within different STEM fields, because technology devices and software applications are reshaping our world and we want it reshaped to fit all its people (Margolis and Fisher 2002; Margolis et al. 2008; Sax et al. 2017; Wilson et al. 2010).

The stereotype of computer majors as geeks or computing as a male-dominated profession pervades our social media and societal biases. This stereotype is particularly damaging to young women and students of color because it leaves them thinking that a computing profession is not welcoming to them (Blickenstaff 2005; Greenwald et al. 2002; Hill, Corbett, and St. Rose 2010; Margolis and Fisher 2002; Margolis et al. 2008; Whitney and Taylor 2018). Positive computer experience in the early years of education has been shown to influence *all* students' future interest in computer-related fields (Margolis and Fisher 2002; Margolis et al. 2008; Sax et al. 2017). These positive experiences include age-appropriate, hands-on technology activities or working on issues that have a positive social impact in students' communities. Also, working on a project with a partner (pair programming) or group enables students to see computing as not just an individualistic enterprise (Klawe, Whitney, and Simard 2009; Sax et al. 2017). When women and students of color see computing as a tool to positively influence society or address social justice issues, they are more likely to be interested in computer science fields as a major or profession (Riegle-Crumb et al. 2012).

Experiences within middle and high school classrooms play an important role in determining what students choose as a college major and/or future career. In some schools, coding experiences are already occurring by accessing different free websites (such as Hour of Code, Scratch, and Codesters), but it is often separate or an add-on to the content instruction. Moreover, many schools cannot afford or don't have access to a computer science teacher (Wilson et al. 2010), so computational thinking becomes part of an added after-school experience (e.g., Lego Robotics, Girls Who Code, Black Girls Code). If a computer science class is taught, it is usually a high school elective or advanced placement course. Both demonstrate examples where only a select few students can access the experience (Boulden et al. 2018). By integrating computational thinking within your content area, you are transforming the lives of your students by bringing digital equity to your classroom and school, thereby opening more future career paths for them.

1.2 Computational Thinking in Practice

Papert (1980) pioneered the idea that programming can influence how children learn to think conceptually about mathematical topics. Papert had students direct the movements of a turtle by coding commands in BASIC in the LOGO environment. During these lessons, he observed children engaging in "animated conversations about their own personal knowledge as they try to capture it in a program to make a Turtle carry out an action that they themselves know very well how to do" (Papert 1980, 28). He argued that in becoming a programmer, the child "acquires a sense of mastery over a piece of the most modern and powerful technology and establishes an intimate contact with some of the deepest ideas from science, from mathematics, and from the art of intellectual model building" (Papert 1980, 5). Writing a computer program that works is an incremental and iterative process that begins and advances in small steps, sometimes changing direction and sometimes returning to previous spots. It is not a clean and sequential process; rather, it is an interactive and adaptive process that takes many revisions, such as a written piece of work (Brennan and Resnick 2012; Vee 2013). It is critical that programmers develop strategies for figuring out, dealing with, or anticipating problems. Programmers need to learn how to test and debug their code in the same way writers edit their texts. Reading through what the code actually does—not what the author thinks it does—is a skill that enhances learning (Brennan and Resnick 2012, 7).

Skills Needed for Programming

Modern technological advances exploit the fundamental computer science skills of abstraction, sequencing, loops, events, modularizing, conditionals, algorithmic processes, data usage, and scalability (Brennan and Resnick 2012; College Board 2017; Harlow et al. 2016) that form the foundation of requisite coding knowledge. In addition to these skills, we add two processing skills (transference of skills and comprehending the code) to supplement this list.

Abstraction   Abstraction is "the process of generalizing from specific instances" (Lee et al. 2011, 32). "Abstraction reduces information and detail to facilitate a focus on relevant concepts" (College Board 2017, 14) to understand and solve problems. In problem solving, abstraction may take the form of stripping down a problem to what are believed to be its bare essentials. Abstraction is also commonly defined as capturing the common characteristics or actions into a set of instructions that can be used to represent all other instances, thus leading to the automation of the task (Lee et al. 2011, 33).

Sequencing   A fundamental concept in coding is the ordered list of individual steps or instructions to be executed by the computer for a particular activity or task. Sequencing puts "commands in the correct order so that the computer accomplishes a specific task" as required (Harlow et al. 2016, 340). "Like a recipe, a sequence of programming instructions specifies the behavior or action that should be produced" (Brennan and Resnick 2012, 3).

Loops   Loops enable the same sequence of steps or instructions to be run multiple times—that is, a piece of code that can be repeated a specific number of times (Brennan and Resnick 2012; Harlow et al. 2016). The speed of a computer allows this repeated set of instructions to be executed in nanoseconds. With automation, the computer is instructed to execute a set of repetitive tasks quickly and efficiently compared to the processing power of a human, thereby enabling a labor-saving process.

Events   An event is one thing that causes another thing to happen. It is an essential component of interactive programming (Brennan and Resnick 2012). Event-driven programming is different from call functions or subroutines because it is always listening for interruptions (e.g., keyboard or mouse input) instead of having a set order of executable statements.

Modularizing   Modularizing is the ability to build something large by putting together collections of smaller parts; these smaller parts are often called subroutines or functions and can be called up several times with a sequence of instructional steps (Brennan and Resnick 2012).

Conditionals   Conditionals in code (e.g., statements such as if-then-else or when) tell the computer to make decisions based on certain conditions. Conditionals support the expression of multiple outcomes. For example, when the green flag is clicked, the game begins, or if the left arrow is pressed, then an object moves one step to the left (Brennan and Resnick 2012; Harlow et al. 2016).

Algorithmic processes   Algorithms are a step-by-step set of instructions that can be applied more generally—not just to one specific computational problem that you are working on at the moment. Algorithms are tools for developing and expressing solutions to computational problems (College Board 2017). Within algorithms, there may be operators that support mathematical, logical, and/or string expressions and that enable the programmer to perform numerical and/or string manipulations (Brennan and Resnick 2012).

Data usage   Defining variables involves storing, retrieving, and updating data values (such as keeping score in a game or updating the value of a variable) (Brennan and Resnick 2012). Data usage is widely applicable in coding because you have to store values for many different variables that can be retrieved later in the program. Data usage might help you keep track of the value in order to determine a mathematical calculation or know where to draw the next line in a pattern.

Scalability   Scaling up is the ability to take what you have done with a smaller set of data and see if it works with a larger set of data. With scalability, the same code can handle data of different sizes and/or variables of different values. A common problem with scalability is that your program may run in a reasonable amount of time with a small set of data but when you scale up your program it may take far too long so it is no longer useful.

Transfer of skills to new situations   To grab code, apply it in other programs, and use it appropriately in new situations is a skill set that requires a deeper knowledge of code usage. It is one thing to write code that works; it is another to select and/or employ the same concepts or adapt pieces of code in a new context. That transference of skills shows deeper levels of understanding of the coding concepts and demonstrates a fluency for coding. The analysis of code to examine how and why it works is a reflective metacognitive practice that validates whether the code adaptations, in a new context, were correct (Lee et al. 2011). A programmer who is able to explain what a particular piece of code does but is unable to meaningfully use it in a new context does not fully understand or is unable to transfer the concept that grounds the piece of code (Brennan and Resnick 2012). To transfer coding language and usage to a new situation demonstrates students' comprehension of the coding concepts.

Reading, understanding, and updating previously written code   When working in the computer industry, learning how to read, understand, and build on other people's code is an important skill. Brennan and Resnick (2012) found that when middle school students interacted with, reused, and remixed code available to the Scratch online community, they developed "critical code reading capacities" (Brennan and Resnick 2012, 8) and enabled students "to explore different ways of knowing, such as critiquing, extending, debugging, and remixing as well as fluency with different concepts and practices" (Brennan and Resnick 2012, 21). Many students see little reason to revise their code if the program is working, but by sharing different strategies for coding, they begin to see ways to make their program more efficient. Brennan and Resnick (2012) found that when creating programs in Scratch and then sharing them with their peers (an authentic audience), they valued "that others were engaging with and appreciating their creations, whether by entertaining others, engaging others, or educating others" (Brennan and Resnick 2012, 11). Sharing their written code provides students with an external motivator to focus on revising their code to be more efficient or more easily understood (Lee et al. 2011).

Teaching computer programming skills to all middle and high school students has been facilitated by the development of graphical user interface programming environments that allow students to code by clicking, dragging, and dropping block commands into a coding area, thereby making it easier for all students to try programming and feel successful doing it (Harlow et al. 2016; Kafai and Burke 2014). Computer programming can exercise creative thinking, innovation, and design skills that transcend disciplines. However, we must be wary of learning to code for coding's sake; simple coding does not require computational thinking. As Voogt et al. put it, "To focus on programming as the primary instantiation of computational thinking, and to expect programming alone to result in more refined thinking . . . would be a mistake both conceptually and pedagogically. The focus [of computational thinking] should be on the higher-level concepts being learned and the multiple domains in which they can be applied" (Voogt et al. 2015, 718). Computer scientists (e.g., Bell et al. 2009; Cuny 2011; Wing 2008) believe that learning to code should be combined with instruction in computational thinking. By having students apply computational thinking when programming, we can engage students in solving authentic and complex real-world problems.

1.3   Integrating Computational Thinking into the Classroom

We understand the pressures you are under as teachers—the need to increase students' test scores, match student learning objectives to state and national content standards, provide support and structure to students who are experiencing trauma or anxiety, enable healthy social and emotional growth, and produce educated citizens for a fully functioning democratic society—so we do not want you to see this as an additional task. We want the activities related to computational thinking to be value-added for you and your students. We want to help you think about ways you can integrate computational thinking into what you are already doing.

In the 1990s and early the following decade, students often learned the Microsoft Office suite (Word, Excel, and PowerPoint) as a separate course. Now, those word processing, spreadsheet, and presentation skills are an integrated component of teaching and learning. We believe that just as the Google platform has transformed how and what students are learning and producing in their classrooms, the integration of computational thinking will likewise be a common experience for students of all ages. We also believe that computational thinking and coding is too large a skill and concept to be left to the computer science teacher or as a stand-alone class. As we think about integrating computational thinking into our teaching, it is good to familiarize ourselves with the different ways to integrate content.

Drake and Burns (2004) describe an integrated curriculum as one that makes connections that cross disciplines and experiences. There are three approaches to integrating your content: multidisciplinary, interdisciplinary, and transdisciplinary. The essential difference between the three approaches is the degree to which the various disciplines remain separate entities.

- A *multidisciplinary* integrative approach focuses the subject matter around a central theme. This is often seen in a combined English and social studies or science and mathematics themed lesson. For example, students may read books or stories written during the Great Depression of the 1930s while the social studies teacher talks about the major historical events during that time, or students may learn about volume and mass during science class by using different materials and formulas, while during math class the focus is on their derivation and computation. In these examples, the content is still distinct and separate but there are connections that are specific to each subject area.

- An *interdisciplinary* integrative approach primarily organizes the curriculum around common learning across the content. Common skills and concepts from the disciplinary standards are embedded to emphasize the interconnectedness of the learning. For example, in section 2.2 of chapter 2, on Andrade-style art, a student would need to understand the mathematical concepts of the degrees of a circle, angle measure, and coordinate plane within the context of the artist's style in order to generate that form of art.

- A *transdisciplinary* integrative approach crosses many disciplinary boundaries, with the learning experience or the curriculum organized holistically around students' questions and concerns. Many teachers may see this materialize in personalized learning or student-negotiated project-based learning that transcends disciplinary boundaries. For example, a student might be interested in investigating the effects of global warming trends. The teacher, in collaboration with the student, maps out a learning plan that could include the different topics within science, math, literature, and history that are involved in the investigation. The exploration of the effects of global warming could not be separated into discrete content areas, for the information that is to be gathered, explored, and worked on informs and builds on itself.

These three categories of curriculum integration form a continuum from *multidisciplinary* integration, representing the most discrete way to integrate content, to *transdisciplinary* integration, representing a complete holistic unification of content that is student driven. Teachers can incorporate any of these approaches to integrate content, whether in a classroom or across a team, and they can be used across the K–12 curricula (Drake and Burns 2004).

1.4   Book Preview

This first chapter of our book presents the research that grounds and supports the activities and rich tasks that are provided in chapters 2–6. Going forward, each chapter presents learning activities and rich tasks that promote computational thinking across different content areas in the middle and high school curricula. We included examples of learning tasks that enable any beginner to create a working program (low threshold) but are flexible enough to satisfy the needs of advanced programmers (high ceiling and wide walls).

We provide examples of coded programs and suggestions for related activities that do not require the use of digital technology to explore different real-life issues and authentic experiences. We have found that hands-on learning and paper-and-pencil activities enable students to develop a concrete understanding of the abstract principles needed for creating code and other digital artifacts. We incorporate learning theory and apply pedagogical strategies to help engage students in meaningful and developmentally appropriate low-threshold/high-ceiling activities and rich tasks. These learning experiences are characterized by relevant and integrative curricula that are taught and assessed in a variety of ways. The activities and tasks in this book are applicable to different grade levels and connect directly to professional organizations' content standards. Although the activities we present are tested and ready for use in classrooms, we prefer to think of them as seeds for further curricular development. The following paragraphs describe the foci of chapters 2–7.

Chapter 2: Creating Algorithmic Art   In this chapter, middle and high school students learn to create algorithms that generate expressive abstract images in the styles of Victor Vasarely, Josef Albers, Edna Andrade, and Wassily Kandinsky. As artists, they celebrated the power of simple shapes, geometrical properties, and abstraction within their art. Here, principles of algorithmic art are introduced within rich tasks that integrate computer programming with visual art and geometry. We also present the distinctions between algorithms, programs, and artifacts, as well as the concept of *abstraction* in the contexts of art, geometry, and computer science. We demonstrate how students can use the Codesters or Scratch languages to draw these geometrical works of art.

Chapter 3: Applying Graph Theory to Analyze Literature and Social Networks   Here, students learn how to construct topological graphs that clarify the relationships between characters in different novels and the patterns of disease propagation. This chapter is based on Moretti's (2011) essay "Network Theory, Plot Analysis," in which graph theory clarifies the interactions between characters in Shakespeare's *Hamlet*, *King Lear*, and *Macbeth*. Moretti represents each character from a work of literature by a point (or vertex), and characters that share a social relationship are connected by a curve (or edge). We use his idea of graph theory to analyze a character's social network in different works of literature, such as J. K. Rowling's Harry Potter series. This activity also helps students understand abstract models (a graph) through the organization of information into a discrete structure. The chapter includes examples of how this lesson can be used with different literary texts and how the concept of graph theory transfers across contexts and content to be used to understand social networks, disease propagation, and other complex phenomena.

Chapter 4: Using Abstraction, Iteration, and Recursion in Labyrinths and Mazes   In this chapter, we describe and show how labyrinths and mazes are different in structure. Students learn an iterative algorithm for generating a Cretan-style labyrinth. Then, using paper and pencil, students create their own labyrinths of different sizes. These hands-on activities include background information on labyrinths in different areas of the ancient world, their use and meaning during medieval times, and the development of multicursal mazes during the Italian Renaissance. Students learn to apply abstractions in order to graph mazes and create new ones, and then to solve them using a recursive depth-first search algorithm.

Chapter 5: Simulating the Different Laws of Physics in Video Games   Students apply Newtonian physics (e.g., laws of motion, universal gravitation) along with the law of reflection to create different computer games. Using team-based programming with Codesters and/or Scratch, students create games that simulate the motion of objects or projectiles within a confined space or near the earth's surface.

Chapter 6: Critically Examining and Analyzing Data   In this chapter, students and teachers learn how to locate, analyze, and present empirical data pertaining to critical issues affecting our society today. The chapter specifically focuses on using a primary data source to investigate questions about local temperature trends. Students download data files from a US government website (e.g., www.ncdc.noaa.gov/cdo-web/) and then use Google Sheets and/or Python to manage, process, analyze, and interpret the data.

Chapter 7: Incorporating Computational Thinking into the Classroom   We conclude in chapter 7 with examples from teachers who incorporated computational thinking into their classrooms based on the ideas presented in this book.

We also discuss how you can access different resources to include computational thinking in your own teaching. For example, Scratch is a free, online, visual programming language designed for users of all ages that allows them to create their own games, interactive stories, or animations (see www.scratch.mit.edu) and share those creations with an online community. In Scratch, users form interactive computer programming scripts by dragging and dropping program blocks that link together like puzzle pieces. Codesters, another online programming language (see www.codesters.com), has all the same benefits as Scratch programming environments. It uses a Python-based text editor instead of blocks, so users can type the lines themselves and use Python commands outside the drag-and-drop options. There is also interest in promoting computational thinking without computers. Tim Bell and his colleagues from the University of Canterbury in Christchurch, New Zealand, have created the CSUNPLUGGED website (see www.csunplugged.com). They offer some great suggestions for lessons that help promote computational thinking and computer science principles without using computers. We also have a supplemental website (teachingcomputationalthinking.com) that contains the executable programs that we discuss in our chapters.

1.5 Going Forward

At its essence, computational thinking is a humanistic process. We solve problems in our lives every day. We design methods that enable us to organize, manage, and recall information for efficiency. We look for patterns in our problems as a strategy for scaling up to solve larger and/or more complex problems. Computational thinking employs many of those methods in systematic ways. It is a set of thinking skills, habits, and approaches that are integral to solving complex problems that rely on abstractions and algorithmic processes (Wing 2008), as well as a reflective process for analyzing the appropriateness of those methods. But, like communication, numeracy, and critical thinking skills, computational thinking is too important to relegate to one specific content area or class. Moreover, we contend that students will understand and value computational thinking most when its relevance is demonstrated across the widest possible range of subjects within learning experiences that are developmentally responsive, authentic, challenging, and empowering. Whether you take small steps or large ones to integrate computational thinking, it is something that can transform students' learning experiences in schools.

2 Creating Algorithmic Art

In this chapter, we discuss how students can create algorithms that generate original artwork using the Scratch and/or Codesters environments. Practical tasks are designed to connect students with abstract and conceptual art in the style of Wassily Kandinsky, Edna Andrade, Josef Albers, and Victor Vasarely.

Art takes many shapes and forms, and it is a way to express emotions and beauty. Abstraction involves interpreting, understanding, and processing something in a way that exposes its core concepts and truths. In art, abstraction can mean using geometric shapes and figures to represent more complex objects, feelings, and emotions. In coding, abstraction can mean taking a task and breaking it down into executable, algorithmic steps to communicate an idea to the computer in a way that it can understand. These two definitions of abstraction do not seem related at first glance, but in this chapter we encourage students to study abstract art styles in a way that allows them to transfer those ideas into coded masterpieces. Our perspective is that computational thinking represents a formalization of human creative expression. By abstracting in the coded sense, students will exercise computational thinking methods and better understand abstraction and algorithmic processes in the art sense—abstract algorithmic art.

Some artists use geometric shapes and patterns (e.g., circles, rectangles, grids) to form their art. Wassily Kandinsky, a Russian painter in the early 1900s, had overlapping geometric shapes in his art. One of his most well-known pieces is a grid of concentric circles. Edna Andrade, an American artist, was one of the first to create optical illusion art, in the 1960s. She was one of the pioneers of the Op Art movement and used many circles, or what appeared to be circles, in her works. Josef Albers, a German-born American artist and educator, used shades and hues to color his abstract art. He helped develop modern art education in the 1900s. Victor Vasarely, a Hungarian-French artist, was another Op Art pioneer, known for stretching the lines in a grid to create the illusion of other shapes. In this chapter, we are going to imitate these artists' styles in both unplugged and computer-based activities.

Art created on a computer is different from other art media in two major ways: the computer uses code to create art, and the art is displayed mainly via light from a computer screen. Throughout history, artists have used different media, such as paint, watercolor, pastel, pencil, and ink. In the digital age, light from a screen is used to create art. Think about how the screen on your computer or phone shines in the darkness. Your screen is made up of thousands of tricolored lights called pixels. You will program these lights to turn on and off to display your art on the screen.

Learning Activity 2.1: Codesters and Scratch Programming Languages

In this chapter, we are going to be demonstrating code using Codesters[1] and Scratch. If you have never coded in either of these languages, check out the Scratch coding tutorial at scratch.mit.edu or the Codesters tutorial at codesters.com for how to program in these languages. You can create a free account through their websites and complete their tutorials to become acquainted with the platform. An hour or two of going through their tutorials will increase your ease with programming in these languages. We also recommend trying out the different Hour of Code coding modules at hourofcode.com to learn beginning computer programming content and to build muscle memory for computational thinking.

We also have unplugged tasks that use other media (such as construction paper, colored pencils, markers, and paint) to create these art forms. The algorithms and computational thinking concepts will be the same, and the results will look similar. The difference is that these unplugged activities do not use code and are not displayed in a digital format, but with either plugged or unplugged media, guiding students through the thought process behind the creation of these art forms is at the heart of computational thinking. The following questions outline the process of interpreting, understanding, and creating algorithmic art.

Students interpreting the art:
- What do students notice as they look at the art?
- What processes did the artist employ to create the art?

Students' understanding of creating the art:
- How would the student create the art?
- What steps are repeatable when creating the art?

Students creating the art:
- What tools are needed to create this art form?
- What steps would the students take to replicate this art form either with art supplies or with a computer?

Each of the artistic styles discussed in this chapter takes you through an example of interpreting, understanding, and creating the art by using computational thinking.

2.1 Kandinsky Art

Kandinsky's art style involves a bunch of geometric shapes that overlap each other. If we can create lines of code that will draw one shape, we can reuse that code to draw many shapes. We want to use different colors, sizes, and positions so that the shapes will scatter across the screen. We will use commands to randomize for these values, which means the computer will choose where the shape is placed. The code will be creating the art.

To simulate Kandinsky's style, we will use

- **loops** to draw many shapes and
- **sequencing** to choose different colors, sizes, and locations for each shape.

Learning Activity 2.2: Kandinsky Unplugged

In this activity, students create their own version of a Kandinsky work of art. Let your students pick or create their own shapes of different colors. Using construction paper, paint, magazine cutouts, markers, and other items, have the students place the shapes randomly on a canvas (e.g., a piece of paper, a poster board), or as a group project you could choose to create a class mural on which students randomly place a shape of their choosing.

First, let's design the algorithm (see algorithm 2.1). We want to have lots of shapes placed on the canvas in various colors, locations, and sizes, and we can have steps that choose these colors, locations, and sizes. From these three pieces of information, we can draw a shape. If we repeat those instructions X times (choosing new random values with each repetition), then we will have made Kandinsky-style art.

Algorithm 2.1: Kandinsky Art Algorithm

```
repeat X times:
    choose a random color
    choose a random location
    choose a random size
    create a shape of that size in that location with that color
```

In figure 2.1, you can see the algorithm in the Scratch environment. We set the sprite to a ball, which you can see in the example output in figure 2.2. A sprite is a character within the Scratch environment that you can program to move and draw, among other functionalities. Your students can play around with the editable fields of this environment in the following ways:

- Changing the number in the `repeat` block will determine the number of balls drawn.
- Changing the sprite to a different object will modify how the art is seen. In this program, the sprite is a ball.
- The `go to` block covers the entire drawing area. By shrinking the range of the numbers in this command, your students can restrict the balls to appear in only part of the screen.
- The `change color effect` block has a drop-down menu for the different colors, which allows students to change the transparency, brightness, pixelation, mosaic, and other fun effects instead of color. Changing the numbers in this line will affect how much each ball can differ from the one previously drawn.
- The `change size` block makes the ball bigger or smaller, so changing the numbers there will affect how much the sprite can grow or shrink.

The `clear` and `stamp` commands are what erase and draw the balls, respectively. Note that the `clear` command is outside the `repeat` loop so that it only erases once, at the beginning of the program, whereas the `stamp` command is inside the loop so that the ball is drawn each time it is moved and modified.

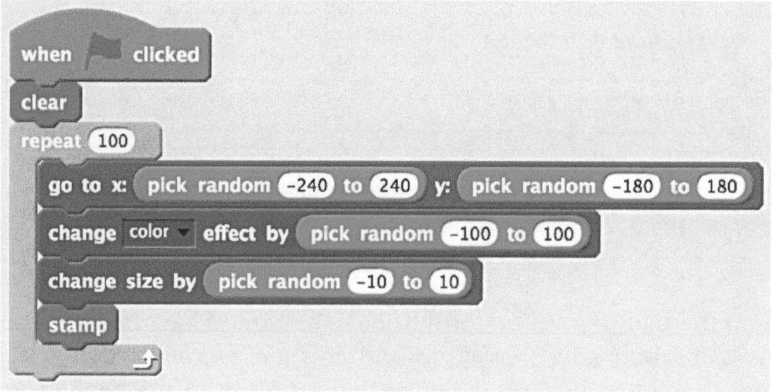

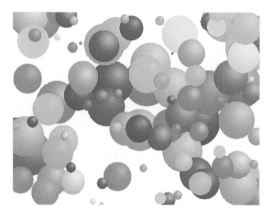

Figure 2.1
The Kandinsky-style Scratch algorithm.

Figure 2.2
An example of the output from the Kandinsky-style Scratch algorithm.

Now we will code this algorithm in the Codesters environment, a Python-based animation language, to draw 100 random squares. Later in this section, we will discuss how you can modify the algorithm to draw other shapes.

We need to look at how the program stores the pieces of information we need. Location is stored as a coordinate pair (x, y). You can think of the coordinates as in the game Battleship: when you state a location such as B5 in Battleship, you are using two coordinates (a letter and a number) to specify the horizontal and vertical placement of a location. It works the same way in Codesters, except we use two integers: the first coordinate (called x) is the horizontal placement and the second coordinate (called y) is the vertical placement. The location $(0, 0)$ is in the center of the drawing area, and x and y can range from –250 to 250. Figure 2.3 shows the coordinate grid that Codesters uses. It includes a square centered at location $(125, 125)$, a circle at $(125, -125)$, a star at $(-125, -125)$, and a triangle at $(-125, 125)$. The size of the square is stored as an integer representing the length of each side. Color is a bit more complicated, so let's investigate what it entails.

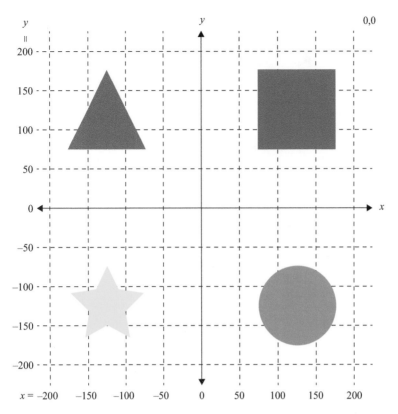

Figure 2.3
An example of a coordinate grid with coordinates from –250 to 250 on the *x* and *y* axes.
Image: Courtesy of Codesters.

In coding, colors are separated into red, green, and blue parts. If all three parts are shining their fullest, the pixel appears white. If all are turned off, the pixel appears black. All the colors you can imagine can be represented as a combination of these three light parts. For example, combining red and green makes yellow. This is the opposite of combining paint colors: the more paint colors you mix together, the closer to brown and black you get; the more light colors you add together, the closer to white you get.

We choose how much red, green, and blue go into each pixel by choosing a number for each one. The numbers are represented in hexadecimal form for the Codesters project. This is base 16, so each digit can be represented as 0-9 or a-f (for 10–15, where a represents 10 and f represents 15). Each of the red, green, and blue parts is represented with two hexadecimal digits, as low as 00 and as high as ff. We write all three parts consecutively with a pound sign at the beginning, so the color #000000 is black and #ff0000 is red. What colors would #0000ff, #ffff00, and #888888 represent? (Answers: blue, yellow, and gray.)

Program 2.1 gives the Codesters algorithm to create Kandinsky-style squares and figure 2.4 gives an example output from the program.

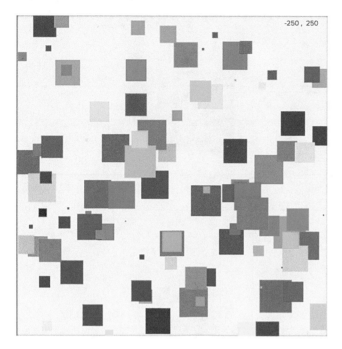

Figure 2.4
An example of the output from the Kandinsky-style Codesters algorithm. Image: Courtesy
of Codesters.

Program 2.1: Kandinsky-Style Codesters Art

```
# lines that start with a pound sign are comments
# import the random number generator library module
import random
# define a list of digits possible for hexadecimal
# colors with a variable named chars
# the next list should be on one line of code
chars = ['0', '1', '2', '3', '4', '5', '6', '7', '8', '9', 'a', 'b',
'c', 'd', 'e', 'f']
# create a loop that runs 100 times
# the variable i will hold values 0-99
for i in range(100):
    # create a variable named color
    color = "#"
    # create a loop that runs 6 times
    # the variable j will hold values 0-5
    for j in range(6):
        # the color variable is updated to add
        # random digits from our chars list
        color += chars[random.randint(0, 15)]
    # call up square module or subroutine with
```

```
# sprite=codesters.Square(x, y, width, color)
# the next command should all be on one line
sprite=codesters.Square(random.randint(-250, 250), random.randint(-250,
250), random.randint(1, 50), color)
```

The first line of executable code (import random) allows us to use the Python random library, which helps us choose random numbers for the location, size, and color of each square. The second line (chars= . . .) defines a list, named chars, of digits possible for our hexadecimal colors. Then comes a for loop that executes 100 times. You can have your students change the 100 to a different number to see more or fewer squares appear. Note that the rest of the lines after this are indented. This is important because it means that these lines are inside the loop (i.e., these lines are executed 100 times).

Learning Activity 2.3: Counting Possibilities

How many different pieces of art can the Kandinsky-Style Codesters Art program produce? If there are 100 shapes on the screen, each with a random color (the red, green, and blue parts will each have $16 \times 16 = 256$ options because they are represented as two hexadecimal digits), at a random location on a 500×500 coordinate grid (going from –250 to 250 on the x axis and –250 to 250 on the y axis), with a width between 1 and 50, that is $100 \times 256 \times 256 \times 256 \times 500 \times 500 \times 50 = 20,971,520,000,000,000$ possibilities! That's almost 21 quadrillion possibilities, or about 2.1×10^{16}.

For the next line, inside the for loop, we create our random hexadecimal color. We start by declaring a variable named color and setting it to be a string containing the pound sign. This variable will eventually store the entire hexadecimal color. With Codesters, as with its base language, Python, a # at the beginning of the line starts a comment, a # inside quotation marks makes it a string variable (a sequence of characters), and we are defining a string that stores a hexadecimal value representing the color. To create a random color, we loop six times and choose a random digit each time from our chars list to add to our color variable. The computer randomly chooses an integer from 0 to 15 and uses it to index into the list, where the integers 0–9 will index to their corresponding characters, 10 will index to a, and 15 will index to f. It adds that character to the end of the color string variable. Your students should not change the 6 in the loop, because hexadecimal colors need to be exactly six digits long, but they can play with the options for the randomized color. All the options should be between 0 and 15, and the first number should be less than the second number (to produce a valid range from low to high). For example, if they change the number 0 to 10 in the line color += chars[random.randint(0, 15)], then the characters chosen can only be in the a-f range (which are high values). This will produce lighter colors. Conversely, if the students change the second number from 15 to 5 (color += chars[random.randint(0, 5)]), then this will produce darker colors.

Learning Activity 2.4: Beyond Squares

Codesters has a button on the left pane called Shapes, which produces a list of options. Drag and drop the Circle command into the text window to create a circle. If you replace the Square command with the Circle command, then the art will show all circles instead of squares. Your students can then explore how they could randomly choose either `circle` or `square` for each of the 100 iterations of the loop. Let them send jpegs or screen captures of their art to share with their peers and discuss some of the choices they made in the art. Together you can look into using those jpegs to display on school monitors between announcements or on the computer labs' computers as a screen saver.

The last command in the algorithm is to create a square. As seen in the comment that starts with the # symbol, the inputs to create a square are the *x* and *y* coordinate values at the center point of the shape, the width (or side length), and the color. If you move your cursor over the drawing area of the Codesters program, you will see the coordinate points update in the upper-right corner. The middle of the drawing area is the location (0, 0), and both axes range from –250 to 250 from left to right and from bottom to top. This is why the random integer we choose for the *x* and *y* coordinates has that range. Your students can change the first digit in both ranges from –250 to 0 to see all the squares appear in the first (upper-right) quadrant. The width is set to a value between 1 and 50. You can have your students change that range as well to see the effects of larger or smaller squares.

Learning Activity 2.5: Kandinsky Circles

Kandinsky's most well-known art piece is a grid of concentric circles. For this coded activity, let students explore how to create concentric circles in Codesters. Hint: You can keep the colors random, but you will want to manually set the values for size and location. See figure 2.5 as an example of what it should look like.

You can run the program multiple times without changing the code and it will produce different output. This is because it's coded art.

2.2 Andrade Art

One of Edna Andrade's well-known styles of optical illusion is to make you see circles when there are none. If you do an online search for Edna Andrade's images, you will see examples of these Op Art pieces. Show them to your students and ask them to draw an imitation of this style. Some of them may draw a bunch of lines going out in a circle for a small radius, then a ring of lines tilting the other way outside it, then another ring of lines tilting at a different angle, and so on. Other students may draw a zigzagging line from the center to the edge and repeat it at different angles. Have your students share their drawings with each other and talk about the different approaches. If you were to code this, what would the steps be? What information would you need to know before you could start drawing? What set of directions can you give someone else that would

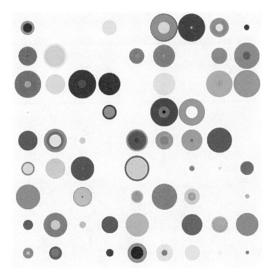

Figure 2.5
Kandinsky-style concentric circles. Image: Courtesy of Codesters.

allow them to draw it? This is the computational thinking process of abstraction, to transform the observation and understanding of the art into a series of steps that can form an algorithm.

We choose to code Andrade's style by drawing zigzagging line segments that all originate from the center point. The zigzags are identical copies of each other but positioned to point at a different angle from the center. You can think of this as applying rotational geometry, or as fanning out from an initial position. The result is that if you connect the corresponding elbows of all the zigzag lines, they would form a circle. In fact, from afar you may think that the drawing does have circles included; it is only on closer inspection that you can see that they are really lines radiating out from a central point.

To simulate Andrade's style, we will use

- **abstraction** to interpret Andrade's style as zigzags;
- **data usage** to store angles and distances for the zigzags;
- **scalability** to choose how many zigzags to draw; and
- **loops** and **sequencing** to draw the zigzags.

To develop an algorithm to draw such an art piece, we start in the center of the screen and draw identical zigzagging lines outward, each starting at a different angle. In order to draw one zigzag line, we need to know the direction and length of each leg. This should be the same for all the lines, so it needs to be decided at the beginning of the program. We use randomness to calculate this, so the program will create a different piece of art each time it runs. Algorithm 2.2 gives the pseudocode for the algorithm.

Algorithm 2.2: Andrade Art Algorithm

```
choose random angles and distances for the zigzag
choose X number of lines
repeat X times:
   start at the center of the screen
   turn to face a new direction
   loop through the angles and distances to draw the zigzag line
```

Learning Activity 2.6: Zigzag Art

Take construction paper and let your students cut out a zigzag pattern. Then have them make identical copies of that zigzag until they have enough to spread out in a circle (all the pieces starting from the center point). Have them glue all the zigzags in place. Then tell them to step back and look at the piece from across the room. Can they see the concentric circles? To demonstrate why they see it, let them use a geometry compass to measure the distance from the center to one of the zigzag elbows and trace a circle at that radius. The circle should go through the elbows of all the other zigzags, too. This is the circle they see from afar.

In the `turn to face a new direction` step, we want all the lines to be spaced evenly. This will produce the best optical effect. In Codesters, angles are measured in degrees (where 360 degrees is a full circle), so we make two decisions: we choose a number of lines that is evenly divisible by 360, and we calculate the starting angle to be in increments of (360 / number of lines). This increment needs to be an integer with no decimal part so there will be no rounding errors in our program.

You can see the Scratch code in figure 2.6. Program 2.2 is the Codesters version of the algorithm and an example output is seen in figure 2.7.

Program 2.2: Andrade-Style Codesters Art

```
# import the random number generator from library
import random
# set the background color to blue
stage.set_background_color("blue")
# create a default sprite to draw with
sprite = codesters.Sprite()
# hide the sprite so you can see where it draws
sprite.hide()
# set the pen width to 4 pixels
sprite.pen_width(4)
# set the number of lines to draw to 24
num_lines = 24
# create a list of random angles
```

```
# the next command should all be on one line
angles = [random.randint(25, 75), random.randint(-75, -25), random.randint(25, 75),
random.randint(-75, -25)]
# set total_angles to the sum of the angles list
total_angles = sum(angles)
# create a list of random distances
# the next command should all be on one line
distances = [random.randint(50, 100), random.randint(50, 100), random.randint(50,
100), random.randint(50, 100)]
# create a loop that runs num_lines times
# the variable i will hold values 0-(num_lines-1)
for i in range(num_lines):
    # make sure we don't draw
    sprite.pen_up()
    # move to the center of the drawing area
    sprite.go_to(0, 0)
    # turn to draw a new line
    sprite.turn_right((360 / num_lines))
    # ready to draw
    sprite.pen_down()
    # loop for each angle in the angles list
    # the variable index will hold values 0-3
    for index in range(len(angles)):
        # turn the angle stored in the angles list
        sprite.turn_right(angles[index])
        # move the distance from the distances list
        sprite.move_forward(distances[index])
    # return to the starting angle
    sprite.turn_left(total_angles)
```

The first executable line imports the random number generator from the library so that the program will be able to choose random numbers. Then we set the background of the screen to blue. You can have your students change that to a different color if they want, or the line can be excluded to leave the default background. The next two lines create a default sprite (`sprite = codesters.Sprite()`) and hide it (`sprite.hide()`). The default sprite looks like the Codesters logo, which you will notice appears for a split second when you run the program. That is because when the sprite is created, but before it is hidden, it shows up on the screen. It appears so fast you may not even see it—that is how quickly the program executes the lines of code. We hide the sprite because we want to see the lines being drawn as it moves around. To see that the program draws underneath the center of the sprite, you can comment the line that hides the sprite by adding a pound (#) symbol at the beginning of the line.

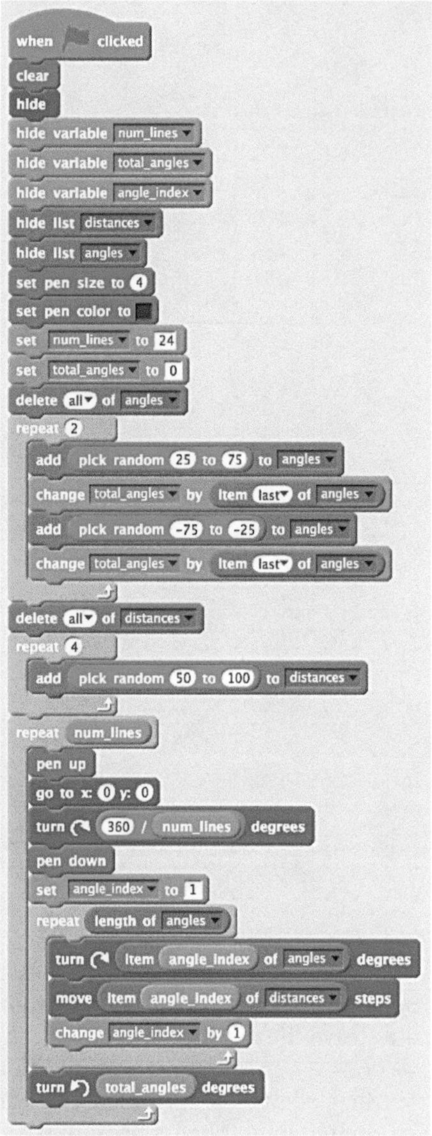

Figure 2.6
The Andrade-style Scratch algorithm.

Learning Activity 2.7: When the Number of Lines Is Not Divisible by 360

In this coded activity, students are asked to explore what happens to the spacing between the lines when they use a number that is not divisible by 360.

Set the number of lines to 19. What do you notice about the difference in the spacing? Why is that? What happens when the number of lines is set to 7 as compared to 19? How does the spacing between the first and last lines change?

Figure 2.7
An example of the output from the Andrade-style Codesters algorithm. Can you see the circles? Image: Courtesy of Codesters.

The next line sets the width of the sprite pen to 4. You can have your students play with the thickness of the zigzag lines by making this number larger or smaller. Then we set the number of lines to 24, which your students can change to another positive whole number that evenly divides into 360. If the number does not evenly divide into 360, the program will still run, but there will be a gap between the first and last lines drawn that is larger than the gaps between the other lines. This is because there was a large remainder left after dividing the number of lines into 360, and that remainder is the number of extra degrees between the first and last lines drawn.

Learning Activity 2.8: More Codesters Fun

Besides changing the values in the code given, you can have your students add code to make their program unique. Have them try one or all of the following tasks:

- Choose a color pen to draw with in the Andrade-Style Codesters Art code. It defaults to black, but use a command like `sprite.set_color("green")` to draw in a different color. How would you make every other line alternate colors? (Hint: Remember that i is a counter variable. If i is even, use one color; if i is odd, use the other color.) How would you choose a random color? (Hint: Review section 2.1 on Kandinsky art.)
- Add or remove angles and distances. If you add more of each, with a lower range of distances, then there will be shorter lines with more zigzag turns.
- Share the output with each other or with the class. Explain what you did, why, and what you learned by changing the code.

Next, we create the angles that determine the structure of the zigzag lines. These angles will be an array of four values. An array is a list of values and is used so that we can capture multiple pieces of information with one variable name. Each has a range of 25–75 degrees, where the program will choose a random integer within that range. The values alternate between positive and negative, which enforces the zigzag behavior. When you turn right at a positive angle, you are turning clockwise; when you turn right at a negative angle, you are really turning left (counterclockwise). Since we are using a loop to make our code cleaner and more efficient and scalable, we need to use the same command for both types of turns. This is why we turn right all the time, at positive and negative angles, instead of alternately turning left and right. You can have your students modify the ranges and/or the signs of these values to see the effects. We want to know the total of all the angles at which we turn because we want to return to the center of the screen and reset our angle to where we started. This way we can build from there to draw the next line. We then set a `total_angles` variable to the sum of the angles in the list. Even though there is a mixture of positive and negative angles, adding them together will correctly calculate the angle away from the initial direction. We then create a similar array of distances. Distances cannot be negative, so all four values are set to be within a range of 50–100. This is an arbitrary range that your students can play around with; it is large enough to be visible and take up most of the drawing area but small enough that it does not go far off the drawing area. Note that the number of angles and number of distances should match (in this case, there are four of each). If they are unbalanced, your program may not run properly.

Now we enter a loop that runs for each line that is drawn. The variable i is a counter that automatically increments with each line drawn. For the first line, i will have value 0. For the last line, i will have value `num_lines−1` (which in our case will be 24−1, so the loop for our program will run with i values from 0 to 23, or a total of 24 times).

Inside the loop, before we start drawing the line, we need to make sure we are positioned correctly. The way Codesters works is that you can move your sprite at any time. If the pen is down while you move, it will draw a line following your movement. If the pen is up, nothing will be drawn. So, the first thing we do is lift the pen and make sure the sprite is in the center of the screen (at location (0, 0)). We then turn right (rotate clockwise) for our increment of `360 / num_lines` (calculated earlier in this section) to get to the angle where our line should begin.

Now we are finally ready to draw the line, so we put down our pen. Then, for each angle and distance we randomly set, we turn right and move forward. After we have finished drawing the line, we turn left to undo all the right turns, so we have reset our zigzag angles and are ready for the next line to be drawn.

To see the randomness effect of drawing different angles and distances, your students can run the program multiple times without changing the code.

2.3   Albers Art

Josef Albers liked to create concentric squares where each square had a different color hue. Together, the colors created a tasteful palette that earned Albers his fame. To create an art program in his style, we draw concentric squares and use patterns with hexadecimal colors described in section 2.1 to create the color hues. We will employ computational thinking to explore and observe different patterns of colors and placements of squares to better understand Albers's abstract art.

To simulate Albers's style, we will use

- **data usage** to store information about the colors;
- **loops** to draw the concentric squares; and
- **abstraction** to interpret the pattern of color hues and square locations and sizes.

In order to imitate Albers's style of art, we want the squares to be overlapping, with the smaller inside squares having their centers located lower than the larger ones. Since they are overlapping, and the last one drawn appears on top, we need to draw the largest square first. We have all the squares centered left to right on the screen, but their widths decrease as we go along. For our example code, we chose to have six squares, with the largest having a side length of 480 and each square shrinking in decrements of 80 units.

Learning Activity 2.9: Albers Art Unplugged

In this activity, students create their own form of Albers-style art.

Hand out printer paper to your students. Ask them to cut out five rectangles of different sizes. Then let them choose three colored markers or pencils and color all five rectangles (each one differently) using those three colors. Some rectangles will need to be a mixture of two or more colors. The students then glue the rectangles on top of each other, with the largest at the bottom and the smallest on top. Each student's work will look different because each chose different colors, but each work will have some continuity of color within itself because all the rectangles were colored with three markers.

We also want the colors to change for each square, but unlike in the Kandinsky example earlier in the chapter, we do not want to choose completely random colors for each shape. Instead, we want there to be a pattern to the colors, a way to connect them from smallest to largest. To create this effect, remember that hexadecimal colors are represented in the format #1234ab, where the six digits have values in the range 0-9 and a-f (i.e., 10–15) and the first two digits represent the red part, the middle two represent the green part, and the last two represent the blue part. We will use the same character list as in the Kandinsky example to show the color options. For each of the red, green, and blue parts, we will choose a starting character and a delta. A delta is a change in the value. For example, if a value was set to 10, a delta of 2 would make it 12 and a delta of –3 would make it 7. The starting character is in the 0-9 range, and the delta will have options 0 (no change), 1 (incremental change), or –1 (decremental change). As an example, if the red part started at 8 and had an incremental change of 1, it would show the pattern 88, 99, aa, bb, cc, dd in the six rectangles drawn.

We set the starting range to be 0–9 for the red, green, and blue colors, not the full spectrum of hexadecimal digits. This is because we do not want the colors to go past f (the largest digit). In the highest case, the color part will start at a (10) and increment to f (15). We start at 0 because the numbers above and below zero are valid indexes into a list. In Codesters, you can use negative numbers to index from the back of the list: an index of –1 is the last thing in the list, –2 is the second-to-last thing in the list,

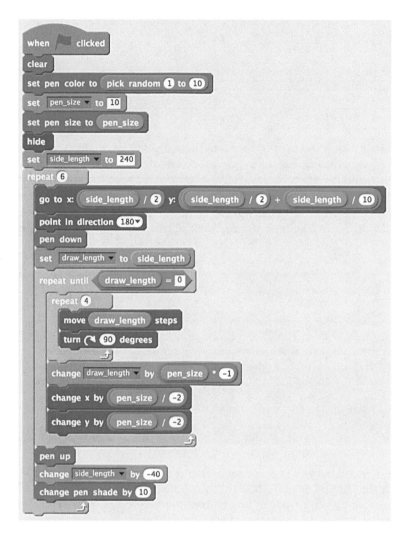

Figure 2.8
The Albers-style Scratch algorithm.

and so on. In our case, decrementing from 0 will land you at f. If a color started at 2 and decreased, its six colors would be 22, 11, 00, ff, ee, dd.

　　Program 2.3 gives the Codesters code for the Albers-style art. The Scratch version is shown in figure 2.8. Note that Scratch does not have an easy way of drawing a filled-in shape, so we create a variable for pen width and draw lots of squares inside each other.

Program 2.3: Albers-Style Codesters Art

```
# import the random number generator library module
import random
# define a list of digits possible for hexadecimal
# color with a variable named chars
```

```
# the next list should be on one line of code
chars = ['0', '1', '2', '3', '4', '5', '6', '7', '8', '9', 'a', 'b', 'c', 'd',
'e', 'f']
# set the start value for the color's red part
red_start = random.randint(0, 9)
# set whether red will get darker, lighter, or stay the same
red_delta = random.randint(-1, 1)
green_start = random.randint(0, 9)
green_delta = random.randint(-1, 1)
blue_start = random.randint(0, 9)
blue_delta = random.randint(-1, 1)
# create a loop that will have i values from 6 to 1
for i in range(6, 0, -1):
    # set the color based on the variables above
    color = "#" + chars[red_start + (i * red_delta)] * 2
    color += chars[green_start + (i * green_delta)] * 2
    color += chars[blue_start + (i * blue_delta)] * 2
    # draw a square of the color calculated
    sprite = codesters.Square(0, (6—i) * -20, i * 80, color)
```

The first executable line includes the random number generating library so that we can compute random numbers. Then we define a list of chars made up of the 16 hexadecimal digits. The next six lines set the red, green, and blue starting values and deltas, as described. We compute the deltas here (as opposed to later inside the loop) so that the color changes an equal amount for each box drawn. This produces the smooth pattern of color hues as the squares get smaller.

Then we start a loop that will execute six times. We set i to be a loop variable that holds the values of 6, 5, 4, 3, 2, and 1, for each iteration of the loop. Notice that the range looks different here: it has three numbers in the parentheses instead of the usual two. The first is the starting number, the second is just after the ending number, and the third is the increment, so it will start at 6, stop before 0, and decrease by 1 for each iteration. We needed to set it up this way because the width of the squares is dependent on this number and, as described earlier, we need to draw the largest square first, so we want the loop to start with the largest number.

Inside the loop, we create our color by forming a hexadecimal string. We calculate the red, green, and blue parts based on the starting value and delta of each, using i to make sure the value is different for each iteration. We then multiply it by 2 so that we have duplicate digits. This works because in Codesters you can multiply a string by an integer to repeat it: "hello" * 2 becomes "hellohello", and in our case "3" * 2 becomes "33".

The last line in the program draws the square. The center of the square is at x coordinate 0, which means it's centered on the drawing's complete area. The y coordinate of the center point becomes lower with each square drawn, so it is based on the i variable. The width of the square is also based on i, because our squares should get smaller each time through the loop. The last input is the color we calculated.

You may notice when you run the program multiple times that the colors change. For the most part, the squares form a spectrum of hues. You may also notice that occasionally you get one solid square. That happens when all three colors have deltas set to 0, which should have a 1 in 27 (1/27) chance of happening. This is because there is a 1 in 3 (1/3) chance of getting a delta of 0 and it happened for all three color parts, which is a 1 in 3 times 1 in 3 times 1 in 3, equaling a 1 in 27, chance ($1/3 \times 1/3 \times 1/3 = 1/27$). You will also occasionally see a sharp difference in color between two rectangles. In figure 2.9, there is a clear difference between the three largest and three smallest rectangles. This happens when one or more of the color parts wrap around from the low end of the spectrum (0) to the high end (f).

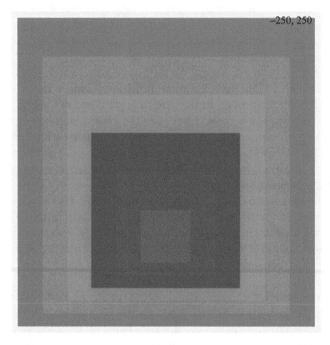

Figure 2.9
An example of the output from the Albers-style Codesters algorithm. Image: Courtesy of Codesters.

2.4   Vasarely Art

Victor Vasarely was well known for taking parallel lines and curving them into other shapes. To imitate his style, we will take a grid of colors and use Bézier curves to give the illusion of a circle.

A Bézier curve connects two endpoints by using two control points. Each endpoint starts off pointing to one of the control points and then curves to meet the other endpoint. So, if the control points move farther away from the endpoints, the line will be more curved. If the control points are on opposite sides of the direct path between the endpoints, the curve will be S shaped.

Learning Activity 2.11: Vasarely on Paper

To simulate Vasarely's style of art on paper, have your students take construction paper and use a graphing compass to draw a circle on it. Then have them draw grid lines surrounding (but not inside) the circle. To connect the lines through the circle, have them use yarn that starts at the two disconnected edges of the circle and use a cup to bend the yarn into a curve through the circle. Then have them glue the yarn in place. Then have them glue yarn over the grid lines on the outside of the circle as well to finish their Vasarely masterpiece.

To create the illusion of grid lines being bent, we will need to draw three sets of lines: the curves that make up the circle illusion; the lines that extend from the endpoints of the curves to the edge of the drawing area; and the grid lines outside the curves' reach.

To simulate Vasarely's style, we will use

- **abstraction** to interpret Vasarely's style as a grid with the grid lines curved in places and to recognize that this will involve drawing three sets of lines;
- **data usage** to store information about the curves and lines;
- **subroutines** to draw three logically different sets of lines; and
- **modularization** to use symmetries to draw many lines from few inputs and to reuse code to draw logically different sets of lines.

Algorithm 2.3 shows how we will draw each of the three sets of lines.

Algorithm 2.3: Vasarely Art Algorithm

```
choose random circle and curve parameters
choose a random scale for the grid lines
repeat for the circle's range:
   draw the curve lines
   draw the grid lines that connect to the curves
repeat for the range outside the circle:
   draw the grid lines
```

The first two lines of the algorithm involve choosing random values so that the sizes of the grid lines, circle, and curves are determined by the computer. This way, you will see something different each time you run the program.

The two other parts of the algorithm loop through two ranges: the area inside the circle's radius and the area outside it. We split these parts into separate loops because we have to perform different actions: inside the circle's range, we need to draw the Bézier curves inside the radius and the partial grid lines outside the radius; outside the circle's range, the grid lines run all the way across the screen.

Now we are ready to write the algorithm in Codesters (Scratch does not have a built-in way to draw curves, so we will not use it for this activity). Program 2.4 gives the code for the Vasarely-style art, and figure 2.10 shows an example of the output that is drawn on the computer screen.

Program 2.4: Vasarely-Style Codesters Art

```
# import the math library module
import math
# import the random number generator from library module
import random
# set a random radius
radius = random.randint(5, 25) * 10
# set the distance between grid lines
scale = random.randint(1, 5) * 10
# set the sharpness of the curve
curve = random.randint(1, 5) * 10
# set the height of the curve
fraction = random.randint(2, 8)
# set the coordinates within range of the circle
coords = range(int(-scale / 2), -radius, -scale)
# create a function called draw_lines
def draw_lines(x, y1, y2, c):
    # draw the four lines using the subroutine
    # codesters.Line(x1, y1, x2, y2, color)
    sprite = codesters.Line(x, y1, x, y2, c)
    sprite = codesters.Line(-x, y1, -x, y2, c)
    sprite = codesters.Line(y1, x, y2, x, c)
    sprite = codesters.Line(y1, -x, y2, -x, c)
# loop through the coordinates
for coord in coords:
    # set coord2 so it is on the circle's edge
    coord2 = math.sqrt(radius * radius—coord * coord)
    # calculate the height of the curve
    height = -radius + ((radius + coord) / fraction)
    # draw four Bézier curves using subroutine
    # codesters.Curve(x1, y1, cp1x, cp1y, cp2x, cp2y, x2, y2, fill, color)
    # the next command should be on one line
    sprite = codesters.Curve(coord, coord2, height, curve,
height, -curve, coord, -coord2, None, "red")
```

```
    # the next command should be on one line
    sprite = codesters.Curve(-coord, coord2, -height, curve,
-height, -curve, -coord, -coord2, None, "red")
    # the next command should be on one line
    sprite = codesters.Curve(coord2, coord, curve, height,
-curve, height, -coord2, coord, None, "red")
    # the next command should be on one line
    sprite = codesters.Curve(coord2, -coord, curve, -height, -curve,
-height, -coord2, -coord, None, "red")
    # call the function above to draw grid lines
    draw_lines(coord, -coord2, -250, "green")
    draw_lines(coord, coord2, 250, "green")
# loop through the area outside the circle
for x in range(coords[-1]—scale, -250, -scale):
    # call the function above to draw grid lines
    draw_lines(x, -250, 250, "blue")
```

Note that the indentation in the program is essential for it to run correctly in Codesters. Code that is part of a function (def), a loop (for), or a conditional (if) statement needs to be indented. Space at the beginning of a line is how the computer can tell where a function, loop, or condition begins and ends, so the spaces that you add can change when and how many times that line of code executes.

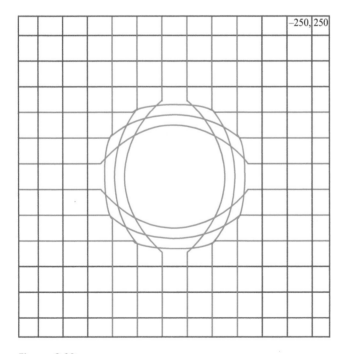

Figure 2.10
An example of the output from the Vasarely-style Codesters algorithm. Image: Courtesy of Codesters.

The first two lines of the Codesters algorithm import `math` and `random` libraries. The imported random library allows us to use the computer's random number generator. The math library allows us to take the square root of a number, among several other math functions. To find the square root of a number, you call a function `sqrt` and the computer runs the already written code to find the square root.

Then we create some variables (e.g., `radius`, `scale`, `curve`, `fraction`, and `coords`) and give them values. We set the variable `radius` to a random multiple of 10 between 50 and 250. This will be the radius of the circle area. We make the variables `scale` and `curve` a random multiple of 10 between 10 and 50 so that the computer sets the size. The variable `scale` is the distance between grid lines, so the larger the `scale`, the fewer grid lines there will be. The variable `curve` is the distance between the control point and the center of the endpoints, so the larger the `curve`, the more rounded the arc will be. The range of the variables `radius`, `scale`, and `curve` is something that your students can change. We then set a `fraction` variable to a random integer between 2 and 8. The height of the curves is somewhere between that of the endpoints and the far edge of the circle, and the `fraction` variable will determine where in that range the arc will stretch.

Next, we create a list of coordinates within the circle. Remember that (0, 0) is the center of the drawing area. We decided to draw the grid lines to straddle the center of the drawing area because having lines down and across the middle of the screen would complicate the curvature within the circle's radius (either making it unsymmetrical or requiring two curves for each center line), so we start at half the `scale` value and move `scale` units until we reach the value of the `radius`. For example, if the `scale` variable is set to 10 and the `radius` variable is set to 50, `coords` would be [5, 15, 25, 35, 45].

Next, we create a function called `draw_lines`. A function is a set of commands that can be executed from anywhere after the function is defined in your code and can be executed any number of times. The function we create is to draw lines. Since our circle is centered at (0, 0), our grid pattern is going to be symmetrical around the x and y axes. So, given three coordinates, x, $y1$, and $y2$, we can create four lines: the vertical line between $(x, y1)$ and $(x, y2)$; the vertical line between $(-x, y1)$ and $(-x, y2)$; and the two horizontal lines formed when those x and y coordinates are swapped. Later in the code, this will allow us to call this function with three coordinate numbers and will draw four lines based on those numbers. Figure 2.11 shows the four lines formed from the x coordinate 20 and y coordinates 30 and 60. The vertical lines are from (20, 30) to (20, 60) and (–20, 30) to (–20, 60), and the horizontal lines are from (30, 20) to (60, 20) and (30, –20) to (60, –20). The x and y axes are also drawn, so that you can see how the lines are oriented.

The last input to the `draw_lines` function is the color of the line drawn. The input is named c, but we will be passing colors ("red," "green," or "blue") to this function so it is able to draw in whatever color we pass to it.

Learning Activity 2.12: Vasarely Colors

Ask your students how they could use the Kandinsky logic to make each line and curve drawn with a random color, or use Albers logic to create different hues of colors.

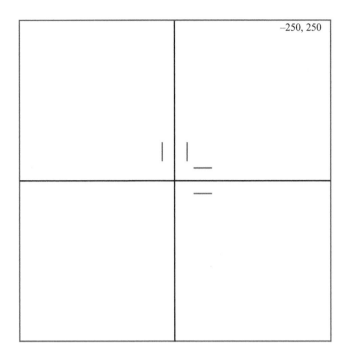

-250, 250

Figure 2.11
The four lines drawn with x coordinate 20 and y coordinates 30 and 60. Image: Courtesy of Codesters.

Now comes the loop. We go through each coordinate point (named `coord`) in our coords list and use the equation of a circle ($r^2 = x^2 + y^2$) to solve for the other coordinate (`coord2`). Since we have a radius variable (r) and a coord (x), we can use $\sqrt{r^2 - x^2}$ to calculate the y variable. We then use those two coordinates to draw four curves. The logic behind having four of them is the same as for the lines: the symmetries along the axes allow us to switch the x and y signs and coordinates to draw more than one curve for each coordinate point. Two of the curves will be reflections of each other across the x axis, like looking at a reflection in calm water; the two other curves are formed if you rotate those curves 90 degrees. Figure 2.12 shows an example of four curves drawn from one pair of coordinates. The Codesters Curve function takes the following format:

```
sprite=codesters.Curve(x1, y1, cp1x, cp1y, cp2x, cp2y, x2, y2, fill,
"color")
```

The two endpoints of the curve are ($x1$, $y1$) and ($x2$, $y2$). The control points are ($cp1x$, $cp1y$) and ($cp2x$, $cp2y$). We set the fill (the color of the area under the curve) to None, but it can be set to a color. The last input is the color of the line.

The endpoints are always some variation of `coord` and `coord2` (with the order and sign taking care of the symmetries), and our control points are always a variation of `height` and `curve` (again with the symmetries). This is because we want the endpoints to be on the edge of the circle and want the curve to lean away from the center of the circle. Changing the order or sign of the variables `curve` and `coord2` and/or changing

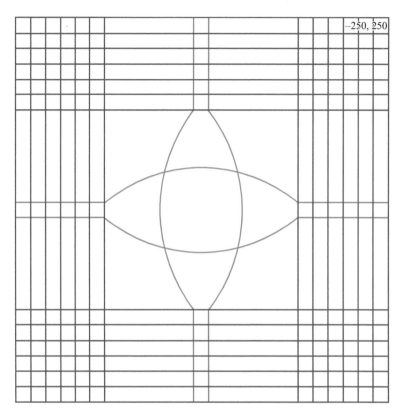

-250, 250

Figure 2.12
The four curves drawn from one iteration of the Vasarely loop. Image: Courtesy of Codesters.

the values of height and curve will create different patterns of curves. This will often make the curves intersect each other and can possibly go outside the bounds of the circle. For example, changing all the instances of height to curve will make the pattern look like a grid that was pushed out of the circle, and changing all instances of curve to height will cause loops that look like drawn curtains. Your students can play with these values, as tweaking them can create a fun Spirograph effect.

After the curves are drawn, there are two calls to our draw_lines function to draw the lines from the curve endpoints to the edge of the drawing area.

Finally, there is a separate loop that goes through all the coordinate points not used by the circle (since the circle's radius can be as small as 50 units, there may be plenty of extra space). It calls draw_lines to create the lines that cross the full drawing area.

Note that we used three different colors for the three sets of lines drawn (the curves, the grid lines that connect to the curves, and the grid lines that don't touch the curves). This is so that you can see which parts of the code draw which lines in the drawing window. Encourage your students to change the colors even more by making each of the four curves a different color or everything one color.

Learning Activity 2.13: Combining Artists' Styles

After going over two or more of these Op Art artists (Kandinsky, Andrade, Albers, and/or Vasarely) with your students, have them combine art styles from different artists into new masterpieces, letting them choose what aspects they want to implement from each artist and how they will combine them. This can lead to a deeper understanding of both the artists' styles and the code that mimics them, and requires computational thinking to transfer knowledge from multiple sources into a novel work of art.

2.5 Summary

In this chapter, you have seen four different Op Art artists' styles simulated with computer programs. You can see how their different styles were transformed into code and how randomness was used to allow the computer to be creative. These are examples of how your students can apply computational thinking to observe artists' styles and characteristics of their art pieces that can translate into algorithms and code. People can program computers to create art, and these activities are aimed to spark your students' interest in both the art styles and the programming tools they can use to create art.

Applying Graph Theory to Analyze Literature and Social Networks

In this chapter, we introduce topological graphs as a way to incorporate abstraction in the analysis of literary works. By using graphs to visualize the relationships between characters in the text, we provide practical tasks that offer new ways to interpret plays, short stories, and novels. Likewise, we show how graphs can describe social networks that in turn reveal how ideas, as well as communicable diseases, are spread through society.

Within the liberal arts classroom, computational thinking occurs in how we gather information from the text, how we make connections within the text (whether they be between the characters in the story or the interactions of historical figures within a period of history), how we draw conjectures or predictions, or how we represent the information we have learned from the text. Interpreting works of literature, historical events, or social interactions employs critical thinking skills, decision-making processes, and drawing connections or conjectures. Many different perspectives can coexist in the interpretation of the text or historical event, just as there exist many mathematical and computational strategies to help you achieve a solution to a problem. We provide examples of using computational thinking to gather and digest information in ways that can be abstracted into a visual aid (namely, a topological graph) that leads to analyzing the resource to produce a more nuanced and deeper understanding of the material.

Topological graphs represent the connections or relationships between pairs of objects (see figure 3.1 as an example). They can be used to visually represent the relationships between characters in a story, to connect characters with places and events, to keep track of known evidence and information in a mystery plot, and much more. Topological graphs are made up of two parts: points and the lines connecting them. The points, called vertices (singular: vertex), represent the elements in the set. The lines, called edges, represent relationships between vertices. If the relationship is mutual, then the edge is undirected (meaning it is not an arrow). This is the structure for a social media site like Facebook, where two people have to mutually agree to be friends in order to view each other's posts. If the relationships are not mutual, then the edges are directed (meaning they point from one vertex to another). The structure for Twitter's social media site is not mutual, because you can follow one user and see their posts without their having to follow you back. Ask your students how a different social media platform would be represented in a graph. For example, Snapchat's structure (at the time of this writing) is a combination of directed and undirected edges, because friends are established mutually (undirected) but subscriptions are directed.

Topological graphs can hold additional information. Edges could be assigned a numerical weight (such as the capacity of a pipe or the amount of energy needed to get

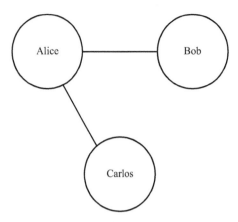

Figure 3.1
An example of a topological graph. Alice has edges to Bob and Carlos, but Bob and Carlos are not directly connected to each other.

from one location to another) or color coded (such as distinguishing between friends and adversaries). Vertices could be sized according to a scale (such as the number of albums sold) or have special distinctions (such as a double-walled vertex signifying a killed character).

In this chapter, we show examples of these graphs and the logical conclusions about the story that you can draw from them. We also use topological graphs to describe how to track the spread of diseases through a population and the spread of ideas through the structure of social networks.

Learning Activity 3.1: A Spider's Web Morning Greeting

A Spider's Web Morning Greeting is an example of a topological graph.

- Holding a ball of yarn, a student greets someone across the circle and gently rolls the ball to that person while firmly holding onto the end of the yarn.
- The student who receives the ball of yarn greets another student across the circle and rolls the ball to that student, making sure to hold onto the unraveling strand with one hand.
- This continues until everyone has been greeted and the yarn has created a web across the circle.

Each person is a vertex in this graph, and the yarn represents the edges between the vertices. This activity is a great visual to demonstrate vertices and edges for students. Take a moment to ask the students who they are connected to in this graph, how many edges are connected to them, and how this relates to who they greeted.

- To unravel the web, students greet each other in the reverse order until the ball of yarn is wound up again.

(Responsive Classroom 2013)

3.1   Graph Example: *Harry Potter and the Sorcerer's Stone*

In this section, we use the first book in J. K. Rowling's Harry Potter series as an example of how to analyze a work of literature with topological graphs. These activities are adapted from Moretti's (2011) essay "Network Theory, Plot Analysis," in which he used graph theory to clarify the interactions between different characters in Shakespeare's *Hamlet*, *King Lear*, and *Macbeth* and in Dickens's *Our Mutual Friend*. In this essay, each character from these works of literature is represented by a point (or vertex), and characters who share a social relationship are connected by a curve (or edge).

Algorithm 3.1 shows the steps we will take to analyze the book by using a graph.

Algorithm 3.1: Creating a Graph from a Book

1. Read through the book and log the interactions between the characters.
2. Make decisions to define the interactions you want to graph, and tally the number of those interactions between each pair of characters.
3. Create a vertex for each character who has at least one interaction, and connect the pairs of interacting characters with an edge.
    a. This can be done manually on paper or can be created in a presentation program (such as Microsoft PowerPoint, Apple Keynote, or Google Slides).
    b. You may want to store more information in the vertices and/or edges of the graph. We give examples and discuss these options later in this section.
4. Make observations about the graph. Use it to raise new questions and search the text for answers. Use its data as evidence to support a claim. Use it to analyze the complex structure of the relationships between the characters in the book.

You can perform these steps many times with the same text, making different decisions each time to visualize new data and varying aspects of the book. In this section, we use *Harry Potter and the Sorcerer's Stone* (Rowling 1998) to create several examples of different graphs and a glimpse into the analyses you can write about them.

To create a graph from literature, we will use

- **abstraction** to focus on certain aspects of the text that we want to represent visually;
- **data usage** to gather information from the literature to display visually in the graph;
- **sequencing** (concept) to perform a series of instructions to gather data from the literature and display it in a graph; and
- **conditionals** (concept) to decide whether an interaction qualifies as something that should be displayed in the graph.

Creating a Graph

First, we go through *Harry Potter and the Sorcerer's Stone* and mark when characters interact with each other. Here is an excerpt of the interactions recorded from chapter 11 of the book:

Harry Potter and the Sorcerer's Stone Chapter 11 Log

Madam Hooch spoke to the Quidditch teams.
Lee spoke to the crowd.
McGonagall spoke to Lee.
Hagrid spoke with Ron and Hermione.
Fred spoke to Harry.
Dean spoke with Ron and Hagrid.
Lee spoke to the crowd.
McGonagall spoke to Lee.
Hagrid spoke to Seamus.
Ron spoke with Hermione.
Ron and Hermione saw Snape.
Hermione knocked Quirrell over.
Hermione set Snape's robes on fire.

The next step is to tally how many interactions each pair of characters have with each other. There are some subjective decisions that need to be made, which can produce productive discussion and/or creative license for your students. Below are examples of decisions that we made for this particular example. You may find that you need to answer similar questions with your story and that your decisions may differ from ours.

- What defines an interaction between two characters? We defined it as speaking (dialogue) with each other. This means that if a character was present in a scene but did not speak, they were not included. If nonverbal interactions took place (e.g., seeing a character from afar, listening to a conversation from behind a door, or knocking someone over), they were not included.
- What will the edge weights (the thickness of the line) represent? We kept track of the number of conversations between the characters and used that as the edge weight. In figure 3.2, you will notice that Harry and Ron converse the most in the book (their edge is the thickest), whereas Harry and Dumbledore only converse thrice. The length of the conversation has no bearing, so even though Ron and Harry have many shorter conversations and Harry and Dumbledore have fewer but longer dialogues, the graph will show the total number of conversations. One could choose to count in sentences or words if the context made that sensible.
- What if more than two people are conversing at once? This is a bit tricky because an edge cannot connect more than two vertices in a topological graph. We used the context of the conversation to decide. For example, when Harry, Ron, and Hermione are speaking together, we added all three pairwise edges between them, but when Harry and Ron are pressing for information from Hagrid and Hermione is present but silent, we only added edges between Hagrid and Harry and between Hagrid and Ron. Harry, Ron, and Hermione were not talking with each other in this context, even though all were present and a conversation was taking place.
- What if there is dialogue without a clear recipient? We excluded these from the graph. For example, when Dumbledore is addressing everyone in the Great Hall, when Percy is addressing all the first-year students, or when Vernon Dursley overhears the exclamations of an unnamed wizard, we do not include these speaking parts in the graph.

You may have additional questions that come up for a different piece of literature. This process includes a lot of computational thinking as you decide what data makes the most sense to abstract (and visualize) in a graph or try out different restrictions and rules to graph and see how each one affects the graph and reveals something different to analyze about the text.

The excerpt of the chapter 11 interactions, with our decisions, ends up being counted as follows:

Harry Potter and the Sorcerer's Stone Chapter 11 Tally

McGonagall and Lee: 2
Hagrid and Ron: 1
Hagrid and Hermione: 1
Fred and Harry: 1
Dean and Ron: 1
Dean and Hagrid: 1
Hagrid and Seamus: 1
Ron and Hermione: 1

This may be easier for your students to record in a spreadsheet, although it is doable on paper. After all interactions have been tallied, it is time to make the graph. Each character will be a vertex, and each pair of characters in the tally will have an edge between them. The tally count will be the edge weight. We chose to show the edge weight as the thickness of the line drawn. One could also label each edge with a number, as we will demonstrate later in this section. The complete graph is in figure 3.2.

You may ask your students for their reactions as they look through the graph. For example, it may be surprising that Professor Snape and Draco Malfoy never speak to each other in the book, even though it is a well-known fact that Draco is Snape's favorite student. It may also be a surprise that Professor Snape does not have a speaking part with any professors except Quirrell. Another surprise may be the absence of characters: Crabbe and Goyle are with Draco most of the time, but they never have a speaking part and therefore are not represented in this graph.

One way to analyze this graph is to look at the number of edges connected to a vertex. This is called the *degree* of a vertex. Harry is the most connected character with degree 27, followed by Hagrid with 17, Ron with 13, and Professor McGonagall with 11. These numbers can signify many things. The higher numbers mean more developed characters, as we get to see how they behave with different groups of people (for example, Professor McGonagall speaks very differently with Dumbledore than with Neville). The numbers can also point to power dynamics: Professor McGonagall has more interactions with the students than other professors not because she is their favorite but because she is their head of house and is Dumbledore's right-hand woman. You can have your students use this graph of degrees to help analyze the book. For example, this graph can point to some interesting similarities between Professor Snape and Neville (e.g., both have a respectable graph degree of 7, both are indirectly involved in many events and conversations between Harry, Ron, and Hermione, and both have caught the three sneaking around the castle and have tried to stop them).

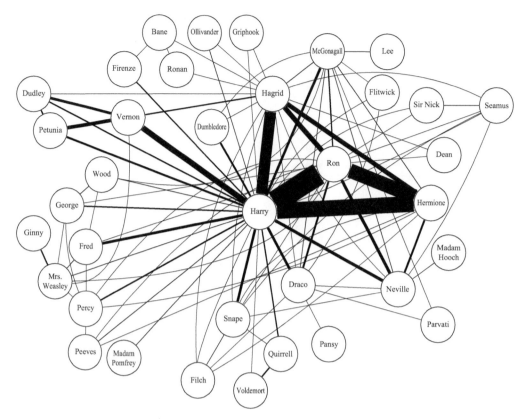

Figure 3.2
A graph of the conversations in *Harry Potter and the Sorcerer's Stone*.

Learning Activity 3.2: Graph Essay

Ask your students to write an essay about either (1) how the graph does not accurately represent the relationship between two characters or (2) how the graph illuminated an unexpected relationship between two characters. For example, a student could make an argument that Hagrid is a more important part of the book (and Harry's life) than Harry's best friend, Ron.

Cleaning a Graph

You will notice that the graph is quite messy. To clear things up a bit, we created a second graph, made up of only the edges that have weight greater than 1 (i.e., when characters had more than one conversation with each other). This excluded a few secondary characters from the graph (such as Parvati Patil and Pansy Parkinson). The result is shown in figure 3.3. This more clearly shows the important characters in the book and the relationships between them. Harry is clearly the main character, having the most connections of anyone. There are many characters who converse more than once only with Harry, and then there are two more interconnected *subgraphs*: sets of characters

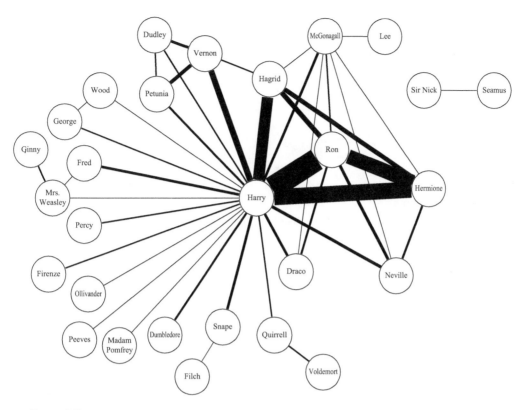

Figure 3.3
A graph of characters with more than one conversation in *Harry Potter and the Sorcerer's Stone*.

and the conversations between them. One is among Dudley, Hagrid, Harry, Petunia, and Vernon. This is Harry's Muggle family, whom you get to know in chapters 2–4 of the book, and Hagrid is the only wizard who interacts with the family (much to their chagrin). The other, more prominent subgraph is among Draco, Hagrid, Harry, Hermione, Neville, Professor McGonagall, and Ron. This subgraph is also where the thickest lines (most conversations) reside, so one could argue that these characters are the most important ones in the book. The three thickest lines form a triangle between Harry, Hermione, and Ron, which gives a visual representation to the three main characters, who are best friends. Hagrid is the other character with multiple thick line connections, showing how the three main students befriend and confide in him more than they do with their professors or roommates.

These graphs have illuminated and visualized relationships between the characters. Using abstraction and algorithmic design, your students can also create these visual aids to help their analysis and interpretation of literary works.

> **Learning Activity 3.3: Cultivating Curiosity**
>
> It is likely that once your students really dig into the topological graphs, they will end up with more questions about the text than they had previously. To help answer some of their questions, encourage them to reference the text to answer them and/or to revisit the decisions they made to create the graph. You can also have them explore other related works (e.g., they may be curious about how the movie adaptation of the book would line up with the text if graphed in the same way, or whether there are common characteristics of graphs produced from different works by the same author).

Graph by Chapter

If you separate the graph by chapters, you will see the character arcs more clearly. For example, Harry, Vernon, Petunia, and Dudley engage in all the interactions in chapters 2–3, so they would be the only vertices in a graph for those chapters of the book. During the transition chapters when Harry is introduced to the wizarding world, he interacts with many new characters (and often for the only time). This graph would have more vertices, but the edge weights would be smaller. Isolating chapters or groups of chapters like this can help you to visualize the plot structure (exposition, conflict, rising action, climax, falling action, and resolution) and the differences in writing style among various phases of the book.

By separating the topological graphs by chapter, you may also be able to categorize characters. For example, *bookend* characters, who only appear in the beginning and ending chapters, would include the Dursleys and Dumbledore; *exponential* characters, who have a slow start but gradually become more important, include Hermione; *full-arc* characters, who have an important role throughout the novel, include Hagrid, Harry, Professor McGonagall, and Ron. This is a different way to visualize the character arcs in the book.

As an example of graphing by chapter, figure 3.4 shows a graph of the words spoken in chapter 1. You will notice that the graph has two disconnected subgraphs, called *components*: Vernon and Petunia talk to each other but to no one else; Hagrid and Professors Dumbledore and McGonagall speak among each other, and Dumbledore speaks briefly to Harry. The edges in this graph are directed, so there can be more than one edge between two characters. In mathematics, this is called a *digraph* (i.e., a graph that has directed edges between the vertices). For example, Vernon and Petunia have two edges between them, pointing in different directions. The edge pointing from Vernon to Petunia represents that Vernon speaks to Petunia in the chapter. The edge weights in this graph are the number of words spoken by each character.

There is some interesting analysis to be done in this graph. It is only an introduction to the book and a snapshot in the timeline of the story, but it is quite revealing:

- Vernon speaks more than four times as many words to Petunia as she speaks to him. This may reveal some stereotypical big-ego personality traits of a person barking orders and always having the last word.
- Look at the edges among Dumbledore, McGonagall, and Hagrid. Dumbledore and McGonagall speak about 10 times more words to each other than to Hagrid. This raises a question: why did J. K. Rowling have Hagrid enter the conversation so late? Let's brainstorm:

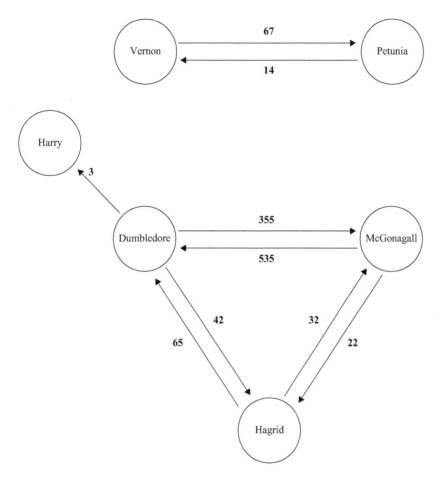

Figure 3.4
A word count graph of chapter 1 of *Harry Potter and the Sorcerer's Stone*.

- It could signify that Hagrid is a minor character. But we know from the other graphs of the book that this is a false proposition.
- It could mean that there is a power dynamic involved. Sure enough, if you look at the dialogue, you will notice that Hagrid addresses Dumbledore as "sir," whereas McGonagall addresses him as "Dumbledore." This confirms the presence of a power dynamic where Hagrid is submissive in the presence of Dumbledore and McGonagall.
- Looking at the number of words spoken between Dumbledore and McGonagall can lead to various interpretations. McGonagall speaks almost 200 more words to Dumbledore in the chapter. This could be interpreted as gender based (where McGonagall gossips about different rumors flying around) or power based (where Dumbledore holds all the cards and reveals them only on a need-to-know basis). Perhaps looking at conversations between these two characters in other chapters of the book would shed more light and supply evidence for one interpretation or the other.

You can have your students create similar graphs and analyses for other chapters in the Harry Potter book and other literary works.

Learning Activity 3.4: Literature Graph

Ask your students to create a graph of the literary work they are studying. Each vertex could be a character in the story, a location, a point of time, or some other aspect of the work. Let the students decide what the edges will represent, whether they will be directed, and so on. The graph could be a map of a family tree, a friendship map, a timeline, a travel log, or something else.

Learning Activity 3.5: Other Resources to Use for Topological Graphs

Here are some ideas for other books or resources (besides the one we already mentioned) to use in which topological graphs can help students analyze the text to make connections between characters in the story or between people in history, or to help follow the plot points of a story or historical event:

- *The Westing Game* by Ellen Raskin
- *Percy Jackson and the Olympians* by Rick Riordan
- *Romeo and Juliet* or *Julius Caesar* by William Shakespeare
- *Eyes on the Prize: America's Civil Rights Years, 1954–1965* by Juan Williams
- *All the President's Men* by Carl Bernstein and Bob Woodward

Evidence Graphs

So far, we have looked at the relationships between characters and the importance of characters in a literary work, but a mystery novel will often contain plot points of evidence leading to a climax where the mystery is solved and all the evidence falls into a coherent timeline. We can use a graph to keep track of these plot devices to help us make an educated decision before reading the climax.

A good way to approach this graph is to list the big questions as they arise in the book: what mystery are we trying to solve? In *Harry Potter and the Sorcerer's Stone*, there are three questions that end up connected in the end:

- What was in the Gringotts safe that was almost robbed?
- What is Fluffy guarding in Hogwarts?
- Who is trying to hurt Harry?

These make up the first column of blocks in figure 3.5. Connected to these are the items in the second column: events and evidence that give clues to the answers. Harry was with Hagrid in Diagon Alley on the day of the attempted robbery, so he may have seen the would-be thief. On Halloween, a troll was set loose in Hogwarts, which was later discovered to be a mechanism to distract attention from an attempted robbery of whatever Fluffy is guarding. During a Quidditch match, Harry's new broomstick is bewitched to try to throw him off. These are examples of the events listed in the second column of the figure.

Lastly, the third column lists all the people present and involved with the events. Let us examine the degree of each character (i.e., the number of edges connecting the character to the second column). The two characters with the highest degree, degree 5,

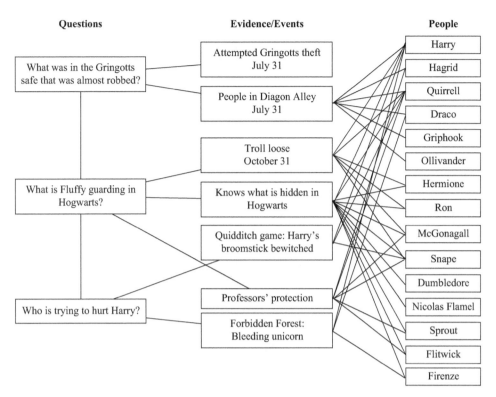

Figure 3.5
A graph of the mystery plot points in *Harry Potter and the Sorcerer's Stone*.

are Harry and Quirrell. In fact, they are the only two characters who are connected to events leading back to all three mystery questions. The main suspect in the novel is Snape, but the major difference is that we know Quirrell was in Diagon Alley on the day of the attempted bank robbery (whereas we don't know this information about Snape). This is a plot point that Harry realizes after he finds Quirrell in the climactic scene in Hogwarts; it is easy to forget it when reading the novel, but the evidence becomes clear when it is displayed in a graph.

Learning Activity 3.6: Applying Computational Thinking to a Mystery

If you teach a mystery novel, have your students create a graph like the ones in figure 3.5 (digital) or figure 3.6 (unplugged) as they are reading. Then, before they reach the climax of the book, have them analyze the graph and guess what the conclusion will be. By abstracting the known facts of the mystery into a topological graph, your students can produce a visual aid that helps them think critically about the book and work past the misleading stumbling blocks that the author uses to keep the climax a surprise (e.g., subjective points of view that inject emotion to cloud judgment) and potentially push them in the right direction to conclude the correct resolution from the clues in the book.

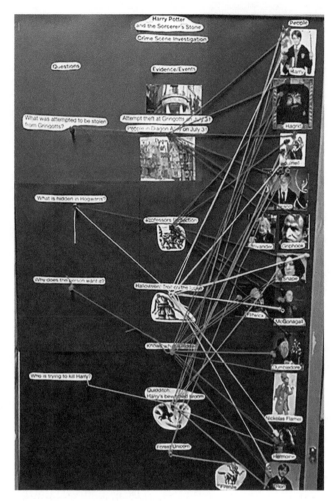

Figure 3.6
An example of the mystery plot points made with pins and string on a bulletin board.

3.2   Social Networking

These topological graphs can serve not only as visual aids for analyzing pieces of literature but also as models for social networks, disease propagation, or the influence of a
powerful family such as the Medici family from Florence, Italy, during the Renaissance
or the Koch brothers in modern US politics. The notion that there are six degrees of
separation between any two people on earth is in essence a social networking problem:
if you graphed each person as a vertex and friendships or acquaintances as edges, then
there would be a path of at most six edge lengths between any two vertices. This reveals
the smallness of the world and how interconnected everyone has become in this age
of technology.

Graphs can be useful tools for creating a visual representation of information. If
you have a team-based assignment, have each student record the number of hours
they work, which tasks they accomplish, and which teammates they work with to

accomplish the task. Then have them graph the team, where the vertices are people (the size of the vertex is proportional to the amount of time worked on the project) and edges connect pairs who worked together on a task (weighted by the number of tasks or some other metric). What do you want a graph like this to look like? Probably vertices of similar size that are very interconnected. Then think about the problem teams you have had: What do their team dynamics look like in a graph? Is one person refusing to work with teammates and disconnecting themselves from others (socially in life and literally in the graph)? Is one person dominating the time and effort put into the project? This can be an interesting way to visualize team dynamics, spot when things go wrong, and show students what is expected of them.

In the case of disease propagation, graphs are used to track the spread of a virus. If vertices represent people (marked as infected by the disease or not) and edges represent pairwise contact between people, you can do several calculations with this:

- observe how the graph changes over time, from a single infected individual to an outbreak;
- see who is most likely to become infected next based on how many connections/ edges they have with infected individuals;
- take known infections and use their common connections to trace the infection back to its source; or
- experiment with how the properties of the graph (e.g., number of vertices, number of edges, average degree of a vertex) influence how quickly the disease spreads.

An application of the disease propagation problem is Conway's Game of Life.[1] A population is represented on a grid, where each square/cell is marked as alive (black) or dead (white). The eight squares surrounding each cell are considered its *neighbors*. The following rules are applied to the population to see whether the death spreads over time:

- *Underpopulation*   Any cell with one or zero live neighbor(s) dies.
- *Surviving*   Any cell with two or three live neighbors lives on to the next generation.
- *Overpopulation*   Any cell with more than three live neighbors dies.
- *Reproduction*   Any dead cell with exactly three live neighbors becomes alive.

Given these four rules and a starting state of the population, you can see the population change over simulated generations of time. An example of a transition from one generation to the next is given in figure 3.7. There are known patterns that are classified as still lives (unchanging), oscillators (two or more patterns that rotate), and spaceships (move in a direction across the grid/world). You can simulate Conway's Game of Life yourself: allow your students to set the original state by choosing which cells in a grid are alive and dead; have them move to the next generation of the simulation by looking at each cell in the grid and using the preceding four rules to determine whether it is alive or dead in the next generation; and keep calculating new generations to see how the pattern of live and dead cells changes over time. What characteristics of the starting grid cause the population as a whole to die, flourish, or migrate?

As you can see, there are lots of applications of topological graphs. Every field of study and class that you teach has data that can be represented in a graph, analyses that can be observed from the graph, and conclusions that can be drawn from the graph that wouldn't have been exposed as clearly outside a graph format. Collecting

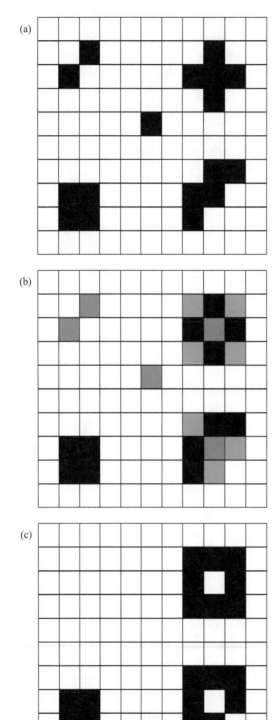

Figure 3.7
An example of how Conway's Game of Life works. (a) An initial configuration of live (black) and dead (white) cells. (b) The changes according to Conway's rules: the blue cells are added and the red cells die. (c) The resulting configuration after one generation.

and abstracting information from a piece of literature, a spreadsheet, or another source often brings clarity to something that could otherwise be overwhelming or messy.

> **Learning Activity 3.7: TeleGraph**
>
> Play a game like Telephone but allow students to share the message with more than one of their classmates. You start by telling one student a one-sentence message, which they then spread to other students, who can then spread it to more students, until everyone in the class has heard at least a version of it. Have the students write down on a piece of paper what they heard and who they heard it from. You can now draw a graph of the path of the message through the classroom and pinpoint where the message changed along the way. You can do this in two different ways: you can have the students tape their message and who they heard it from on flip chart paper or type the message and who they heard it from in a Google Sheets file. If a student hears two different messages from two different people, then there will be two edges pointing to that student's vertex.

3.3   Summary

Creating algorithms or moving ideas into abstraction is an important aspect of many problem-solving skills because it helps us visualize the relationships between the characters in a book, provides an objective perspective on the data, and transfers this skill to analyses of other books. It applies computational thinking to literary works to help students think critically about the work and achieve a deeper understanding of its plot, character relationships, and character development.

In this chapter, we presented algorithms for analyzing different parts of *Harry Potter and the Sorcerer's Stone* and produced topological graphs from the output of these algorithms.

4 Using Abstraction, Iteration, and Recursion in Labyrinths and Mazes

In this chapter, we include activities and algorithms to create labyrinths. These hands-on activities include background information on labyrinths in different areas of the ancient world, their use and meaning during medieval times, and the development of multicursal mazes during the Italian Renaissance. Students learn to apply abstractions in order to graph mazes and create new ones, and then solve them using a recursive depth-first search algorithm.

This is part of a maze of twisty little passages, all alike.
There is an emerald here the size of a plover's egg!

—Will Crowther's computer game *Adventure*

Examples of labyrinths and mazes can be found in diverse corners of the world, spanning the course of history from the late Bronze Age to the modern era. Most people use the words *labyrinth* and *maze* interchangeably to mean a devilishly confusing network of passages. The word *labyrinth* likely refers to the Minoan civilization on the Greek island of Crete. Matthews (1922) notes that the prefix *labrys* denotes the double-edged axe used by the Minoans as a tool, weapon, and religious symbol. Double-edged axes were also discovered by archaeologists amid the ruins of the Palace of Knossos (constructed in 1900 BCE). The suffix *inth* refers to a place. Thus, *labyrinth* might refer to the Palace of Knossos, the "Palace of the Double-Edged Axe." The word *maze* can be traced back to the thirteenth-century English word *mæs*, which means something that causes confusion or deception.

Following the taxonomy of Kern (2000), we define a *labyrinth* as a unicursal, circuitous path or passage. Here, *unicursal* means that only one path can be followed; no branches to other paths exist. The word *circuitous* means that the one path orbits around the central goal in an irregular fashion, making it difficult for a traveler to predict the direction of the next turn. Three distinct styles of labyrinths are Cretan (figure 4.1), Roman (figure 4.11), and Christian (figure 4.12). All are unicursal, but they are conceptually more interesting than either regular spirals (figure 4.2), where the turns follow consistently in the same direction, or periodic meanders, which appear in some classical frieze patterns (figure 4.3). "Threading" a unicursal path is an easy task: one enters the labyrinth and advances forward. Though the path twists and turns, the persistent walker inevitably reaches the goal without making a single decision.

In contrast, we define a *maze* as a network of paths that contains at least one *junction*: a location where three or more paths join. Figure 4.4 depicts the plan of the hedge maze at Hampton Court, which contains eight junctions (can you find them?). At each junction, the maze walker must decide which branch to follow: some branches might

Figure 4.1
A Cretan labyrinth.

Figure 4.2
A spiral is not a labyrinth.

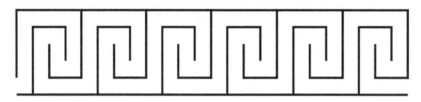

Figure 4.3
A frieze is not a labyrinth.

Figure 4.4
The maze at Hampton Court.

lead to other junctions, some to dead ends, and one or more to the goal. Solving a maze usually requires following an initial path, backtracking at dead ends, and then exploring alternative paths until the goal is discovered. Because more than one course can be followed, a maze is said to be *multicursal*. It is desirable to avoid retracing the same path over and over again. Later, we will describe some algorithms that enable one to thread any maze efficiently.

We use this nomenclature to explore how these designs and puzzles intersect different curricular subject areas. We will demonstrate how labyrinths, mazes, and other computational puzzles can introduce computational thinking principles into lessons in art, world history, mythology, literature, and mathematics.

4.1   Cretan Labyrinths

The Cretan labyrinth (figure 4.5) is a ubiquitous cultural symbol. Schuster and Carpenter (1996) and Kern (2000) document the migration of this design around the globe. The earliest example that can be accurately dated appears on a clay tablet (c. 1200 BCE) that was unearthed from the ruins of a Mycenaean palace in Pylos, Greece. Petroglyphs of similar design found in Galicia (Spain), Sardinia (Italy), and Cornwall (England) may be older, but they are more difficult to date reliably. Rock carvings of Cretan labyrinths belonging to the Iron Age are distributed through the Mediterranean region (from Syria and Turkey to Spain and Portugal) and up to the British Isles. Cretan labyrinths are abundant in artifacts that date from the golden age of Greece (500–300 BCE). For example, the British Museum displays a collection of post-Minoan bronze and silver coins that were recovered from the Palace of Knossos, many of which were embossed with Cretan labyrinths. The conquests of Alexander the Great (in 327 BCE) may have delivered the design to India, if it was not already there. Kern (2000) catalogs numerous examples of Cretan labyrinths in Indian manuscripts, rock carvings, and temple reliefs. It appears that these designs migrated farther east, as labyrinthine patterns decorate Batik fabrics and Sumatran buildings. In the Middle Ages, northern Europeans constructed large labyrinths within their landscapes. The British cut turf labyrinths up to 20 meters in diameter into fields of grass, and Scandinavians created "Troy towns" by aligning boulders to follow the contours of the Cretan design. Although evidence of labyrinths in the Americas is limited, petroglyphs that depict Cretan labyrinths were carved into rock walls by the Pueblo tribes of Arizona and New Mexico. (Cretan labyrinths also appear on traditional baskets woven by the Pima tribe.) An intriguing mystery concerns the age and origin of these North American "Cretan" petroglyphs (Schuster and Carpenter 1996). Did knowledge of the Cretan labyrinth travel across the Pacific from Asia or across the Atlantic from European explorers? Or did these tribes independently discover the Cretan design, perhaps long before the arrival of the European explorers?

Figure 4.5
The earliest depictions of Cretan labyrinths had a rectangular form. This includes the labyrinth found in Pylos, as well as those found on Cretan coins minted before 200 BCE (Schuster and Carpenter 1996).

Although the designs of Cretan labyrinths did not change over time and region, their cultural significance did. For the Greeks, the labyrinth symbolized the inventiveness and skill of Daedalus, the legendary engineer who built for King Minos of Crete the life-sized labyrinth that concealed and caged the Minotaur. In the Greek legend, Theseus of Athens, the son of King Aegeus, sails to Crete in order to slay the Minotaur.[1] After landing on Crete, Theseus wins the heart of Ariadne, King Minos's daughter, who gives her lover a clew (or ball) of golden thread. With this device, Theseus enters Daedalus's labyrinth without fear of getting lost. He consequently "threads" the labyrinth to its center, slays the Minotaur, and then traces the thread back to the entrance, without becoming eternally lost.

Learning Activity 4.1: Internet Labyrinth Hunt

Organize an internet scavenger hunt for websites that display images of labyrinths found around the world. Important labyrinths to seek are

- the Pylos labyrinth, Greece;
- the Hollywood Stone, Ireland;
- Holmengrå, Norway;
- Oraibi, Arizona;
- Pompeii, Italy;
- Boscastle, England;
- Troy towns in Scandinavia;
- Pansaimol, India; and
- Purmatang Purba, Sumatra.

Describe the similarities or differences across the different labyrinth images.

What cultural meanings might these labyrinths hold for the people who created them?

Although the word *labyrinth* is rooted in the history of Crete, the ancient Greeks used it to refer to other buildings with complex networks of passages. The Greek historian and traveler of the ancient world Herodotus (484–425 BCE) describes in *The Histories* his visit to the temple of Amenemhet III in northern Egypt and refers to this edifice as a "labyrinth" ($\lambda\alpha\beta\upsilon'\rho\iota\nu\theta o\varsigma$).[2] Though this structure is believed to have been reduced to ruins during the Roman era, independent reports from other classical authors, such as Strabo (c. 23 CE), Diodorus (c. 30 BCE), and Pliny (c. 79 CE), confirm the former existence and complexity of this ancient monument (Matthews 1922).

An apparent paradox, however, is how the unicursal passage shown in figure 4.1, in which it is impossible to become lost, became associated with the confusion of the Egyptian labyrinth and Daedalus's creation, both of which are clearly implied to be multicursal. There are competing theories here. Kern (2000) suggests that the unicursal design conforms to the steps of an intricate ancient dance that might in turn be inspired by the apparent wanderings of the planets in the sky. (The word *planet* actually means "wanderer.") Another theory is that the unicursal labyrinth, with its surprising twists and turns, is a metaphor for the confusing passageways found in the Egyptian temple and the Palace of Knossos, and more abstractly for the unpredictability of one's future. Thus, the Cretan labyrinth may be the simplest possible two-dimensional representation of indeterminacy and uncertainty.

The design of the Cretan labyrinth was also celebrated in ancient India. The epic poem "Mahabharata," perhaps the longest poem ever written, describes an ancient war between two families: the Pandavas and the Kauravas. The narrative mentions a specific military formation, called a *chakravyuha*, in which soldiers arrange themselves in a spiral around their leader for his protection. The chakravyuha is depicted in much Indian art as a modified Cretan labyrinth that is augmented with a spiral around the center. The shape is also placed at the entrances of houses as a charm to repel evil spirits. The Cretan labyrinth also appears in Indian manuscripts as a charm to reduce the pain associated with childbirth (Kern 2000).

Learning activity 4.1 provides an opportunity for students to use technology to discover the distribution of Cretan labyrinths around the world, and their cultural significance in different historical eras. For secondary classrooms, the books by Kern (2000) and Matthews (1922)[3] are valuable supplements.

Algorithms That Generate Cretan Labyrinths

Learning activity 4.2 is more challenging than it first appears.[4] Why is it easier to recall a spiral (see figure 4.2) or a set of a dozen concentric circles than the Cretan labyrinth (see figure 4.1)? The answer may be that the labyrinth has a greater degree of complexity than the other objects, and simpler things are easier to memorize than complex ones. (For example, it is easier to memorize a five-digit zip code than the first 15 digits of π.) Information storage and retrieval is a common and important computational task for both humans and machines. Although memorization by rote alone does not promote conceptual understanding (Hilgard, Irvine, and Whipple 1953; Katona 1940; Simon and Newell 1971), the challenge to memorize may inspire students to discover patterns, concepts, and abstractions. For example, the task of memorizing a 12-by-12 multiplication table with 144 entries is initially daunting. However, once students discover patterns in the values (e.g., the symmetry induced by the commutative property, the simple rules for multiplying numbers by 1, 2, 5, 9, and 10), the task becomes feasible. Conceptual abstraction is an important step in learning (Bransford, Brown, and Cocking 2000; Papert 1980; Sousa 2016).

Learning Activity 4.2: Redrawing the Labyrinth—Take 1

This activity helps demonstrate the need for an algorithm in order to create this labyrinth.

- Give each student a sheet of unruled paper.
- Project an image of the Cretan labyrinth (see figure 4.1) for one minute.
- Invite your students to study and remember the labyrinth's shape, without writing notes, in order to redraw it.
- Then turn off the projector. Ask your students to replicate the design from memory.
- Afterward, ask your students the following questions: "What strategy did you apply to redraw the labyrinth?," "Was it successful or not, and why?," and "What was difficult about redrawing the figure?"

Abstraction is also an essential component of computational thinking (Wing 2006, 2008). It can be a filtering process, where one selectively discards bits of information deemed to be irrelevant for the task at hand. Only essential information is retained. For example, Roger Tory Peterson developed a system for identifying birds and other forms of wildlife that uses a minimal set of *field marks* that distinguish each animal species from the others (Peterson 2008). Alternatively, abstraction can be a recognition process, where one discovers common features and the relationships between them. (We will return to this approach when we study mazes later in the chapter.) Abstraction can also lead to algorithmic representations, which are often simple to recall. An example of the latter is the algorithm used to tie one's shoelaces. Collectively, these different views of abstractions are conceptual precursors to the data structures and algorithms on which computer programs are based. However, they are also valuable problem-solving tools in their own right.

We now apply these ideas to show how to draw a Cretan labyrinth on demand. The easiest method reduces the Cretan labyrinth to a small set of *features*, a *kernel*. The full design then emerges from the kernel as one applies a simple algorithm, demonstrated in algorithm 4.1. Schuster and Carpenter (1996) speculate that different cultures around the world have used it for millennia.

Algorithm 4.1: How to Draw a Cretan Labyrinth

Procure a blank sheet of paper and a pencil.
1. Below the center of the page, draw the seed, or kernel, of the labyrinth, as shown in step 1 in figure 4.6. The kernel consists of a cross, four quarter circles (each placed in a quadrant of the cross), and four points, each placed in the center of each quarter circle. (You should practice so you can draw the kernel from memory.) The latter four points, plus the four endpoints of the cross and the eight endpoints of the quarter circles, define 16 *features* that will serve as anchor points for eight arcs, which are drawn in steps 3 through 9.
2. Connect the upper end of the cross with the upper-right endpoint of the upper-left quarter circle, as shown by the small red "frown" in step 2 of figure 4.6.
3–9. For each remaining step, identify the uppermost pair of unused anchor points, one from the right side of the figure and one from the left side, and then connect each pair with a circular arc that extends above the drawing, shown as a red arc in each step of figure 4.6.

Note that the kernel (step 1 in figure 4.6) is easy to remember because of its four-fold symmetry. Because steps 3–9 are iterated in sequence, one arc being drawn after the other, this kind of algorithm possesses what is called an *iterative* structure. Once your students have practiced the algorithm and memorized the kernel, they can be asked to draw the "seven-circuit" labyrinth, as described in learning activity 4.3. The relative ease of this second effort should be a compelling justification for the use of abstraction as a cognitive method. The appendix includes a computer program, written in Processing, that draws a seven-circuit Cretan labyrinth on a computer screen (see appendix A.1). The program draws the elements of the labyrinth in a different manner, after the design has been decomposed into a family of semicircles, quarter circles, and the central cross.

1.

2.

3.

4.

5.

6.

7.

8.

9.

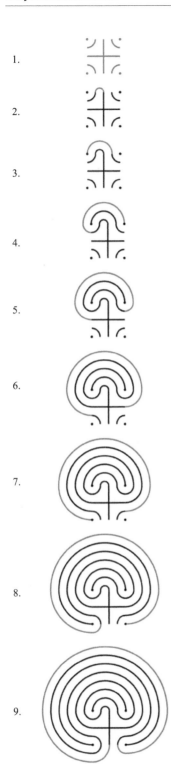

Figure 4.6
A nine-step algorithm for generating a Cretan labyrinth with pencil and paper. The new elements to be drawn in each step are highlighted in red (Schuster and Carpenter 1996).

The result of this process is technically called a "seven-circuit" Cretan labyrinth because the maze walker crosses the labyrinth's medial axis[5] seven times while walking from the entrance to the goal (see figure 4.7). In summary, the Cretan labyrinth is a simple design described by a kernel with fourfold symmetry followed by the construction of eight parallel arcs. A fundamental principle of computer science is that no object, or dataset, is more complex than the simplest algorithm that generates it.[6]

The drawing algorithm 4.1 can be modified in several interesting ways. First, if in step 2 one connects the upper endpoint of the cross with the upper endpoint of the upper-right quarter circle, then, after following the remaining steps, one generates the mirror image of figure 4.1. Alternatively, by omitting the four quarter circles in step 1, the subsequent steps generate a *three*-circuit Cretan labyrinth. Next, for variety, add an extra set of quarter circles to the kernel in step 1 to obtain an 11-circuit Cretan labyrinth (see figure 4.8). Finally, replacing the original quarter circles by right angles, with sides parallel to the arms of the cross, yields the rectangular Cretan labyrinth (see figure 4.5). Learning activity 4.4 helps students learn this algorithm in greater depth.

The 9-step algorithm for constructing the labyrinth provides a scaffold for building it. Scaffolds are pedagogical techniques used to teach children to build on knowledge from an already created schema, such as adding multidigit numbers using their addition facts, tying their shoes, or pronouncing new multisyllable words by using phonetic recall of simpler words. Simplifying a complex problem by breaking it into pieces or steps stands on its own as an important principle of computational thinking, called *divide and conquer*. Usage of divide and conquer accelerates the completion of many tasks, especially those that involve large amounts of data. Another everyday application occurs when one presorts the pieces of a jigsaw puzzle into separate heaps according to the pattern printed on the piece or by the presence of a straight edge, indicating that it belongs on the boundary of the assembled puzzle.

Figure 4.7
A seven-circuit Cretan labyrinth with passages numbered as they are visited. The kernel of the labyrinth is highlighted in red.

Figure 4.8
An 11-circuit Cretan labyrinth, with the kernel highlighted in red.

Path Length Estimation

The next activity focuses on how to measure the length traversed in a labyrinth. All that is required is a meter stick and some yarn. Measuring the lengths of straight line segments with a ruler or meter stick appears in the second-grade *Common Core State Standards for Mathematics* (CCSSI 2010); computing the circumference of a circle appears in the seventh-grade standards. Length estimation and measurement are important practical applications of mathematical knowledge. The extension of these concepts to curved paths (and trajectories) is a challenging topic that many students will encounter in calculus and physics. The seventh-grade Common Core requirements can be augmented with methods for measuring the lengths for different paths. In this context, we are interested in measuring the path length of the Cretan labyrinth. We present several direct and indirect methods for doing this:

1. Inspired by the myth of Theseus and Ariadne, one might place one end of a strand of yarn at the labyrinth's entrance, curl it through the design, and mark the point on the yarn that touches the center. (It might help to pin the drawing to a corkboard and use additional pushpins to fix each turn of the yarn.) Then remove the yarn and use a meter stick to measure the linear distance between the beginning of the strand and the mark that corresponds to the labyrinth's center. A similar method might be used to measure the circumference of a circle.

2. The drawing of the Cretan labyrinth in figure 4.1 was generated by assembling the central cross, 10 semicircles, and 10 quarter circles of various radii with respect to five different centers: the four points that belong to the kernel and the center of the goal. Using the formula for the circumference of a circle ($C = 2\pi r$), students can determine the lengths of the walls that delineate the path through the labyrinth. (Don't neglect the lengths of the central cross.) Once the dimensions of the walls have been computed, the distance of the path will be bounded between two lengths: the sum of the lengths of inner walls around each twist and turn and the sum of the lengths of the outer walls. One can then estimate the path length by computing the average of these two numbers.

3. An alternative indirect method estimates the same length as a ratio of the total area of the labyrinth to the passage width. This "area method" is best understood with the aid of a rectangular Cretan labyrinth drawn on graph paper, as shown in figure 4.9. In this figure, the labyrinth is 13 units high and 15 units wide, so the area of the smallest enclosing rectangle equals $A = 13 \times 15 = 195$ square units. A maze walker would need to step through all but seven of the enclosed squares to reach the center. (We ignore this discrepancy for now.) If the total area A is divided by the path width of $w = 1$ unit distance (u.d.), we obtain an estimate of the total path length:

$$L = \frac{A}{w} = \frac{195\,(\text{u.d.})^2}{1\,\text{u.d.}} = 195\,\text{u.d.}$$

(The actual path distance traveled also depends on the widths of the turns taken by the maze walker around each corner. Here we assume each corner turn proceeds through the path center.)

This value can also be verified by counting the squares inside the labyrinth: each interior square contributes 1 unit distance to the path length. (This estimate is actually 7 units too large, because of the difference in area between the smallest enclosing rectangle and the area enclosed by the labyrinth, shaded in orange in figure 4.9.) This method can also be applied to labyrinths with different geometries.

For a circular version of the Cretan labyrinth, one might attempt to circumscribe the design by the smallest enclosing circle. The construction in figure 4.10 suggests that the diameter D of the enclosing circle is approximately 15 path widths; that is, $D \approx 15w$. Thus, the area of the pink circle is approximately

$$A = \pi \left(\frac{D}{2}\right)^2 = \pi \frac{225w^2}{4} \approx 177w^2.$$

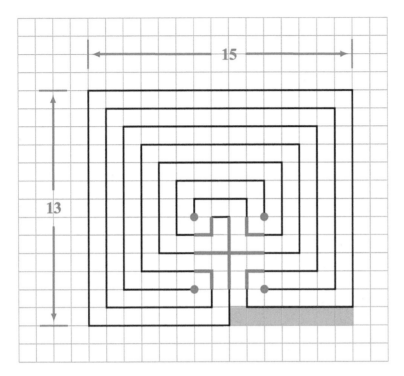

Figure 4.9
Estimating the path length of a rectangular Cretan labyrinth.

If we neglect the area of the portion of the pink circle that lies outside the labyrinth (near the entrance), the area enclosed by the path, $A = wL$, should equal that of the circle. Hence,

$$L \approx \frac{A}{w} = 177w.$$

However, because we did not subtract the area near the entrance and did not account for the nonuniform width of the path around the central cross, this estimate should be regarded as an upper bound of the actual path length.

4. For a life-size example, construct a Cretan labyrinth on the playground and apply learning activity 4.5.

4.2 Roman Labyrinths

Students of European history learn that the Roman civilization celebrated many of the same gods and heroes as the ancient Greeks, including the legend of Theseus, Ariadne, and the Minotaur. In Roman art, however, Daedalus's labyrinth was most often presented in square or rectangular form, on a larger scale. Approximately 50 examples survive to the present day (Kern 2000, 85). Most exist as decorative floor mosaics distributed throughout the Mediterranean region, Gaul (France), and Great Britain. Although they are inlaid into floors, the passage widths are usually too narrow

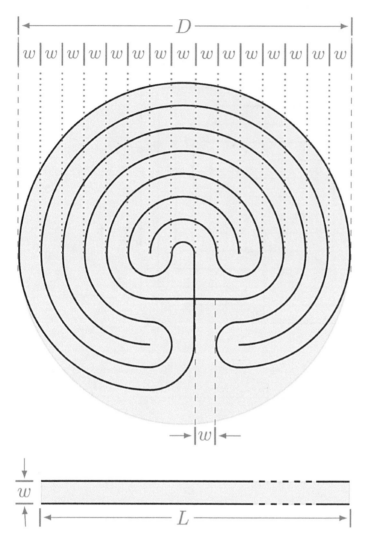

Figure 4.10
The "area method" for path length estimation, applied to a circular, seven-circuit Cretan labyrinth. The pink region indicates the smallest circle that encloses the labyrinth. The area of the circle is approximately the same as the total area enclosed by the path. The latter can be represented as an elongated rectangle of width w and length L, shown in the lower figure.

for human traffic. Figure 4.11 depicts a typical unicursal Roman design copied from a mosaic in Cremona, Italy, c. 50 CE. (The original mosaic depicts a heroic image of Theseus slaying the Minotaur in the labyrinth's center.) Most Roman labyrinths are subdivided into four quadrants, like this one. Here, the entrance leads directly into the first quadrant. Only after the path has covered every unit of area in the first quadrant does it progress to the second and so on.

The designs of the second and third quadrants are nearly rotational copies of the first. The fourth quadrant, however, breaks the symmetry with a subtle twist that is required for the path to reach the center. (Ask your students to find it.)

> **Learning Activity 4.5: Drawing a Large Labyrinth and Estimating Its Path Length**
>
> Take your class outside with a box of sidewalk chalk.
>
>   As a group, construct a large, seven-circuit Cretan labyrinth (e.g., about 30 feet in diameter) with passages wide enough to walk through. Ask the students to predict how many steps are required for a designated maze walker to reach the center and invite them to take turns traversing the path.

Although less common, there exist examples of Roman labyrinths that are contained within circular boundaries. These designs were also usually based on four quadrants, with the unicursal path running from one quadrant to the next in essentially the same manner.

Labyrinths played other roles in Roman culture. In *The Aeneid*,[7] the poet Virgil describes an elaborate sequence of games that Aeneas hosts on the island of Sicily in memory of his deceased father, Anchises. The final game consists of a mock battle between the sons of the nobility, mounted on horseback:

> So complex the labyrinth once in hilly Crete, they say,
> where the passage wove between blind walls and wavered on
> in numberless cunning paths that broke down every clue,
> with nothing to trace and no way back—a baffling maze.
> Complex as the course the sons of Troy now follow, weaving
> their way through mock escapes and clashes all in sport
> as swiftly as frisky dolphins skim the rolling surf,
> cleaving the Libyan or Carpathian seas in play.
>
> Virgil (2006), *The Aeneid*, book V, lines 649–654

This *Lusus Trojae*, or Trojan ride, was a traditional rite of passage for the sons of Roman nobles that was practiced as early as c. 80 BCE, as confirmed by other Roman works, such as Suetonius's *The Lives of the Caesars* (Doob 1990). Kern (2000) speculates that the ceremony was precisely choreographed so that each horse and rider followed a prescribed labyrinthine path that was traced on the ground.

4.3   Christian Labyrinths

A remarkable change in labyrinth design occurred in the ninth century as labyrinths were adopted as a Christian symbol. The "Jericho labyrinth" depicts a seven-circuit, square Cretan labyrinth symbolizing the Battle of Jericho. Perhaps the seven circuits of the design provided a meaningful symbol for the seven laps that were taken around this city:

> And it came to pass on the seventh day, that they rose early at the dawning of the day, and compassed the city after the same manner seven times; only on that day they compassed the city seven times. And it came to pass at the seventh time, when the priests blew with the horns, that Joshua said unto the people: "Shout; for the Lord hath given you the city."
>
> Joshua 6:15–16

Prior to the ninth century, Cretan labyrinths appeared in stone, floor mosaics, and on the backside of coins. The "Jericho labyrinth," however, was drawn with pen and ink

Figure 4.11
The layout of the Roman labyrinth found in the Villa Cadolini in Cremona, Italy, c. 50 CE. Here, the passages are colored to help visualize the order in which each quadrant is visited—(1) blue, (2) green, (3) yellow, (4) pink—and the approximate symmetry of the first three quadrants. Note that paths in the darker shade are traversed before the lighter ones. Note also that the structure of the fourth quadrant differs significantly from the preceding three.

on parchment. This labyrinth was actually drawn on one page of a larger devotional book called a *computus* (Latin for computation), in which priests would compute the dates for Easter in the current and future years. Parchment was a scarce resource, so computuses often contained more than just computations; priests also used them to pen devotional writings, annals, and occasionally a labyrinth, which became a Christian symbol.

During the ninth century, the design of labyrinths that were drawn in computuses evolved to become the circular, 11-circuit design that appears in figure 4.12. The earliest known example might be a drawing in a computus found in the monastery of St.-Germain-des-Prés in Paris, which places Satan, instead of the Minotaur, in the labyrinth's center (Kern 2000, 112). Like Roman labyrinths, its design is partitioned into quadrants. However, the path enters and exits each quadrant before all 11 circuits are encompassed. The lower two quadrants are actually visited three times during the entire traversal, while the upper two are each visited four times. Although the meanderings appear chaotic, there is a subtle symmetry present: the first half of the traversal is an inversion of the second half. Consequently, the turns taken when leaving the labyrinth from the center are taken in exactly the same order and direction as when entering the labyrinth from the entrance.

The passing of the first millennium was accompanied by a fervent rise in religiosity that is reflected in the erection of elaborate cathedrals in the High Gothic style. The flying buttress as an architectural innovation enabled towering structures. The loads were transferred laterally, so the supporting walls could now include large windows

Figure 4.12
A Christian labyrinth based on the design at Chartres Cathedral. Each quadrant is colored in a manner similar to that in figure 4.11.

of stained glass. The architects of the age were likely proud of their achievement, and some incorporated labyrinths into their designs, perhaps with association to Daedalus. These church labyrinths often were inlaid into the pavement. Surviving examples can be found in France (Arras, Bayeaux, and Chartres) and Italy (Lucca and Ravenna). Fascinating information about the history and significance of Christian labyrinths is presented in Wright (2001).

> **Learning Activity 4.6: Estimating Path Lengths (continued)**
>
> Apply the area algorithm to estimate the path length of the Cremona labyrinth (see figure 4.11) and the Chartres labyrinth (see figure 4.12).

4.4 Mazes

The earliest known examples of *multicursal* mazes are three drawings on parchment by Giovanni Fontana, a Venetian doctor, c. 1420 (Kern 2000, 138–139). Two display a circular design, one with seven circuits and the other with 10; the other maze is rectangular. What distinguishes these drawings is the innovative use of junctions (or branches). Moreover, the inscriptions on some of the drawings suggest that the purpose of each drawing was for entertainment. Fontana may well be the inventor of the maze as a puzzle. Mazes subsequently became more secular, appearing in drawings, woodcuts, and formal gardens.

In subsequent subsections, we will explore how principles of computational thinking can be used to thread mazes of arbitrary complexity. Before proceeding, it is helpful to note that each maze we consider includes the following features:

1. A single *entrance*.
2. A single *goal*.
3. One or more *junctions*, where three or more paths merge.
4. An arbitrary number of *dead ends*.

Learning Activity 4.7: Maze Recognition

Ask your students to label a variety of mazes (see figure 4.20) using the four-color scheme used in figure 4.13. This exercise will help them develop pattern recognition skills and will aid in subsequent activities.

(It is certainly possible to design mazes with multiple goals and entrances, and the methods that we describe can be applied to these variations. However, to simplify the discussion, we do not consider them here.) Figure 4.13 identifies each type of feature by using colored circles. Note that this maze has eight junctions (labeled in blue) and six dead ends (labeled in red). It is important that students be able to recognize these features in other mazes before proceeding.

We view the process of threading the maze as a *computational process*. In this context, each feature represents a *decision point* in the computation. By this, we mean that a certain action must be taken when the "maze walker" (or *agent*) arrives at each feature. Specifically, the entrance (marked with a green circle) in figure 4.13 represents the initial state of the computation. Here, the decision is whether to begin or wait. Once the computation begins, the agent enters the maze and proceeds along the initial passage to the next decision point. Marching forward, the agent reaches the first junction (labeled with a blue circle immediately above the entrance). Junctions are the most important decision points. At each junction, the agent must decide which branch to follow next. The number of choices corresponds to the number of paths that meet. We will call this number the *degree* of the junction. In this example, the current junction has degree 3, and thus the agent can either (1) turn left, (2) turn right, or (3) turn completely around and exit the maze. If the agent were to turn left, it would follow

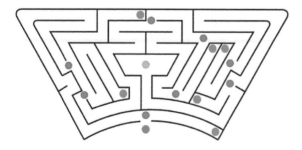

Figure 4.13
The maze at Hampton Court, with prominent features (decision points) highlighted: the entrance in green, junctions in blue, dead ends in red, and the goal in gold.

a twisty path and arrive at a new junction, also of degree 3. If instead the agent turns right, then it follows a curved path along the lower edge of the maze. This path leads to a dead end, indicated by a red circle. Each dead end is also a decision point: either the agent turns around and *backtracks* to the previous junction or remains there. The last type of decision point is the goal. Here the agent stops (or celebrates) and the computation terminates.

Thus, the act of solving every maze (indeed every puzzle under the sun) is akin to executing a computer program. Let's explore different algorithms for threading a maze.

Random Walk

The random walk (algorithm 4.2) is the simplest algorithm for solving any finite maze. By the laws of probability, it is guaranteed to deliver the agent to the goal.

Algorithm 4.2: Random Walk

Perform the following actions until the goal is reached:
1. If the agent is at the entrance, then enter (or reenter) the maze and proceed until the next decision point is reached.
2. If the agent arrives at a dead end, then turn around and return to the previous decision point.
3. If the agent arrives at a junction, choose a branch at random and proceed to the next decision point.

Learning Activity 4.8: Threading a Maze with a Random Walk

Ask your students to apply the random walk algorithm to the Hampton Court maze, using a board game token to indicate the current location of the agent. The roll of a six-sided die can simulate the random choice in step 3: for example, for junctions of degree 3, let the agent turn left if the roll is 1 or 2; turn right if the roll is 3 or 4; and turn completely around, returning to the previous decision point, if the roll is 5 or 6. With one token for each student, the simulation turns into a competitive race game.

Unfortunately, the random walk algorithm is not very efficient, as it may send the agent back and forth along the same paths many times before deciding to discover an unexplored region of the maze.

Wall Following

Wall following is a simple computational process: the only interesting decision occurs in step 1. The act of following a wall around a dead end performs the desired action of turning the agent around and backtracking. Also, the algorithm (algorithm 4.3) ensures that no path is traversed more than once in the same direction, an efficiency improvement over the random walk algorithm. However, wall following is only guaranteed to succeed for a certain type of maze. To see this, let's examine the *counterexample* shown in figure 4.14. If the agent were to follow the right wall as it entered the maze, then it would follow a counterclockwise circuit along the rectangular boundary of the maze, return to the entrance, and then exit the maze before discovering the goal. (What would happen if it followed the left wall instead?)

Learning Activity 4.9: Threading a Maze by Wall Following

Ask your students to apply the wall following algorithm to the Hampton Court maze. Does the algorithm work for this maze? How does the algorithm differ if the right wall is followed rather than the left?

The maze in figure 4.14 is an example of what we might call a *disconnected maze*: one in which it is possible to draw a closed loop that contains some passages but does not intersect any walls. If a maze is disconnected, then wall following may not work. Figure 4.15 demonstrates that the maze in figure 4.14 is disconnected, as the blue dashed loop separates the goal from the entrance without crossing any interior walls.

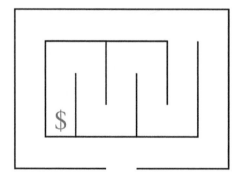

Figure 4.14
A maze that stymies the wall following algorithm, where the $ symbol is provided to represent the goal of the maze.

Learning Activity 4.10: Maze Classification

Ask your students to answer the following question: "Is the Hampton Court maze connected or disconnected?" It turns out that it is indeed disconnected, but wall following works anyway because both the goal and the entrance are exterior to the loop that disconnects this maze. Thus, wall following works sometimes if a maze is disconnected.

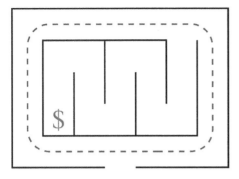

Figure 4.15
The dashed loop demonstrates how the maze in figure 4.14 is disconnected.

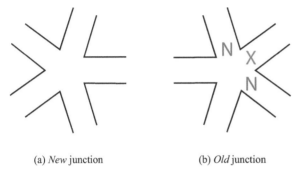

(a) *New* junction   (b) *Old* junction

Figure 4.16
(a) Since this five-way junction has no labels on its threshold, it has not yet been visited. It is therefore classified as a *new* junction. (b) This five-way junction has been visited twice, as is evident by the presence of two Ns on its thresholds. It is therefore classified as an *old* junction. Note also that every old junction contains exactly one threshold with an X, which denotes the path by which the agent arrived during its initial visit.

Trémaux's Algorithm

An efficient algorithm that will enable an autonomous agent to thread any maze is a valuable tool. According to Édouard Lucas (1891), an answer was discovered by Charles Pierre Trémaux, a nineteenth-century French engineer. In order to apply this algorithm (algorithm 4.4), we assume that the agent can place marks or labels in the maze. Since the junctions represent the significant decision points in solving the puzzle, we should only need to mark the ends of the passages where they meet a junction.

Here we follow Even (1979) and adopt two distinct symbols: N for new and X for exit. Labels are applied at a junction only by the agent, as the junction is visited. It is important to stress that when applying the algorithm, every junction that is visited will have exactly *one* path that is labeled with an X; no more, no less. Junctions that have no labels are said to be *new*; those with two or more labels are said to be *old* (as seen in figure 4.16). In addition to the labels, the agent is required to maintain one bit of memory: it must remember whether it is *advancing* or *backtracking*.

Before   After

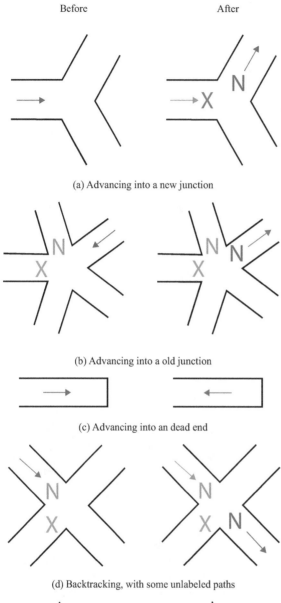

(a) Advancing into a new junction

(b) Advancing into a old junction

(c) Advancing into an dead end

(d) Backtracking, with some unlabeled paths

Figure 4.17
Applying the labels at path thresholds by using Trémaux's algorithm. In each pair of illustrations, the left drawing displays the state of the junction immediately before the agent has arrived and the right drawing shows the state immediately after the agent has moved onward. Green arrows indicate where the agent is advancing; red arrows indicate where the agent is backtracking.

(e) Backtracking, with no unlabeled paths

Algorithm 4.4: Trémaux's Algorithm

1. Enter the maze and *advance* to the next decision point.
2. Until the goal is reached, perform the following actions at each decision point:
   a. If the agent *advances* into a *new* junction, then
      i. Place an X at the end of the current passage;
      ii. Select a new path; place an N at its entrance; and
      iii. *Advance* to the next decision point (figure 4.17(a)).
   b. If the agent *advances* into an *old* junction, then
      i. Place an N at the end of the current passage;
      ii. Turn around; and
      iii. *Backtrack* (figure 4.17(b)).
   c. If the agent *advances* into a *dead end*, then
      i. Turn around; and
      ii. *Backtrack* (figure 4.17(c)).
   d. If the agent *backtracks* into an *old* junction with one or more unlabeled paths, then
      i. Select a new (unlabeled) path;
      ii. Place an N at its entrance; and
      iii. *Advance* to the next decision point (figure 4.17(d)).
   e. If the agent *backtracks* into an *old* junction with no unlabeled passages, then
      i. Select the path that is labeled with an X.
      ii. *Backtrack* (figure 4.17(e)).
   f. If the agent exits the maze through the original entrance, then give up. The goal cannot be reached.

Trémaux's algorithm takes some practice to learn and requires care and discipline. Consequently, we present a variety of learning activities here. Be aware that if the algorithm is not followed exactly, then, at best, extra exploration may be required. At worst, the goal will not be found. The essential steps are shown in figure 4.17. In each part, the left drawing shows the state of a decision point (junction or dead end) immediately *before* the agent arrives; the right drawing shows the state of the decision point immediately *after* the required actions are executed. Green arrows (vectors) indicate the location and orientation when the agent is advancing (marching in the direction of the arrow) and red arrows show the same when the agent is backtracking. As noted, two kinds of marks are used to record the decisions made so far. (The marks enable the agent to avoid unnecessary traversals. At a maximum, each path is traversed once in each direction.) Each old junction (one that was visited earlier in the process) has exactly one threshold labeled with an X and one or more labeled with an N. Steps 2a, 2c, 2d, and 2e are usually easy to learn. Step 2b, however, is tricky, and many students have difficulty adhering to it because the temptation to select an unlabeled path is, unfortunately, strong. Another common error is to place a second X at the exit of the current path instead of an N. Remind your students that exactly one X is allowed at each junction.

Steps 2a and 2d require that the agent select an unlabeled path for subsequent exploration. Since the choice of this path is arbitrary so long as it is unlabeled, there are often many orders in which the different parts of a maze can be visited. In certain circumstances, one might desire that the maze be explored in a consistent way. In order to accomplish this, we define an agent to be *right bearing* if it always selects the rightmost choice that is available. Similarly, we define an agent to be *left bearing* if it always selects the leftmost option available. Figure 4.19 shows the markings that a right-bearing agent inscribes at each threshold as it begins threading a given maze with Trémaux's algorithm. Because of space limitations, only marks for the first half of the algorithm are shown. A complete history is presented in a more compressed form in figure 4.18.

We recommend that the algorithm be learned in phases, first with paper and pencil exercises (learning activity 4.11) and then in a gymnasium or on a playground using mazes constructed with painter's tape or sidewalk chalk (learning activity 4.12). Finally, if possible, we recommend that you take your class on a field trip to a life-size or corn maze in your area (learning activity 4.13).

Learning Activity 4.11: Trémaux with Paper

Practice Trémaux's algorithm in small groups, with mazes on paper and colored markers. Additional examples of mazes are available in the online resources. For extra practice, encourage your students to create their own mazes and then trade copies of them with other students.

Learning Activity 4.12: Threading Minimazes

Minimazes (seen in figure 4.20) are mazes with a small number of decision points but are still interesting for practicing algorithm 4.4. Each minimaze can be re-created on a gymnasium floor with painter's tape or outside using sidewalk chalk. Each maze can fit in a 12 foot × 12 foot area with passages 2 feet wide. Snapp and Neumann (2015) describe a simple game that students can play to help them learn the finer points of Trémaux's algorithm using embodied learning.

Learning Activity 4.13: Field Trip to a Life-Size Maze

Practice Trémaux's algorithm in a life-size maze (such as a corn maze). Here, marks can be inscribed into the earth at the path ends by using a stick or sharp rock. It is helpful for you to divide your class into groups of four to six. To minimize confusion, each group should choose a unique pair of marks to use in place of N and X.

Trémaux's algorithm is an example of what computer scientists call a *depth-first search*. In the following subsection, we will see that this algorithm can be applied to a wide variety of puzzles and other problems, not just mazes.

Other Algorithms

There are two other maze-threading algorithms to use:

- Tarry's (1895) algorithm is a variant of Trémaux's algorithm that relies on three symbols instead of two. It can be elegantly implemented using pebbles.
- The *breadth-first search* algorithm developed by Moore (1959) extends the work of Bellman (1958) and Ford (1956) to find the path through the maze that uses the fewest junctions or the shortest path length.

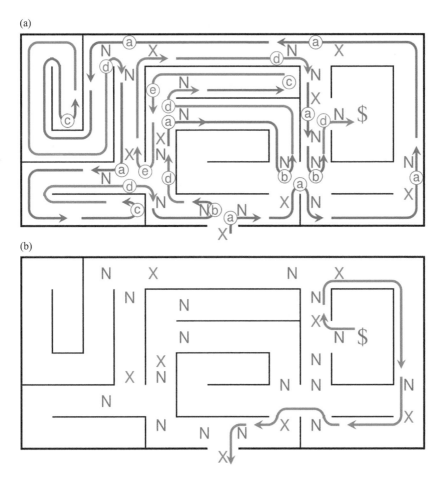

Figure 4.18
A demonstration of Trémaux's algorithm on a challenging maze, where the $ marks the goal of the maze.

(a) The path followed by a right-bearing agent is represented by a sequence of colored arrows: green arrows correspond to forward movement, red arrows to backtracking. Each decision point is labeled with a letter a through e inside a circle, in accordance with the case applied in step 2 and illustrated in figure 4.17. The symbols that the agent draws in each threshold (X and N) are also shown.

(b) After the agent has arrived at the goal, it can efficiently return to the entrance by selecting the path labeled with an X at each junction.

4.5 Graph Theory

In chapter 3, graphs were introduced as an abstraction for representing social networks and analyzing the relationships of characters in fictional works. In this section, we develop this abstraction further in the context of mazes and combinatorial puzzles. Expressing mazes in the language of graphs enables one to extend Trémaux's elegant algorithm, also known as a *depth-first search*, to a wide range of problems. Variations of this algorithm are employed by Google for crawling through the World Wide Web as indexes of websites are constructed and ranked for their search engine.

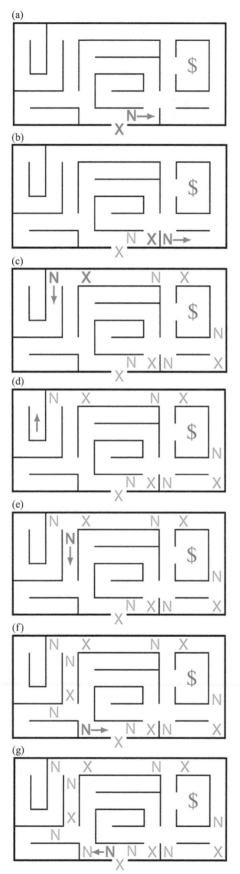

Figure 4.19

An example of Trémaux's algorithm with a right-bearing agent. A $ symbol is provided to represent the goal of the maze.

(a) The agent enters the maze and applies step 2a.

(b) Step 2a is applied at the six-way junction.

(c) Step 2a is applied three more times.

(d) Step 2c is applied at the first dead end encountered.

(e) Step 2d is applied, as one path was unlabeled.

(f) Steps 2a, 2c, and 2d are repeatedly applied to help solve the maze.

(g) Step 2b is applied, turning the agent around and backtracking.

Figure 4.20
Seven different "minimazes" for practicing Trémaux's algorithm. See learning activity 4.12.

In order for this section to be self-contained, we restate the essential definitions and concepts. Computation depends on data, meaning information, which can appear in many forms. For efficiency and ease of interpretation, it is helpful to collect this information in a few standard structures, or "containers." The simplest structure is a *set*, which mathematicians define as a collection of objects without any order and without repetition. Sets containing numbers are common in mathematics. Small sets of numbers are denoted using curly braces. For example, the set of odd natural numbers less than 6 can be written as {1, 3, 5}. The values 1, 3, and 5 are called the *elements*, or *members*, of this set. Since a set is an *unordered* collection, the same set could be written as {3, 5, 1}, {5, 3, 1}, and other combinations. The collection {1, 1, 3, 5, 5} is not a set, because the elements 1 and 5 are repeated. (Such a collection is called a *multiset*.) Sets are valuable because they are abstract. A set can be an unordered collection of *anything*: points on a plane, fictional characters, US presidents, countries, cities, postage stamps, pizza toppings, ice cream flavors, soft drink brands, chess pieces, English words, and so on. We often use a capital letter to denote a set, such as $A = \{1, 3, 5\}$, and the notation $5 \in A$ to indicate that "5 is an element of A." The number of elements contained in a set is called its *size*, or *cardinality*, which is denoted using two vertical bars; for example, $|A| = 3$, because A contains three elements. The set with zero elements, denoted by $\emptyset$ or { }, is called the *empty set*. Computer scientists and mathematicians use symbols in blackboard bold font to describe sets of basic numbers: $\mathbb{N} = \{0, 1, 2, \ldots\}$ denotes the *natural numbers*,[8] $\mathbb{Z} = \{\ldots, -1, 0, 1, \ldots\}$ the *integers*, $\mathbb{Q} = \{n/d : n, d \in \mathbb{Z}, d \neq 0\}$ the *rational numbers*, and $\mathbb{R}$, the real numbers.

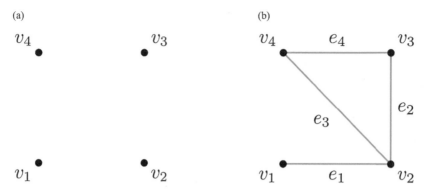

Figure 4.21
A depiction of a graph $G = (V, E)$ that consists of four vertices and four edges.

(a)   A set $V = \{v_1, v_2, v_3, v_4\}$ of four vertices.

(b)   The graph $G = (V, E)$ consists of a set V (see (a)) with a set of edges E. Here, $E = \{(v_1, v_2), (v_2, v_3), (v_2, v_4), (v_3, v_4)\}$.

Learning Activity 4.14: Learning about Graphs

Each student is given plain paper and a box of crayons or colored pencils. Ask the students to perform the following sequence of actions:

1. Draw a red vertex (dot) somewhere on your paper.
2. Draw a green vertex, a brown vertex, and a blue vertex.
3. Connect the green vertex and the blue vertex with an orange edge.
4. Connect the blue vertex and the red vertex with a purple edge.
5. Connect the green vertex and the brown vertex with a black edge.
6. Compare your paper with your neighbor's. How are they similar? How are they different?

Sets are an important building block for other useful data structures. As an example, we define a *graph* as a pair of two sets (V, E). Here V denotes a set of vertices (e.g., points that represent an abstract set) and E denotes a set of edges (also called links or arcs) that connect pairs of vertices belonging to V. A simple example is shown in figure 4.21, where V consists of the four vertices v_1 through v_4, shown in figure 4.21(a), and E consists of the four edges, shown in figure 4.21(b), that connect the pairs (v_1, v_2), (v_2, v_3), (v_2, v_4), and (v_3, v_4). In this figure, the vertices and edges are abstract; they can mean almost anything. All that we have here are four things (represented by the vertices) and four relationships between pairs of things (represented by the edges). Each edge in particular defines an *adjacency* between a pair of vertices. Thus, in figure 4.21(b), vertices v_1 and v_2 are said to be *adjacent* because there exists an edge (i.e., e_1) that links them; likewise, v_1 and v_4 are *not* adjacent. An edge that connects to a certain vertex is said to be *incident* to that vertex. Likewise, the latter vertex is said to be *incident* to that edge. Thus, in figure 4.21(b), edge e_1 is incident to vertices v_1 and v_2, and vertex v_2 is incident to the edges labeled e_1, e_2, and e_3. The number of edges that are incident to a vertex defines its degree. Thus, the degree of v_2, written $d(v_2)$, equals 3. When drawing a graph, edges can be curved and can intersect at arbitrary points. If a graph can be drawn on a piece of paper such that its edges only meet at vertices, then that graph is said to be *planar*.

Because graph theory is so fundamental to computer science, we recommend that it be introduced in the earliest possible grade. Gibson (2012) provides a range of graduated activities geared to children from ages 5 through 17. Based on his study, we offer learning activity 4.14 as an introductory classroom exercise for learning about graphs as abstract structures.

Let's return to the maze at Hampton Court (see figure 4.13). We defined the concept of a decision point: a location in a maze where the agent determines what course to take next. Since the computational events are confined to these decision points, the shape and length of the intervening passages are irrelevant. Algorithm 4.5 presents an iterative procedure that converts a maze into an equivalent graph and learning activity 4.15 has students practice converting between a maze and a graph. Figure 4.22(a) shows the plan of the Hampton Court maze, which we assume is given.

Algorithm 4.5: Abstracting the Graph from a Given Maze

1. Identify each decision point in the maze (the entrance, the goal, the junctions, and the dead ends) and represent each by a vertex. (See figure 4.22(b).)
2. Decision points that delineate a common passage are said to be *adjacent*. Connect each pair of adjacent decision points with an arc (or edge) that conforms to the geometry of each passage. (See figure 4.22(c).)
3. Either erase the walls or imagine that they have disappeared. What remains is a graph where the decision points are its vertices and the twisty arcs are its edges. (See figure 4.22(d).)
4. Redraw the graph with simpler edges but such that all vertices and connections are preserved. (See figure 4.22(e).)

Learning Activity 4.15: Reducing Mazes to Graphs

Ask your students to reduce the maze in figure 4.18 to a graph. Conversely, give them a graph (e.g., figure 4.22(e)) and ask them to construct an equivalent maze.

The outcome of step 1 can depend on one's interpretation of the maze. For example, figure 4.23 shows a maze where four paths meet. The presence of the gap between each pair shown in (a) invites two possible interpretations: either this represents a pair of junctions, each of degree 3 (b), or a single junction of degree 4 (c). In the end, it may not matter, because the two interpretations are topologically distinct. In performing step 4, we chose to orient the edges relative to each vertex to parallel the orientation of the passages in the original maze relative to each junction. This is not necessary, but as we will see, doing so helps one visualize how paths in the graph (figure 4.22(e)) correspond to those in the maze (figure 4.22(c)).

Once the maze has been reduced to a graph, Trémaux's algorithm can be used to find a route from the entrance to the goal. The only difference is that the labels (X and N) that were placed on the threshold of each path are now placed near the ends of each edge. Figure 4.24 illustrates the outcome of Trémaux's algorithm when it is applied to the graph in figure 4.22(e) by both a left-bearing (figure 4.24(a)) and a right-bearing (figure 4.24(b)) agent. In this case, the left-bearing agent is slightly more efficient.

(a)

(b)

(c)

(d)

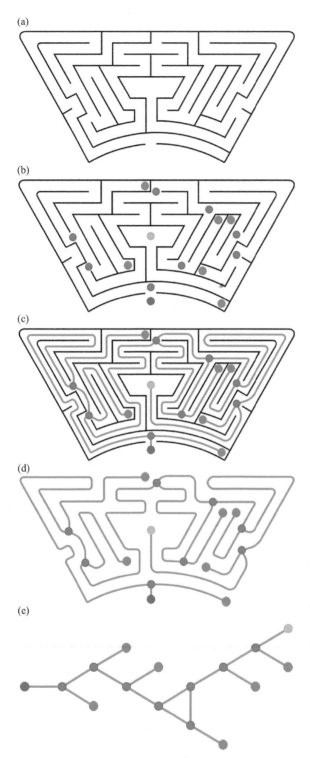

(e)

Figure 4.22
Constructing the graph that is
equivalent to the (a) Hampton
Court maze is a four-step process. First (b), the decision points
are identified (see figure 4.13).
Then (c), pairs of adjacent decision points are connected by arcs
defined by the passages. After the
walls are removed (d), the arcs are
simplified to obtain the equivalent graph in (e).

(a) Step 0: A given maze.
(b) Step 1: Label the decision
     points.
(c) Step 2: Connect adjacent
     decision points.
(d) Step 3: Remove the walls.
(e) Step 4: Normalize the graph.

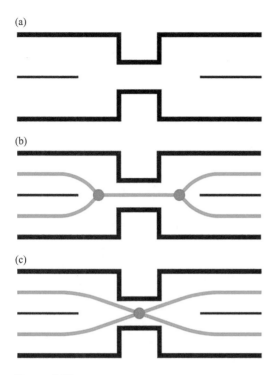

Figure 4.23
A junction with four or more passages can sometimes be interpreted in different ways.

(a) One or two junctions?
(b) Two-junction interpretation.
(c) One-junction interpretation.

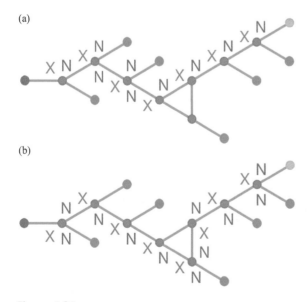

Figure 4.24
Two applications of Trémaux's algorithm to the graph of the Hampton Court maze.

(a) Labels generated by a left-bearing agent.
(b) Labels generated by a right-bearing agent.

It may not be obvious, but the application of Trémaux's algorithm (or any maze algorithm) to a graph is a moment of revelation: we have shown that an algorithm that solves a maze also solves its graph. Since the graph is an abstraction of the maze, solving the problem in the context of the graph is significantly more powerful, because it turns out that there are many similar problems that we would like to solve that can be reduced to graphs from contexts other than mazes. We illustrate this in section 4.6 with a famous example.

4.6 Solving Combinatorial Puzzles with Trémaux's Algorithm

Propositio de lupo et capra et fasciculo cauli:
    Homo quidam debebat ultra fluvium transferre lupum, capram, et fasciculum cauli. Et non potuit aliam navem invenire, nisi quae duos tantum ex ipsis ferre valebat. Praeceptum itaque ei fuerat ut omnia haec ultra illaesa omnino transferret. Dicat, qui potest, quomodo eis illaesis transire potuit.

Alcuin, *Propositiones ad acuendos juvenes* (c. 799)

So reads problem 18 (of 53) written by eighth-century Catholic monk and educator Alcuin of York, from his book of mathematical exercises, *Propositions to Sharpen the Young*. After his distinguished service as a scholar, pedagogue, and deacon, Alcuin was invited by Charlemagne in 781 to teach in a palace school in Aachen, and this book of problems is believed to be a textbook used for this purpose. Alcuin revived the instruction of liberal arts in Western education and was influential in developing the curriculum for the earliest European universities.

But let's return to problem 18 (of 53), which Hadley and Singmaster (1992) translate as

Proposition of a wolf, a goat and a bunch of cabbages:
    A man had to take a wolf, a goat and a bunch of cabbages across a river. The only boat he could find could only take two of them at a time. But he had been ordered to transfer all of these to the other side in good condition. How could this be done?

Here, the implication is that if the wolf and goat are left on the same side of the river and the man is on the other side, then the hungry wolf will devour the goat, and the game is lost. Likewise, the goat cannot be left unattended on the same side of the river as the cabbages because it will eat the cabbages. The puzzle can be solved empirically. Students might visualize the steps using five objects, to represent the man, the wolf, the goat, the cabbages, and the boat. However, we will demonstrate how the principles of computational thinking that we have developed provide a systematic solution to the problem.

First, we use logic to simplify the problem slightly: since the boat can only be navigated by the man, we can always assume that the boat and the man are always on the same side of the river. Thus, there are only four independent entities here: the man (M), the wolf (W), the goat (G), and the cabbages (C).

Every feasible computation we perform is a process that is defined over a set of discrete states. In the example of a maze, the states are defined by the decision points, which in the previous section were eventually mapped to vertices in a graph. *Every* problem that can be approached by computational thinking must be reducible to a discrete set of states. The set of all states is usually called the *state space*. As section 4.4 reveals, *abstraction* is the computational thinking method that leads to the discovery of the state space within a given problem context. Since every problem is different, students will learn abstraction best if the process is practiced over a variety of exercises in different contexts. (For additional examples, see Averbach and Chein 2000; Levitin and Levitin 2011; Wells 1992.) In Alcuin's puzzle, each decision is made by the man immediately before he embarks across the river: does he cross alone or select an available item to cross with him? These choices are constrained by what is present on his side of the river. The moments at which each selection is made constitute the decision points of this puzzle. The acts of propelling the boat across the river and unloading its contents are ancillary. Thus, the states are distinguished by the side of the river the man is on and which of his possessions are within his reach. It is always constructive to ask, "How many states are there?" And it is easiest to answer this question before we consider which states need to be avoided (i.e., those that allow the wolf to eat the goat or the goat to eat the cabbages).

It is often helpful to represent states by using a data container called a list. A *list* defines an ordered collection of objects that allows elements to be repeated. The size of a list is called its *length*. In a sense, a list is the opposite of a set (defined in section 4.5), which is unordered and does not allow repetitions. Lists are often delineated using pairs of parentheses, for example (waffle cone, chocolate, vanilla), which is a list of length 3 that might describe an ice cream cone that is assembled by placing a scoop of chocolate on a waffle cone, followed by a scoop of vanilla on top. Lists are a flexible data structure that we often use without formality. Common examples are shopping lists or lists of chores, where the order in which items appear is significant. In mathematics, students encounter lists as ordered pairs, for example (x, y), where $x, y \in \mathbb{R}$, which label points on the two-dimensional Cartesian plane.[9]

We are now ready to build the state space for Alcuin's puzzle. In principle, each item can be on either the initial (I) or final (F) side of the river, independent of the others. We apply iteration and first consider only the man, representing his state by a list of length 1: (I) denotes that the man is on the initial bank and (F) that he is on the final bank. There are thus only two possibilities, at least so far.

Next, we incorporate the location of the wolf. The locations of the man and wolf together can be represented by a list of length 2, of the form (M, W), where the value of M corresponds to the side of the river on which the man stands and likewise W for the wolf. Since each entity has two possible states, we obtain that there are *four* possible joint states defined by the lists (I, I), (I, F), (F, I), and (F, F), as shown in figure 4.25.

By iteration, we next incorporate the location of the goat, using a combined list of length 3, of the form (M, W, G), where again each symbol can assume the value I or F independent of the others. Eight possible assignments can be discovered, which are shown in figure 4.26.

Finally, we incorporate the location of the cabbage, using a list of length 4, of the form (M, W, G, C). Now 16 possible assignments are discovered, which are tabulated in figure 4.27.

The preceding enumeration could have been shortened by relying on a useful combinatorial concept called the *multiplication principle*. The number of ways that a list of length k, $(x_1, x_2, \cdots, x_k)$ can be constructed equals the product $n_1 \times n_2 \times \cdots \times n_k$, where n_1 represents the number of choices for the first item in the list, x_1; n_2 the number of choices for x_2, and so on, with the proviso that the number of choices available at each step is independent of the choices made so far. Since each of the four items in the puzzle can be in two possible locations (I or F), the size of the state space equals $2 \times 2 \times 2 \times 2 = 2^4 = 16$.

		Wolf	
		I	F
Man	I	(I, I)	(I, F)
Man	F	(F, I)	(F, F)

Figure 4.25
The state space of the puzzle with only the man and wolf under consideration.

Goat = I		Wolf	
		I	F
Man	I	(I, I, I)	(I, F, I)
Man	F	(F, I, I)	(F, F, I)

Goat = F		Wolf	
		I	F
Man	I	(I, I, F)	(I, F, F)
Man	F	(F, I, F)	(F, F, F)

Figure 4.26
The state space of the puzzle with the man, wolf, and goat under consideration yields eight distinct states.

We can now count the number of dangerous or *lethal* states: those in which either the wolf can eat the goat or the goat can eat the cabbage. The man can be separated from all three of his possessions in two ways: (F, I, I, I) or (I, F, F, F). Alternatively, each predator-prey pair can be isolated from the man and the odd object in four ways: (F, I, I, F), (I, F, F, I), (F, F, I, I), and (I, I, F, F). Thus, there are a total of six lethal states that must be avoided, and therefore the remaining $16 - 6 = 10$ states are deemed to be safe.

Note that the puzzle starts in the initial state, (I, I, I, I), and proceeds to the goal state, (F, F, F, F).

The next step is to construct a graph that assigns one vertex to each of the 16 states of the puzzle. In analogy with our graphs for mazes, we can color the initial vertex green, the goal vertex gold, the lethal states red (they are effectively dead ends because no successful solution can travel through them), and the remaining states blue.

Cabbage = I

	Goat = I		Wolf	
		I		F
	I	(I, I, I, I)		(I, F, I, I)
Man				
	F	(F, I, I, I)		(F, F, I, I)

	Goat = F		Wolf	
		I		F
	I	(I, I, F, I)		(I, F, F, I)
Man				
	F	(F, I, F, I)		(F, F, F, I)

Cabbage = F

	Goat = I		Wolf	
		I		F
	I	(I, I, I, F)		(I, F, I, F)
Man				
	F	(F, I, I, F)		(F, F, I, F)

	Goat = F		Wolf	
		I		F
	I	(I, I, F, F)		(I, F, F, F)
Man				
	F	(F, I, F, F)		(F, F, F, F)

Figure 4.27
The state space of the puzzle with the man, wolf, goat, and cabbage under consideration yields 16 distinct states.

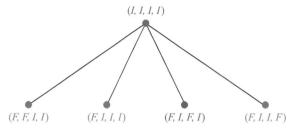

Figure 4.28
The first four possible transitions in the state-transition graph.

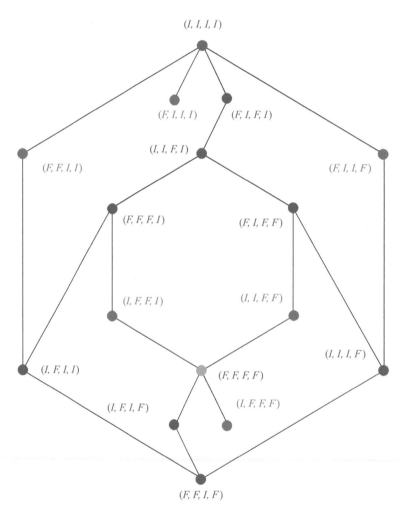

Figure 4.29
The state-transition graph for Alcuin's man, wolf, goat, and cabbage problem.

Two vertices are connected by an edge whenever a legal transition (i.e., river crossing in the boat) facilitates the corresponding change of state in the original puzzle. Since the vertices of the graph represent states of a computation and the edges the possible transitions between the states, the graph under construction is called a *state-transition graph*. We construct it by beginning with the initial state and then systematically construct every possible transition. Begin with a blank sheet of paper and draw the green vertex that corresponds to the initial state (*I, I, I, I*). Then note that since the man can cross with either the wolf, the goat, the cabbages, or alone, there are four initial possible transitions, as shown in figure 4.28. One should then expand each of the four new states (if possible) until every possible transition to every possible state has been revealed. Don't be discouraged if the edges cross or the diagram produced resembles a messy tangle. Repeat the process and try to discover whether the graph can be drawn in a form that is easy to interpret. With care, you might obtain a state-transition graph that resembles figure 4.29.

Our aim is to construct a structure for which Trémaux's algorithm can be applied to discover an efficient solution to the original puzzle. Because the graph involves only 16

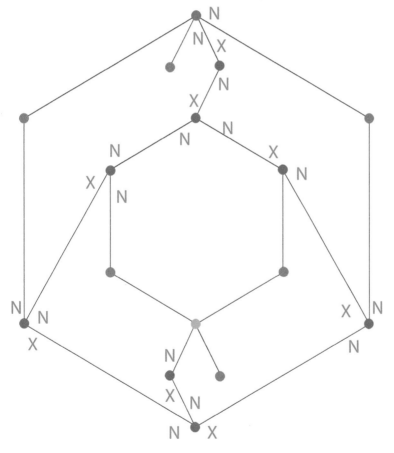

Figure 4.30
Trémaux's algorithm applied to the man, wolf, goat, and cabbage problem by a left-bearing agent.

states (vertices) and 20 transitions (edges), it is not difficult to discover the two optimal solutions. Two paths, each requiring seven steps, pop out:

$(I, I, I, I) - (F, I, F, I) - (I, I, F, I) - (F, I, F, F) - (I, I, I, F) - (F, F, I, F) - (I, F, I, F) - (F, F, F, F)$;

and

$(I, I, I, I) - (F, I, F, I) - (I, I, F, I) - (F, F, F, I) - (I, F, I, I) - (F, F, I, F) - (I, F, I, F) - (F, F, F, F)$.

However, we can also apply Trémaux's algorithm as originally planned, where we backtrack whenever a lethal state is visited during the search (figure 4.30). With a left-bearing agent, Trémaux's algorithm produces a search path with 22 state transitions (several states are visited multiple times). Three of the lethal states are also visited. However, once the agent reaches the goal, it can efficiently backtrack to the initial state by following the edges labeled with an X. Reversing this sequence yields the first of the preceding seven-step solutions.

4.7 Summary

In this chapter, we discussed the difference between labyrinths and mazes, and their historical origins. We explored how to make labyrinths of different circuits and determine their lengths and areas. We also examined how to solve mazes with different algorithms and how to represent these mazes by using graphs. We concluded by solving combinatorial puzzles with Trémaux's algorithm.

5 Simulating the Different Laws of Physics in Video Games

In this chapter, we examine how the different laws of physics are used in the coding of video games and their relation to real-life experiences.

Newton's laws of motion and other physics concepts are abundant in popular video games, from gravitational forces in *Angry Birds* to friction, inertia, and dynamics in car racing games. By building coded video games and experiencing the unplugged activities in this chapter, students can learn a subset of foundational physics concepts. In the games they create, students can tweak different parameters in the code to learn how the laws of physics affect the game. Through these activities, students will gain a better understanding of how the laws of physics shape our everyday lives, our planet, and our solar system.

We have set up this chapter to use collaborative group work in either the unplugged or coding tasks. Collaborative group work helps students achieve a shared goal—a working video game or physics lab experiment. In the realm of computer programming, programs are often too large for one person to do it all. They are usually broken down into smaller units (such as subroutines or modules) that are called up and used within a larger program. When coding in a group setting, people need to know

- which variables are being used (e.g., what variable names you are defining);
- how they are being used (e.g., whether your units are in meters per second or feet per second); and
- how they are being called up in the larger program.

These questions need to be resolved within the group so that the final program can work properly.

5.1 Newton's Laws of Motion

The motions of objects (e.g., particles, cars, basketballs, the rotation of our planet around the sun) influence our lives every day. The study of motion and the related concepts of force and energy make up the field of mechanics. Mechanics is divided into two parts: kinematics and dynamics. Kinematics describes how objects move, and dynamics explains why objects move as they do (Giancoli 2005, 19). In this section, we investigate Newton's different laws of motion and apply them in unplugged and computer-based programming activities and rich tasks.

Newton's First Law of Motion: The Law of Inertia

The first of Newton's laws falls on the kinematics side of mechanics, describing the behavior of all objects in ways that we can observe, control, and code.

> *Newton's first law of motion* states that an object at rest stays at rest until an outside force acts on it and that an object in motion stays in motion in a straight line at a constant speed until acted on by an outside force.

We experience *force* as any kind of push or pull on an object (Giancoli 2005, 72). The tendency of an object to maintain its state of rest or uniform motion in a straight line is called *inertia* (Giancoli 2005, 74). Inertia is the tendency for an object to stay at rest or stay in motion until an outside force acts upon it. Inertia also indicates the mass of an object (Giancoli 2005, 75). For example, a blimp or dirigible airship, has an enormous mass that requires a large force to change its speed and/or direction, yet it is considered weightless.

Speed is a scalar concept that tells us how fast an object is moving, but it does not provide direction. The average speed of an object is determined by finding the total distance traveled, $\Delta x = x_2 - x_1$, divided by the time taken to travel the distance, $\Delta t = t_2 - t_1$:

$$average\ speed = \frac{distance\ traveled}{time\ elapsed} = \frac{\Delta x}{\Delta t} = \frac{x_2 - x_1}{t_2 - t_1}.$$

Learning Activity 5.1: Newton's First Law with a Skateboard

In this activity, students experience Newton's first law of motion by standing on a skateboard (with all skateboard activities the student on the skateboard should wear a helmet for protection).

- If there are no forces acting on them, the student does not move.
- Now have another student (acting as the outside force) push the student on the skateboard.
- The act of pushing is an outside force, so now the student on the skateboard is in motion and will stay in motion until acted on by another force (such as a third student stopping him/her/them or friction—also an outside force—that slows down the wheels of the skateboard).
- Ask the students to describe how these actions on the skateboard are examples of Newton's first law of motion.

In figure 5.1, the example particle is moving in one direction, horizontally (the *x* direction). This is an example of translational motion. The code in figure 5.2 shows an example of Newton's first law of motion. When an object moves along a diagonal or along a path in two dimensions (the change is in both the *x* and *y* directions), you need to consider the *x* direction and the *y* direction separately.

Vectors: Direction and Magnitude

In our everyday language, *velocity* and *speed* or *distance* and *displacement* are used interchangeably, but these different terms have very distinct meanings in physics and mathematics (Giancoli 2005, 20–21). Speed and distance are scalar quantities that measure

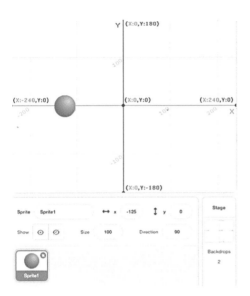

Figure 5.1
An example of a particle moving horizontally.

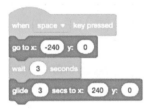

Figure 5.2
An example of the code for showing a particle moving in the horizontal (*x*) direction once a force is acting on it (the glide command). The particle starts at the far left-hand side of the screen (–240, 0) and moves across it to the end of the screen on the right-hand side (240, 0). What is the average speed of the particle going across the screen if it starts gliding at –240 and ends at 240 over 3 seconds?

magnitude only. These scalar quantities do not take into consideration the direction associated with them, whereas both velocity and displacement take direction into consideration. For example, if you say a person ran 5 miles, then that is the distance traveled, but there is no information about the direction. Or if a person is walking at 3 miles per hour, 3 miles per hour is the speed, but no direction was involved. However, displacement has to consider the direction and distance that a person travels, and velocity has to take into consideration the direction and speed (or magnitude) traveled. Speed is only the magnitude of the velocity. For example, if a person is walking *east* at 4 miles per hour against the direction of the moving walkway going *west* at 5 miles per hour, their velocity is going *west* at 1 mile per hour.

On a diagram, we indicate displacement or velocity as a vector. Vectors are quantities that have direction as well as magnitude. Each vector is represented by an arrow;

without an arrowhead at the end it represents just a line. Whether on paper or coded for the computer, the arrow is always drawn so that it points in the direction of the vector (Giancoli 2005, 46).

When vectors are going in the same direction horizontally (left or right along the x axis), you can add them algebraically, or when vectors are going the same direction vertically (up or down along the y axis), you can add them algebraically. For example, if a person biked 80 miles east, $\vec{D}_1$, on the first day and 60 miles east, $\vec{D}_2$, on the second day, the resultant displacement, $\vec{D}_r$, traveled in those two days was 140 miles east. If a person then biked 100 miles west, $\vec{D}_3$, on the third day and 40 miles west, $\vec{D}_4$, on the fourth day, the resultant new displacement, $\vec{D}_{nr}$, is 0 miles. However, the scalar distance traveled was 280 miles in total.

- The displacement of the bike over the first two days is

$$\vec{D}_1 + \vec{D}_2 = \vec{D}_r$$

80 mi + 60 mi = 140 mi where the positive numbers represent an eastward direction.

- As seen in figure 5.3, the displacement of the bike over four days is

$$\vec{D}_1 + \vec{D}_2 + \vec{D}_3 + \vec{D}_4 = \vec{D}_{nr}$$

80 mi + 60 mi + (−100 mi) + (−40 mi) = 0 mi where the negative numbers represent a westward direction.

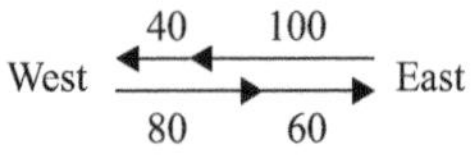

Figure 5.3
Demonstration of vector addition for the bike problem in one dimension.

If the two vectors are not along the same line, then you cannot use simple arithmetic to resolve the resultant vector. You will need to use either trigonometry or the Pythagorean theorem to find the resultant vector. For example, if you have a person walking 4 paces *east* and 3 paces *north*, the resultant displacement is represented by an arrow labeled $\vec{D}_r$, which is resolved by using the Pythagorean theorem. The resultant displacement $\vec{D}_r$ = 5 paces *north of east*. The resultant vector is drawn from the tail of the first vector to the tip of the last vector added. If you have two vectors, one in the x direction and the other in the y direction, then the resultant displacement is the hypotenuse of a right triangle and can be determined by using the Pythagorean theorem (Giancoli 2005, 46–47). Program 5.1 gives an example of this that can be created in Codesters.

In general, a resultant vector $\vec{V}$ that lies in a plane can be expressed as the sum of the two perpendicular components that form the vector. The components are usually chosen to be along the perpendicular directions of the x and y axes. We call this process of finding the components, "resolving the vector into its components" (Giancoli 2005, 49). The vector components are usually written as $\vec{V}_x$ and $\vec{V}_y$ and are added by drawing from the tail of $\vec{V}_y$ to the tip of $\vec{V}_x$. The resultant vector is written as $\vec{V}_x + \vec{V}_y = \vec{V}$.

Program 5.1: Velocity in Codesters

```
stage.set_background("grid")
x_arrow=codesters.Arrow(0, 0, 125, 0, False)
x_arrow.set_color("blue")
y_arrow=codesters.Arrow(125, 0, 125, 125, False)
y_arrow.set_color("red")
velocity=codesters.Arrow(0, 0, 125, 125, False)
velocity.set_color("purple")
```

The output of this program is shown in figure 5.4. The resultant velocity is shown by the arrow (in purple) that points from the origin of the grid to the point (125, 125). This arrow represents velocity by pointing in a direction with a certain length. The x part is shown as an arrow (in blue) that points along the x axis from the origin to (125, 0). The y part is shown as an arrow (in red) that points from the end of the first arrow up, parallel to the y axis. The three arrows together form a triangle, showing how the combination of the arrow pointing right and the arrow pointing up can end at the same spot (and represent the same velocity) as the arrow pointing diagonally. Using the Pythagorean

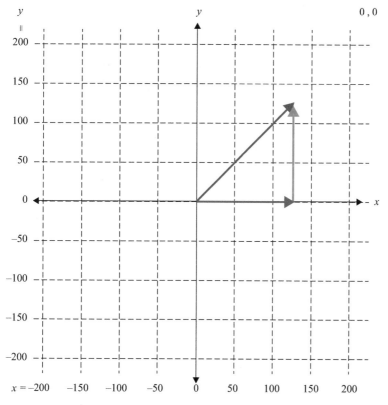

Figure 5.4
The output from the Codesters vector program. Image: Courtesy of Codesters.

Figure 5.5
An example of the output from the Scratch vector program.

theorem $a^2 + b^2 = c^2$, we can compute the velocity from the horizontal and vertical parts. These two arrows each have a length of 125 (which we do not have to compute, because only one coordinate is changing between their endpoints so that change is the arrow's length). We use those lengths for the a and b values in the equation, so $125^2 + 125^2 = c^2$, where c is the velocity of the diagonal vector. By solving for c, we get $c \cong 177$. That means the arrow's velocity is about 177 in the upper-right direction.

To demonstrate how displacement can be broken up into x and y vector parts, we can create a Scratch program. If the displacement is the distance and direction from the center of the drawing area to the cursor, then we draw two arrows to represent the x and y parts of the displacement vector. The output of the program can be seen in figure 5.5, the code for the x part is in figure 5.6, and the code for the y part is in figure 5.7. The x part is represented with a horizontal arrow sprite and will always face right or left (pointing along the x axis from the center of the drawing area). It will reach to the x coordinate of the mouse and will move with the mouse. The same is true for the y part, which is represented with a vertical arrow sprite facing up and down along the y axis. Have your students move their mouse left and right and see how the arrow follows it.

In the Scratch vector program, we will use

- **variables** to keep track of the mouse position;
- **loops** to update the sizes of the arrows; and
- **conditionals** to change the direction of the arrows.

The coded example in program 5.1 shows coordinates that are hard coded to be (125, 125). This is an example of a program that does not have variability; the user would need to edit the code each time they wanted to change the vector positions. In contrast, the code in figures 5.6 and 5.7 has variability because the vector lengths and components are dependent on where the cursor is on the screen and will update when the mouse moves.

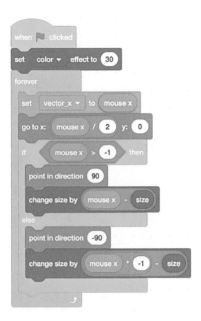

Figure 5.6
The code for the *x*-displacement arrow in the Scratch vector program.

Newton's Second Law of Motion: The Law of Dynamics

Let us switch gears to another law of mechanics, the law of dynamics. The root word "dyn" means *force*, so this topic focuses on the interaction of forces on a mass. Dynamics explain the causes of motion. Now that we understand *how* objects move, we can look at the second of Newton's laws, which explores the question of *why*. What variables are in play to determine the motion of an object?

Newton's second law states that the acceleration of an object depends on the net force acting on the object and is inversely proportional to its mass. The direction of the acceleration is the same as that of the net force acting on the object and is represented by $\Sigma \vec{F} = m\vec{a}$ (Giancoli 2005, 75). This means that if you get pushed while sitting on a chair with wheels, the greater the force used to push you, the greater the acceleration. And the more *mass*ive you are, the lesser the acceleration. Have you ever noticed that a large tractor-trailer truck takes longer to get up to the speed limit than a smaller car? This is because the truck has more mass, causing the effect of acceleration to be smaller.

When there exists a balance of forces on a stationary object, the object remains at rest. When there is a balance of forces on a moving object, there is no acceleration; the object goes at constant speed with the inertia described in Newton's first law.

Conversely, an imbalance of forces causes a mass to accelerate (or decelerate). Say you are in a car stopped at a traffic light and the light turns green. If the driver steps hard on the gas pedal, the car is going to go faster and faster until they let up on the gas. When wind resistance and car speed are in balance or the driver presses the gas pedal at a constant pressure, the car will go at a constant speed.

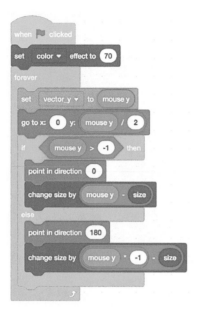

Figure 5.7
The code for the *y*-displacement arrow in the Scratch vector program.

Learning Activity 5.2: Newton's Second Law with a Skateboard

In this activity, students experience Newton's second law of motion.

Ask student A to stand on a skateboard and have another student C hold student A in place. Give student A one end of a coiled spring and hand the other end to student B. Tell student B to pull on the coiled spring until it is stretched out. Student A and student C should feel the force of the coiled spring pulling them. Since student A is being held back by student C, there is a balance of forces and no acceleration. Have student C let go of student A at the same time that student B (still holding the coil) starts walking away from student A. What happens? Why? Have students draw vector diagrams to describe the forces in play in this activity. Have students vary how long the coil elongates. How does the elongation of the stretched spring affect the acceleration? Students should notice that the greater the spring is stretched, the greater the force and the greater the acceleration.

Newton's Third Law of Motion: The Principle of Action-Reaction Pairs

Forces always occur in pairs. If the two forces are of equal strength but in opposite directions, the object goes nowhere. Newton's third law is defined as an "action-reaction" principle (Young and Freedman 2000, 107). Newton's third law of motion states that for every action there is an equal and opposite reaction in a *closed system*. For example, if you let air out of a balloon—whatever path the balloon takes—the exiting air is going in the opposite direction. In a rocket launch, the exiting engine fuel burns down, which forces the rocket to go up. In these examples, the balloon and the enclosed air are a closed system. The rocket and its enclosed fuel are a closed system.

> **Learning Activity 5.3: Newton's Third Law with Two Skateboards**
>
> Have two students face each other, each standing on a separate skateboard, close enough to touch hands. Tell them to push off each other. The push should cause both students to roll away from each other in opposite directions. In this closed system, the student with greater mass rolls away more slowly than the student with lesser mass. Conversely, the student with lesser mass has greater acceleration in the opposite direction.

> **Learning Activity 5.4: Newton's Third Law with a Skateboard and a Fan**
>
> Put a rotating-blade fan on a skateboard. It acts like a ship at sea, the fan blowing the air in one direction and the skateboard moving in the opposite direction. If you attach a piece of cardboard to the skateboard and place it in front of the fan, what happens and why? The skateboard, fan, and the cardboard screen are a closed system, so the skateboard stays stationary. This is an example of Newton's third law: the action-reaction principle. If you remove the cardboard screen, the skateboard starts to move because of an imbalance of forces and therefore accelerates, obeying Newton's second law.

Remember from Newton's second law that mass affects the consequences of the force. If two objects of different sizes collide, the bigger (mass) object rolls in its original direction but slower, and the smaller (mass) object rolls away in the opposite direction.

Let us build a Codesters program called Bumper Rocks (see appendix A.2 for full program) that will have an asteroid and a rock continually move, reflecting off the walls of the computer screen and colliding with each other. We will split the program into smaller subroutines (as seen in programs 5.2–5.6) that enable you to use different computer science skills and incorporate some Newtonian principles. As the rock and asteroid collide, we can determine the angles and forces resulting from a collision (which will allow the objects to bounce off each other). We will take the objects' masses and velocities into account to compute the new paths. The program will also allow you to change the mass of the rock to observe the effects on the forces in play.

> In the Codesters Bumper Rocks collision program, we will use
>
> - **variables** to keep track of the objects and values needed to compute velocities;
> - **functions** and **events** to react to keyboard inputs and collisions;
> - **conditionals** to determine whether an object is at the screen's edge; and
> - **loops** to move the objects.

Start by choosing a background image and two sprites. We want the sprites to start in different locations and to be moving in different directions. As an example, we have the algorithm to create an asteroid and a rock in a space background, a screenshot of which can be seen in figure 5.8.

Figure 5.8
A still frame of the rock and asteroid (with Jupiter in the background) from the Bumper Rocks Codesters program. Image: Courtesy of Codesters.

Program 5.2: Bumper Rocks Setup in Codesters

```
# set the background image
stage.set_background("jupiter")
# create the rock with initial size and speed
rock = codesters.Sprite("rock")
rock.set_size(0.5)
rock.set_x_speed(2)
rock.set_y_speed(-3)
# create the asteroid with initial size, position, and speed
asteroid = codesters.Sprite("asteroid")
asteroid.set_size(0.5)
asteroid.go_to(-200, 0)
asteroid.set_x_speed(-1)
asteroid.set_y_speed(4)
```

The rock and the asteroid start at the same size. In order to see how difference in mass affects collision, we write two functions (program 5.3) so that we can make the rock get bigger or smaller. In our example, we choose to use the "s" key to shrink the rock and the "w" key to grow it. It is good usability for the functions like this to be complementary, so that if you press "s" once and "w" once, the rock should be back to its original size. That is why we set the growth to a fraction.

Program 5.3: Bumper Rocks Keyboard Functions in Codesters

```
# create a function for the 's' key to make the rock smaller
def s_key():
    # make the rock smaller
    rock.set_size(0.8)
# this line makes the code listen for the 's' key
stage.event_key("s", s_key)
# create a function for the 'w' key to make the rock larger
def w_key():
    # make the rock bigger
    rock.set_size(1 / 0.8)
# this line makes the code listen for the 'w' key
stage.event_key("w", w_key)
```

For the next subroutine that is part of the larger Bumper Rocks program, we code the collision function using elastic collisions. In this program, we claim that both momentum ($\vec{p} = m\vec{v}$) and kinetic energy ($\text{KE} = \frac{1}{2}mv^2$) are conserved. This means the objects will not be slowed by forces such as friction and kinetic energy will not be absorbed or converted into heat during the collisions. Remember that momentum is a vector event with magnitude and direction, and energy is a scalar event with only magnitude. The effect in the program is that the total amount of energy will be constant, so the rocks will never stop completely.

The equation used for elastic collision in program 5.4 is derived from the equations for the conservation of total kinetic energy and the conservation of momentum (Young and Freedman 2000, 241). The equation for the conservation of total kinetic energy is written as

$$\text{total Kinetic Energy before} = \text{total Kinetic Energy after}$$

$$(a) \; \frac{1}{2}m_1(v_1)^2 + \frac{1}{2}m_2(v_2)^2 = \frac{1}{2}m_1(v_1')^2 + \frac{1}{2}m_2(v_2')^2$$

where m_1 is the mass of object one, v_1' is object one's new velocity, v_1 is its old velocity, and m_2 is the mass of the other object (object 2), v_2' is the second object's new velocity, v_2 is its old velocity. The conservation of momentum equation is written as

$$(b) \; m_1\vec{v}_1 + m_2\vec{v}_2 = m_1\vec{v}_1' + m_2\vec{v}_2'.$$

By manipulating these two equations (a) and (b) algebraically, we can derive the equation[1] for calculating the new velocities in both the x and y directions to be used in program 5.4. The elastic collision equation is therefore given as

$$v_1' = v_1 - \frac{2m_2}{m_1 + m_2} \frac{\langle v_1 - v_2, c_1 - c_2 \rangle}{\|c_1 - c_2\|^2}(c_1 - c_2),$$

where, in addition to the variables previously defined, c_1 is the center coordinate of one object, and c_2 is the center coordinate of the other object. The angle brackets mean dot product and the double vertical bars mean that we calculate the distance between the two points. We will complete the collision calculations in separate x and y components and look at each dimension individually, because that is how Codesters is set up and it corresponds to the vector component concept we described previously.

Codesters has built-in functions for x_speed and y_speed, but these are really velocities and not speeds, because they include a direction: the x_speed is the velocity in the x direction (right) and the y_speed is the velocity in the y direction (up). If these velocities are negative, that signifies left or downward movement, respectively.

We have to compute the x_speed and y_speed separately for each of the two objects that are colliding, so we will use the preceding equation four times. Let us examine the equation for the x_speed of the rock as an example. In this case:

- v_1 is the current x velocity of the rock.
- m_2 is the size (mass) of the asteroid.
- m_1 is the size (mass) of the rock.
- $\langle v_1 - v_2, c_1 - c_2 \rangle$ needs some unpacking:
  - $v_1 - v_2$ is the rock's velocity minus the asteroid's velocity. We subtract the x and y parts separately, so we will have two values. For example, if the rock has x velocity = 6 and y velocity = –3 and the asteroid has x velocity = –2 and y velocity = 4, then $v_1 - v_2$ will be 6 – (–2) and (–3) – 4, which simplifies to 8 and –7 for the x and y parts, respectively.
  - $c_1 - c_2$ is the rock's center point minus the asteroid's center point. Again, we subtract the x and y parts separately. For example, if the rock is centered at the point (100, 50) and the asteroid is centered at the point (105, 47), then $c_1 - c_2$ will be (100 – 105, 50 – 47), which simplifies to (–5, 3).
  - The angle brackets, $\langle\ \rangle$, signify the dot product of the two vectors. To determine the dot product, you multiply the corresponding parts and sum those products together. This means we take the two x parts (velocity and position) and multiply them. Then we take the two y parts (velocity and position) and multiply them. Finally, we add those two products together.

    In our case, we get ((the rock's x velocity – the asteroid's x velocity) · (the rock's x position – the asteroid's x position)) + ((the rock's y velocity – the asteroid's y velocity) · (the rock's y position – the asteroid's y position)). To use the preceding example velocities and center points, the dot product of $\langle (8, -7), (-5, 3) \rangle$ is expressed as $(8 \cdot (-5)) + ((-7) \cdot 3) = -40 + (-21) = -61$.
- $\|c_1 - c_2\|$ is the distance between the center points of the two objects. This may seem like an odd thing to compute, since the objects are colliding so they must be close enough to touch, but the distance can actually vary depending on the angle of collision and the shape and size of each object.
- $c_1 - c_2$ is the rock's x position minus the asteroid's x position.

Program 5.4 uses the equation in Codesters to calculate the new velocities of the objects after they collide.

Program 5.4: Bumper Rocks Collision Function in Codesters

```
# create a function for collision of the objects
def collision(sprite, hit_sprite):
    # set variables
    size_sum=rock.get_size()+asteroid.get_size()
    x_vel_1=sprite.get_x_speed()
    x_vel_2=hit_sprite.get_x_speed()
    y_vel_1=sprite.get_y_speed()
    y_vel_2=hit_sprite.get_y_speed()
    rock_x=rock.get_x()
    rock_y=rock.get_y()
    asteroid_x=asteroid.get_x()
    asteroid_y=asteroid.get_y()
    # calculate new velocities for 2-dimensional
    # elastic collisions
    # the next seven lines should be on one line
    sprite.set_x_speed(x_vel_1 -
((2*asteroid.get_size())/size_sum) *
((x_vel_1-x_vel_2)*(rock_x-asteroid_x) +
(y_vel_1-y_vel_2)*(rock_y-asteroid_y)) /
((rock_x-asteroid_x)*(rock_x-asteroid_x) +
(rock_y-asteroid_y)*(rock_y-asteroid_y)) *
(rock_x-asteroid_x))
    # the next seven lines should be on one line
    sprite.set_y_speed(y_vel_1 -
((2*asteroid.get_size())/size_sum) *
((x_vel_1-x_vel_2)*(rock_x-asteroid_x) +
(y_vel_1-y_vel_2)*(rock_y-asteroid_y)) /
((rock_x-asteroid_x)*(rock_x-asteroid_x) +
(rock_y-asteroid_y)*(rock_y-asteroid_y)) *
(rock_y-asteroid_y))
    # the next seven lines should be on one line
    hit_sprite.set_x_speed(x_vel_2 -
((2*rock.get_size())/size_sum) *
((x_vel_2-x_vel_1)*(asteroid_x-rock_x) +
(y_vel_2-y_vel_1)*(asteroid_y-rock_y)) /
((rock_x-asteroid_x)*(rock_x-asteroid_x) +
(rock_y-asteroid_y)*(rock_y-asteroid_y)) *
(asteroid_x-rock_x))
    # the next seven lines should be on one line
    hit_sprite.set_y_speed(y_vel_2 -
((2*rock.get_size())/size_sum) *
((x_vel_2-x_vel_1)*(asteroid_x-rock_x) +
(y_vel_2-y_vel_1)*(asteroid_y-rock_y)) /
((rock_x-asteroid_x)*(rock_x-asteroid_x) +
(rock_y-asteroid_y)*(rock_y-asteroid_y)) *
(asteroid_y-rock_y))
# this line makes the program detect collision and
# call the function above
rock.event_collision(collision)
```

We do not want the objects to leave the visible drawing area, so we have them bounce off its four containing sides. Codesters does this automatically but lets us code it so that we know what is really happening (see program 5.5). If it hits a left or right wall (when the *x* coordinate gets too high or low), we change the *x* velocity of the object to move in the other direction. If it hits a top or bottom wall (when the *y* coordinate gets too high or low), we change the *y* velocity of the object to move in the other direction. This keeps the object moving and on screen at all times and appears visually as the objects bouncing off walls.

Program 5.5: Bumper Rocks Movement Function in Codesters

```
# create a function to move the objects and
# bounce off walls
def move(sprite):
    sprite.move_forward(1)
    if sprite.get_x() >= 250 or sprite.get_x() <= -250:
        sprite.set_x_speed(-sprite.get_x_speed())
    if sprite.get_y() >= 250 or sprite.get_y() <= -250:
        sprite.set_y_speed(-sprite.get_y_speed())
```

Finally, we want the objects to move forever, bouncing off the walls and each other until the user manually stops the program. To accomplish this, we use a `while` loop and set the condition to always be true (see program 5.6). This is the Codesters version of a forever loop. In the loop, we call our move function for each object.

Program 5.6: Bumper Rocks Engine in Codesters

```
# have the program run forever
while True:
    move(rock)
    move(asteroid)
```

Now that we have gone over each part of the program, ask your students to play around with it.

- Ask your students how the collisions between the two objects are different from those of the objects bouncing off the walls.
  - Answer: The objects bounce off the walls at the same angle at which they approached it, but collisions change the angle of the objects' velocities.
- Use the "s" and "w" keys to make the rock larger or smaller. How does this affect collisions?
  - Answer: The larger object will have more force to push the smaller one away.
- Which object has the higher velocity coming out of a collision, the bigger one or the smaller one?
  - Answer: The smaller one.

- Your students may notice that sometimes the objects will bounce off each other more than once when they collide, causing what looks like a glitch. Why does this sometimes happen?
  - Answer: Sometimes after a collision, the new velocities do not move the two objects far enough away from each other for them to no longer overlap, causing the collision function to be called again.

Learning Activity 5.5: Creating Video Games

Using Scratch, Codesters, or a programming language of their choice, groups of two to four students can create their own video games that incorporate Newton's laws of motion. Students can decide what they want their game to be and how they are going to use Newton's laws. They will need to storyboard what their video game will look like and do, then divide up and assign work to be completed. Assigning group roles will help facilitate management of the project. In order to finish the project, collaboration will be vital. Since each person will be responsible for a subset of the code, they'll need to determine which variables are needed by which subroutines and where their part fits in the larger program. At the end of the project, let the students describe their finished product and share it with their peers.

5.2 Newton's Law of Universal Gravitation: Law of Mass Attraction

In this section, we define Newton's law of universal gravitation and use it in unplugged and computer-based activities.

Newton's law of universal gravitation states:

> Every particle in the universe attracts every other particle with a force that is proportional to the product of their masses and inversely proportional to the square of the distance between them. This force acts along the line joining the two particles.

Newton's law of universal gravitation answers the question of why an object falls to the ground when it is released. Every object on the earth's surface feels the force of gravitation that draws the object toward the center of the earth (Giancoli 2005, 117). The force of mass attraction is what attracts the object to the earth. It is an example of a force acting through a distance without physical contact (Giancoli 2005, 118). An object falling to the earth is an example of uniform acceleration. All objects, light or heavy, fall at the same rate of acceleration in the absence of resistance such as the air (Giancoli 2005, 32).

The universal law of gravitation also explains why the earth and the planets in our solar system are attracted to the sun and why the moon is attracted to the earth. But for the purposes of the following subsection, we will focus on objects falling to the earth and use a Codesters program to look at the effects of forces due to gravitation. Remember gravitation is a force and gravity (i.e., uniform acceleration) is a consequence of that force. There is a fine distinction between these two concepts (Young and Freedman 2000).

Kinematic Equations: Displacement, Velocity, and Acceleration

Kinematics describes the motion of an object; the root "kine" in kinematic means *motion*. In this subsection, we outline the principles behind equations for displacement, velocity, and acceleration and use them in unplugged and computer-based activities. We have already delineated that displacement and velocity have magnitude and direction. The kinematic equations that govern objects in motion in two dimensions are as follows:

1. *displacement* at any point, $d_a = d_o + v_o t + \frac{1}{2} at^2$ (d_o = original displacement, v_o = original velocity, a = constant acceleration, t = time in seconds);
2. *velocity* at any point, $v_a = v_o + at$;
3. *acceleration* due to gravity (in metric $g = 9.8 \text{m/s}^2$ or in imperial $g = 32 \text{ft/s}^2$).

Learning Activity 5.6: Water Balloon Drop

With two water balloons starting at the same height and the same time, throw one balloon horizontally and drop the other balloon.
   Which water balloon will hit the ground first and why?

Answer: Both balloons will reach the ground at the same time because there is no acceleration in the horizontal direction. The horizontal velocity remains constant and equal to the original velocity from the throw.

Now we will write a Codesters program that will apply our knowledge of displacement, velocity, and acceleration due to gravity in the coding of a basketball program. The path of the basketball is a two-dimensional trajectory, with both horizontal and vertical components that are independent of each other. You can see the full basketball program in appendix A.3, but we will split it up into smaller subroutines (see programs 5.7–5.9) to better understand the different aspects of game and kinematic principles. To set the scene, we first use a basketball court background, place a basketball net, and create a player holding a basketball (program 5.7).

In the Codesters basketball program, we will use

- **variables** to keep track of the ball and net;
- **functions** to shoot the ball and prompt for user input; and
- **conditionals** to determine whether the ball scored.

Program 5.7: Basketball Setup in Codesters

```
# set gravity's strength
stage.set_gravity(10)
stage.set_background("halfcourt")
net = codesters.Sprite("basketballnet", 200, 100)
```

```
# we do not want the net to fall
net.set_physics_off()
net.set_gravity_off()
player=codesters.Sprite("player3", -180, -130)
# we do not want the player to fall
player.set_physics_off()
player.set_gravity_off()
ball=codesters.Sprite("basketball", -150, -130)
# we do not want the ball to fall yet
ball.set_physics_off()
ball.set_gravity_off()
# create a rectangle along the floor
floor=codesters.Rectangle(0, -250, 500, 10, "red")
```

Now let's create a function to shoot the ball (program 5.8) by changing the *x* and *y* velocities. Figure 5.9 shows a screenshot of what this looks like. We prompt the user for these two inputs, so you can run the program as many times as you want and give it different original velocities to see what changes will occur. After we get the inputs, we allow gravity to affect the ball and call the function we just created to shoot the ball.

Figure 5.9
A still frame of the basketball shot in a Codesters program. Image: Courtesy of Codesters.

Learning Activity 5.7: The Effects of Gravitation

Have one student use a slingshot or shoot a basketball at a target. If they don't hit the target the first time, let the other students in the class observe and give feedback on what went wrong and what they can change to fix it. Look for specific advice, such as "You need to pull the slingshot back past your elbow" or "You need to throw the ball higher in the air." Connect these pieces of advice to the x and y components of the velocity vectors. If the ball landed between the student and the target, they need to increase the magnitude of the horizontal and/or vertical components of the velocity. If they shot too high or low, they may need to adjust the vertical component of the velocity.

Program 5.8: Shooting the Ball in Codesters

```
# create a function called shoot
def shoot(x_speed, y_speed):
    # set the ball's speed to make it move
    ball.set_x_speed(x_speed)
    ball.set_y_speed(y_speed)
# prompt the player for inputs
x_vel = int(player.ask("Enter an x-velocity:"))
y_vel = int(player.ask("Enter a y-velocity:"))
# now we want the ball to fall
ball.set_physics_on()
ball.set_gravity_on()
# this calls the function above
shoot(x_vel, y_vel)
```

How will we know if we have scored? We can use Codesters's built-in collision-detection function to detect whether the ball hits any other sprites (see program 5.9). This will detect whether the ball's bounding box overlaps with the bounding box of another sprite. While this is great for detecting whether the ball hits the floor, it doesn't behave the way we want for the basketball net. This is because the net sprite includes the backboard, meaning the bounding box is much larger than the net itself. To give a truer answer, we hard-code the coordinates of a smaller box right at the top of the net. We also check that the ball is moving in a downward trajectory, because shooting a ball up through the net should not count as a score.

If the ball scores, we print a winning message to the screen. If the ball hits the floor, we print a losing message to the screen. In either case, we also stop the ball. The user will need to restart the program to shoot the ball again.

Program 5.9: Detecting a Score in Codesters

```
# create a function for collisions
def collision(sprite, hit_sprite):
    # check for a score
    # the next two lines should be on one line
```

```
    if sprite.get_x() >= 165 and sprite.get_x() <= 215 and sprite.get_y() >= 75
and sprite.get_y() <= 100 and sprite.get_y_speed()<0:
        # stop the ball
        sprite.set_x_speed(0)
        sprite.set_y_speed(0)
        sprite.set_physics_off()
        sprite.set_gravity_off()
        # create a win message
        message=codesters.Text("You scored!", 0, 0, "white")
    # check if the ball hit the red floor
    elif hit_sprite.get_color() == "red":
        # stop the ball
        sprite.set_x_speed(0)
        sprite.set_y_speed(0)
        sprite.set_physics_off()
        sprite.set_gravity_off()
        # create a lose message
        message=codesters.Text("Try again!", 0, 0, "white")
ball.event_collision(collision)
```

Which inputs will shoot the ball into the net? How many attempts does it take your students to score? If you change the value of gravity on the first line of the program, how will that affect the ball? How will you adjust your inputs?

The basketball program gives students a way to see how the acceleration due to gravity affects an object as it falls. It also gives them the ability to consider how the *x* and *y* parts of a velocity will be affected by gravitation's pull. We use functions and built-in collision detection to determine whether the ball scored.

5.3   Reflection

In this section, we discuss reflection and use it in unplugged and computer-based activities. The law of reflection states that the angle of reflection is equal to the angle of incidence with respect to the surface or the perpendicular normal (Giancoli 2005, 633).

Learning Activity 5.8: Air Hockey

Air hockey tables minimize the friction between the puck and the table's surface, so the collisions the puck makes with the walls and paddles are elastic. This means it does not lose any kinetic energy, so it will bounce off at the same angle and with the same speed as it had before the collision. Note that when the puck bounces off the walls, it changes velocity but not speed (because it changes direction). This is another example to distinguish velocity from speed.

To demonstrate reflection, we can code the classic ping-pong game in Codesters. The complete program is located in appendix A.4. The ball has to reflect off the players' paddles and the top and bottom of the screen in order for the game to work. We can split the Codesters program into subroutines (see programs 5.10–5.12) so that your students can work together to complete it:

- One student can get the ball to move at a random angle. If it hits the left or right walls of the screen, it ends the game.
- Another student can get the two paddles to move at the touch of keyboard keys. We do not want the paddles to leave the screen.
- The students will need to work together to get the ball to bounce off the paddles.

In the Codesters ping-pong program, we will use

- **variables** to keep track of the paddles and the ball;
- **functions** and **events** to detect collision and react to key presses; and
- **conditionals** to determine whether the ball hit the paddle.

Program 5.10 gives the code for the ball for the first subroutine of the ping-pong program.

Program 5.10: Ping-pong in Codesters—the Ball

```
# import the random number generator library module
import random
# set a list of speeds that we will choose from
speeds = [-4, -3, 3, 4]
# create the ball and set initial values
ball = codesters.Circle(0, 0, 50, "green")
ball.set_size(0.5)
# set the ball velocity in x and y components
# len(speeds) gets the number of items from the speeds
# list so if students change the number of values in that
# list they do not need to recode the next line
ball.set_x_speed(speeds[random.randint(0, len(speeds)-1)])
ball.set_y_speed(speeds[random.randint(0, len(speeds)-1)])
# create rectangles against left and right walls
left_wall = codesters.Rectangle(-250, 0, 10, 500, "red")
right_wall = codesters.Rectangle(250, 0, 10, 500, "red")
# create a function to detect collision
def collision(sprite, hit_sprite):
    # check if ball hit the left or right wall
    if hit_sprite.get_color() == "red":
        # stop the ball
        ball.set_x_speed(0)
        ball.set_y_speed(0)
        if hit_sprite.get_x() < 0:
            # ball hit left wall
            msg = codesters.Text("Player 2 wins!", 0, 0, "red")
        else:
```

```
            # ball hit right wall
            msg = codesters.Text ("Player 1 wins!", 0, 0, "red")
    # make the program listen for collisions
    ball.event_collision(collision)
```

In the first line of code, we import the random number generator library module so that we can set the ball moving in a random direction. We then make a list of speeds to choose from, which your students can edit to make the ball move differently. Next, we create a green ball in the center of the drawing area and initialize the size and speed of the ball. The velocity is split into its *x* and *y* components, and each part is set to a value randomly chosen from the speeds list.

The following two lines of code create red rectangles that sit on the far left and right sides of the screen, stretching from the top to the bottom of the drawing area. We will use these red walls in our collision detection function, which comes next. This collision detection function will only be called if the ball collides with another sprite. Inside the function, we check to see whether the ball hits one of the two red rectangles. If it did, that means it got past a paddle and the game is over. When that happens, we stop the ball and determine who has won the game; that decision is based on which of the two red rectangles the ball hit. If the ball hits the left wall, we print a message saying that player 2 has won; if it hits the right wall, we print a message saying that player 1 has won. The last line of code attaches the collision function to the ball sprite.

Another aspect of the ping-pong game is creating the paddles. Program 5.11 provides the code for the paddles for the second subroutine.

Program 5.11: Ping-pong in Codesters—the Paddles

```
# create rectangles for the paddles
player1 = codesters.Rectangle(-230, 0, 10, 50, "yellow")
player2 = codesters.Rectangle(230, 0, 10, 50, "gray")
# create a move up function for when w is pressed
def w_key():
    # make sure there is room to move up
    if player1.get_y() < 220:
        player1.move_up(20)
# create a move down function for when s is pressed
def s_key():
    # make sure there is room to move down
    if player1.get_y() > -220:
        player1.move_down(20)
# create a function for when the up arrow is pressed
def up_key():
    # make sure there is room to move up
    if player2.get_y() < 220:
        player2.move_up(20)
```

Program 5.11: Ping-pong in Codesters—the Paddles (continued)

```
# create a function for when the down arrow is pressed
def down_key():
    # make sure there is room to move down
    if player2.get_y() > -220:
        player2.move_down(20)
# make the program listen for the keys
stage.event_key("w", w_key)
stage.event_key("s", s_key)
stage.event_key("up", up_key)
stage.event_key("down", down_key)
```

In program 5.11, we create two paddles to represent the two players in the game. Player 1 is on the left side of the drawing area and player 2 is on the right. Each paddle is drawn as a rectangle. We want the players to be able to move up and down, so we create four keyboard functions. We use the "w" and "s" keys to move player 1 up and down, respectively, and the up and down arrow keys to move player 2. In each function, we call the Codesters built-in move_up or the move_down event on the player to move their rectangle, but only if there is still space on the screen for them to move in that direction. The conditional statement if checks to make sure the player won't go off the drawing area. The last four lines of code in program 5.11 ensure that the program is listening for the four keyboard keys and knows to react to them by calling the functions we wrote.

Now your students are ready to combine their programs. The part they will need to complete together is the logic for the ball to bounce off the paddles. Conveniently, in the first subroutine, your student already set up a collision function to detect when the ball collides with any other sprites. Using program 5.12, we can add this line of code at the beginning of that function (before it checks whether the ball hit the right or left wall) to make the ball bounce off the upper and lower walls.

Program 5.12: Ping-pong in Codesters—Bouncing Off Paddles

```
ball.set_x_speed(-ball.get_x_speed())
```

By negating the x_speed of the ball, we are reversing the direction in which it moves along the x axis. This has the effect of changing it from moving left to moving right and vice versa. Note that we are not changing the y_speed at all, so if the ball is moving down or up it will continue to do so.

Note that, for the program to work, the two students must communicate the following points:

- The two rectangles on the border walls will be the only red sprites in the program. (This enables the end-of-game detection.)
- Player 1 will control the left paddle and will use the keys on the left of the keyboard, and player 2 will control the right paddle and will use the keys on the right of the keyboard. (This enables the end-of-game messages.)

- The students must agree on the relative speeds of the ball and the paddles. (If the paddles are too slow, they may not be able to block the ball in time.)

5.4 Summary

This chapter used unplugged activities and coded programs in Scratch and Codesters to explore physics concepts such as inertia, acceleration due to gravity, reflection, and collision. It included a group programming project that split the work between the students while encouraging communication and collaboration. The activities and exercises empower students to actively learn these foundational concepts of Newtonian physics, and by understanding the physics behind the game, students will better understand the concepts and be able to create a more realistic game.

6 Critically Examining and Analyzing Data

> In this chapter, we discuss how to identify manipulated data, and we demonstrate how to retrieve primary source data from the internet and use algorithms to analyze it.

To be informed citizens in a democratic society, we need to be educated consumers of the information we absorb and use. The electorate's ability to critically examine, analyze, and use data to make good judgments and decisions is paramount to the health of any nation. At the heart of computational thinking is the ability to apply a problem-solving process using different strategies and algorithmic solutions to complex problems. There is nothing more complex and in need of solution than some of the hot topic issues of our day, including questions related to global warming,[1] species extinctions,[2] immigration,[3] school funding,[4] gun violence in the United States,[5] food insecurity,[6] the spread of infectious diseases,[7] and unequal wealth distribution,[8] to name a few. In this chapter, we apply computational thinking to begin to ask questions, critically examine data, and seek answers to one of these complex issues—global warming trends.

We focus our attention on analyzing weather data, but the skills that we apply here can be used to investigate other important issues that currently affect our world. For our example, we gathered primary source data from the US National Oceanic and Atmospheric Administration's (NOAA) National Climatic Data Center (NCDC) website (www.ncdc.noaa.gov/cdo-web/) to examine temperature trends in Burlington, Vermont. Primary source data are publications or data that come from the originating source. Students can download data files from this site, then use a spreadsheet app and/or the Python programming language to process and display the data so they can analyze and interpret the findings. Along the way, students learn the skills necessary to identify credible sources and manipulated presentations of data, and to process and analyze numerical data.

6.1 Elements of a Data Investigation or Inquiry

The elements of a data investigation include

- formulating a question;
- collecting, processing, and displaying the data;
- analyzing, describing, and discussing the results; and
- making inferences and predictions based on the data that help answer the question (Creswell 2012; NCTM 2001; NGSS 2013).

Pose a question of interest   Before starting an investigation, one needs to decide what topic they are going to research (NRC 2012). This decision can be based on many factors, but they should be grounded in a person's interests and/or passions. What topics are important and in need of answers? What issues are affecting people? A research question helps focus the nature of the researcher's work, but what all questions have in common is that data must be collected to answer the questions posed (Creswell 2012; Fraenkel, Wallen, and Hyun 2015; NCTM 2001; NGSS 2013; YPAR 2015).

Determine what data is to be collected for analysis and gather the information   To decide what data to collect, start by doing a background investigation into the issues that surround the question. When students are looking for information that relates to their question, use valid and reliable websites. To determine whether the data on a website is reliable, it should satisfy the currency, relevance, authority, accuracy, and purpose (CRAAP) test (Blakeslee 2004, 2010) (see http://libguides.csuchico.edu/c.php ?g=414315&p=2822716).

What data you decide to collect depends on the questions you are trying to answer (Creswell 2012; NCTM 2001; NGSS 2013). There are five steps to consider when collecting data: (1) determining which participants or data sources will be part of the study, (2) obtaining permission from these individuals or organizations, (3) considering the types of information to collect from the different sources available, (4) locating and selecting instruments to use that capture useful information for the study, and (5) administering the data collection process (Creswell 2012, 141). If your students decide to collect their own data, have them ensure that it is unbiased and that it enables them to answer the questions they are asking. The Youth-Led Participatory Action Research (YPAR) website (http://yparhub.berkeley.edu/investigate-curriculum/) discusses steps students can follow to collect their own data, ensure it is unbiased, and work toward answering their question. When looking for relevant downloadable data that has already been collected, government agencies, nonprofit organizations, nongovernmental organizations, and research groups are a good place to start, as opposed to media outlets or blogs that report their interpretation of the data. Also make sure these agencies, associations, and research groups satisfy the CRAAP test.

Process the data and perform needed calculations   During this step, students determine which mathematical calculations or models to apply that help analyze the data and thereby enable them to find answers to the questions they are asking (NCTM 2001; NGSS 2013). Calculations such as mean (or average), median, minimum value, maximum value, standard deviation, standard error, confidence interval, and linear regression, for example, help tell a story of what is happening numerically with the data.

Display and analyze the results   Displaying the data visually can help the researcher and the audience understand and interpret the data and the results of the data calculations. Tables, bar graphs, histograms, line graphs, scatter plots, pie charts, box-and-whisker plots, and other formats help the researcher analyze and interpret the data. They also enable the audience to understand the results more easily. However, it is important to present the data such that it is easily readable by the audience and does not bias the results or lead to their misrepresentation. The results from the data calculations also provide information about the data for you to analyze to find its meaning.

Discuss and describe the results   After deciding which calculations and/or graphs make the most sense to use with your data, the burden is on using the results to identify and justify the answer to your data investigation question. You will need to develop inferences and predictions based on the analysis of data processing results (NCTM 2001). Guide your audience through the steps taken from interpreting the data to answering the research question. You need to convince not only yourself but the audience that the conclusions are logically sound and justified. Based on the results of your initial question, you may decide that more information is needed and that the conjectures and inferences made for the initial question lead to other questions for investigation.

Learning Activity 6.1: A Classroom Weather Station

- Collect weather data at your school for one month at the same time every day. This weather data could include, for example, temperature, precipitation, sky condition (e.g., sunny, cloudy), and barometer reading.
- Graph the data to see the daily variation in your weather readings. What was the calculated mean for temperatures for each week and for the month? What was the calculated mean for rainfall for the week and the month? Was there a relationship between the rainfall and barometric readings?
- What inferences could be made based on the other weather data you collected? How close were your predictions to the actual results, and why?

6.2   Identifying Manipulated Data

In this section, we provide strategies to identify manipulated data sources sometimes seen in the media. We want students to understand how data can be manipulated to propagate misinformation that confirms a preconceived notion or bias. Unfortunately, some media outlets or political factions misrepresent data to serve their personal interests and agendas. Rather than giving an accurate, robust report on the data, they fall into common traps of omitting information, representing data out of context, exaggerating or minimizing data results, or drawing unjustified conclusions. Alberto Cairo's 2019 book *How Charts Lie: Getter Smarter about Visual Information* is a great resource for understanding how visual displays can be manipulated to give misinformation. Learning activity 6.2 investigates some common ways that information can be misrepresented to draw incorrect inferences.

Learning Activity 6.2: Hunting for Data Misrepresentation

Ask your students to look at examples of data they have seen on different media sources (this can be on social media, websites, newspapers, magazines, video news footage, social networking sites, and so on) and determine whether the source is representing the data accurately and why. Did the manipulated data presentations fit one of the categories of misrepresentation we discussed?

Figure 6.1
President-elect Harry Truman holds up a newspaper that incorrectly declares his defeat. This
media is made available by the holdings of the National Archives and Records Administration.

Sampling procedures   One way to manipulate the data is in how the sample is selected—
that is, who or what data is in the sample and what data or participants are omitted. A
sample is a subset of the data or participants selected from a larger set or population and
is chosen to represent the whole. However, the size of the sample, the location that the
sample is selected from, and the characteristics of the respondents or data can directly
impact the validity of the inferences being made and lead to biased results. Using a limited, nonrepresentative, or biased sample detrimentally affects the generalizations made
to a larger population and leads to inaccurate inferences.

The 1948 US presidential election between candidates Harry S. Truman and Thomas
Dewey is an example of a sampling technique failure that led to an inaccurate prediction. Prior to the election, the Crossley, Gallup, and Roper polls predicted Dewey would
win the presidency, leading the *Chicago Daily Tribune* to publish the erroneous headline
calling the election for Dewey before all the votes were counted (figure 6.1). However,
Truman ended up winning the election instead. The reason for the polls' erroneous
conclusion was that they used a quota sampling technique to select registered voters to
ask who they were voting for. Quota sampling requires that the sample represent different cross sections of the population by having the important characteristics of the
population (e.g., income, gender, race, religion, age, region) proportionally represented
in the sample (Dodge 2003; Nardi 2006). However, this sampling technique did not
enable pollsters to get an accurate representative sample of US voters because there
were many characteristics that were not considered or included in their sample and in
the end biased the results. In this situation, the sampling technique caused an inaccurate prediction for the 1948 presidential race.

Using one data point to generalize to a larger population   Sometimes people draw false conclusions from legitimate pieces of data. For example, an argument was made, by several elected officials in 2019, that global warming was not occurring because Minnesota was experiencing some of the coldest days on record (Pierre-Lois 2019). This illustrates a couple of problematic issues. For one, it mistakes weather for climate. Weather is the short-term meteorological and atmospheric conditions that we experience day to day in our environment. Climate describes weather trends over a long period of time. Questions about global warming should examine data that would illuminate climate trends over time, whereas weather data can only provide a snapshot of the climate in a certain area (i.e., the US Midwest) for a certain amount of time (i.e., one day in winter). Second, it is true that the US Midwest has had some of the coldest days on record in the contiguous 48 states, but a small data sample of one geographical area does not allow a generalization to be made about the whole globe.

Not conducting the full gamut of needed data calculations   This is when the data is being processed when not all the calculations needed to tell the complete story have been conducted. One example of this occurs when calculating the data sampling error. The difficulty with using sampling techniques is that a sample dataset is unlikely to be identical to the larger population that it represents, and no two samples are ever going to be the same in all their characteristics; there will be some variation (Fraenkel, Wallen, and Hyun 2015, 221). Therefore, data collection samples come with a sampling error because we are looking at a subset of the population under study. The sampling error tells you the probable range of outcomes of the larger population based on the bias in the sample data. By calculating and presenting the sampling error, you enable the reader to get a fuller sense of the data.

For example, if the calculated means of two variables are 34 and 48, that seems like a definitive difference. But if the sampling error was ±30, this suggests that the calculated mean of the first variable can be anywhere in the range of 4–64 and the calculated mean of the second variable can be in the range of 18–78, which overlaps by 46 units and is therefore inconclusive as to which is definitively the larger value. It might make you think twice about the reported results about the differences in means.

Using raw data without grounding it in context   Sometimes raw data can be misleading. At first thought, this sounds counterintuitive, because raw data is supposed to be objective and reliable, the foundation for our claims of scientific truth. However, when raw data is not grounded within a context, it can give a misleading impression.

Take figure 6.2 as an example. The first graph (figure 6.2(a)) is the raw data for the number of white and black people killed by police in the United States between 2013 and 2018.[9] Looking at this graph, notice that there were almost twice as many white people killed as black people. But why is it a mistake? Because the raw numbers are not put in the context of the overall US population. If the white and black populations in the United States were of equal size, then the data would be valid. However, there were more than five times as many white people in the United States as black people in 2013–2018.[10] Graphing the number of killings as a proportion of the population for each of these races produces the graph in figure 6.2(b). This presents a very different and more accurate picture, where the black population is being killed at more than three times the rate of the white population. The additional calculation of finding the proportion of the populations more accurately represents the data because it puts the raw data values into the context of the US population. Data like that in figure 6.2(a)

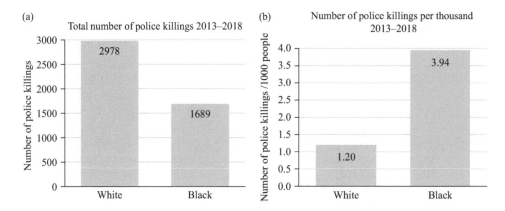

Figure 6.2
(a) The raw numbers of white and black people killed by US police in 2013–2018. (b) The
proportion of white and black US populations killed by police in 2013–2018.

can mistakenly be used to disregard the argument that black Americans are being killed
more frequently than white Americans.

Limiting the amount of data presented   Another way to manipulate the data presentation is to shorten the length of the *x* axis (horizontal axis) or shorten the interval
for collecting data. For example, consider the graphs in figure 6.3, which show the US
murder and nonnegligent manslaughter rate by year.[11] The graph in figure 6.3(a) has
the horizontal axis going between 1999 and 2014 and shows the steady decline of
the murder and nonnegligent manslaughter rate since 2006, but that claim would be
an error if more recent data was included. When the data for the years 2015–2018 is
included in the graph (the most recent data to date; figure 6.3(b)), we see the murder
rate bump up again. This requires that new inferences be made. The conclusion from
the analysis changes from the claim that the murder and nonnegligent manslaughter
rate has been in a steady decline since 2006 to the claim that it has decreased since
2006. Or you could say that the murder and nonnegligent manslaughter rate was in
a steady decline from 2006 to 2014, then rose in 2015 and 2016, but is now on the
decline again.

Exaggerated or minimized data displays on the vertical axis   In addition to omitting
data from the *x* axis, a graph can also be manipulated on its *y* axis. The findings from
a set of data can be stretched and hyperbolized or shortened and dismissed without
technically lying. The most common method of showing an exaggeration or reduction
of the data is in how the data is displayed in graphs. The following examples show
different ways that the vertical axes can be manipulated to tell different stories with
the data processing results. The first example (seen in figure 6.4) shows how truncating
the *y* axis can mislead the reader to draw an incorrect conclusion. The Center for
Responsive Politics reported that female winners in primary elections for the US House
of Representatives raised $1,400,000 on average, whereas male House primary winners
raised $1,585,000 on average.

By changing the *y*-axis data range to be from $1,300,000 to $1,600,000, it looks
like the male candidates raised more than twice as much as the female candidates on

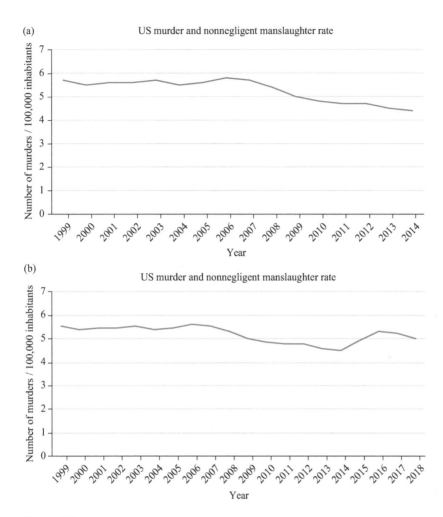

Figure 6.3
(a) A graph of the US murder and nonnegligent manslaughter rate from 1999 to 2014. It omits the data from more recent years. (b) A graph of the US murder and nonnegligent manslaughter rate from 1999 to 2018, with 2018 being the most recent data available.

average, but in reality, the male candidates only raised about 13.2 percent more than the women on average. A more accurate graph of the data is seen in figure 6.5.

The next example shows how truncating the vertical axis can lead readers to think there is wider variation in the data than really exists. By providing the full range of data, in the vertical axis in figure 6.6(b), it looks as though the data is not fluctuating as much.

On the other end of the spectrum, you can enlarge the vertical axis to make the data look not as consequential or not as variable. In figure 6.7(a), the average January temperatures for Burlington, Vermont, look like they fluctuate a little bit but generally align, but in figure 6.7(b) the y axis is set to the data value range and you can see much more fluctuation in the temperatures.

An analogy of exaggerated or minimized data would be like standing in front of a warped mirror: technically it is still your reflection, but it isn't an accurate reflection

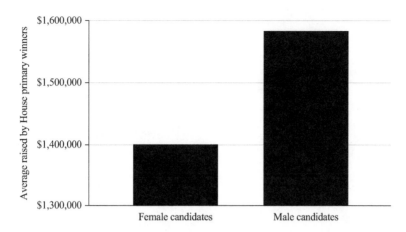

Figure 6.4
Example of exaggerating the difference in values using data on House primary winners.

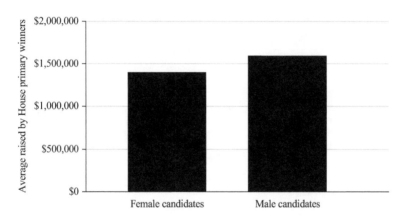

Figure 6.5
A more accurate graph of the data on House primary winners; the *y* axis starts at zero.

of what you really look like. Watch out for these misrepresentations in media, research reports, and slide presentations.

Drawing unjustified conclusions   The scenarios we previously discussed have led researchers and others to draw unjustified conclusions, whether they be from faulty sampling techniques, not performing all the calculations needed to analyze the data, or misrepresenting the data in a visual. The Youth-Led Participatory Action Research (YPAR) website (http://yparhub.berkeley.edu/define-issue/bias/) provides additional resources on ways to detect bias in the media and for learning ways to present unbiased research results.

6.3   Using Data to Analyze Temperature Trends

Global warming and climate change has been one of the most controversial topics argued in US politics in recent years. Arguments have been made that the earth is not

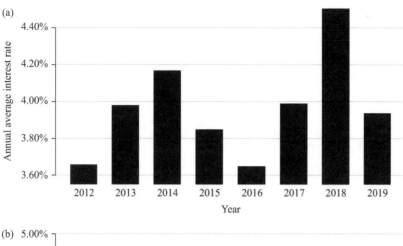

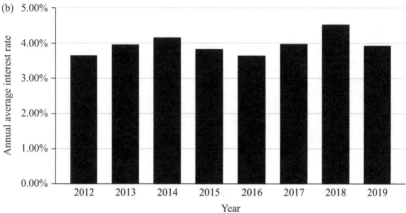

Figure 6.6
(a) A graph of 30-year fixed-rate mortgage rates with the *y* axis scaled to emphasize the fluctuation and (b) a graph of the same mortgage rates with the *y* axis starting at 0 to show the true fluctuation. *Source*: http://www.freddiemac.com/pmms/pmms30.html.

warming, that we are experiencing normal weather fluctuations, or that the science on global warming indicators is not conclusive. Yet, there is publicly available data that has been gathered and can be analyzed. Currently, the US NOAA's NCDC has several decades of weather data available on their website (https://www.ncdc.noaa.gov/cdo -web/) for the public to download. By having students analyze this primary data source, you can empower them to determine whether average temperatures have increased around the world over the last several decades.

Next, we provide an example of using a primary data source to answer the question: *Has the average (or mean) temperature for Burlington, Vermont, changed over the last 78 years and, if so, by how much?*[12] We went to NOAA's NCDC website to download the data needed to determine our answer.

On the Climate Data Online website, click on Search Tool (as seen in figure 6.8) and choose the data you want to download. We chose the dataset "Global Summary of the Month"; selected the date range from December 1, 1940, to December 1, 2019; searched for "Stations"; and entered the search term "Burlington, VT" (as seen in figure 6.9). We chose "Global Summary of the Month" because we wanted to look at monthly averages

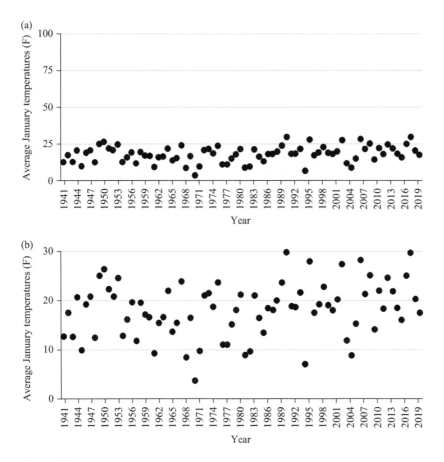

Figure 6.7
(a) Temperatures graphed with an exaggerated y axis. (b) Temperatures graphed with a y axis that matches the range of y values.

over the last 78 years and not the weekly or daily temperatures during this time. You can replace these choices, especially the location, with other variable options that reflect your areas of interest and/or questions you want to investigate.

This leads to a webpage with a map that shows your area of interest with the different weather stations pinned. We selected the Burlington International Airport, VT, US weather station dataset and added it to the cart. When you view the items in the cart, choose the option to download a .csv file (as seen in figure 6.10), as opposed to a .pdf document, because the different spreadsheet programs and Python language read the data in a comma separated value (csv) file format.

After you select .csv files and click Continue, on the next page it will give you more data options that you can select. Based on our research question, we chose "Average Temperature (TAVG)" under "Air Temperature" (shown in figure 6.11), but there are many other options for data variables if you want to look at those data points to answer other questions.

Click Continue to see a summary of the requested data for you to review before clicking the Submit Order button (as shown in figure 6.12). Enter your email address

Climate Data Online

Climate Data Online (CDO) provides free access to NCDC's archive of global historical weather and climate data in addition to station history information. These data include quality controlled daily, monthly, seasonal, and yearly measurements of temperature, precipitation, wind, and degree days as well as radar data and 30-year Climate Normals. Customers can also order most of these data as certified hard copies for legal use.

Browse Datasets
Browse documentation, samples, and links

Certify Orders
Get orders certified for legal use (requires payment)

Check Status
Check the status of an order that has been placed

Find Help
Find answers to questions about data and ordering

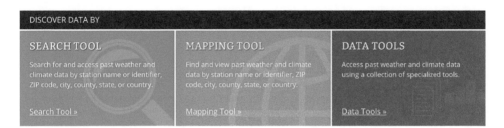

DISCOVER DATA BY

SEARCH TOOL

Search for and access past weather and climate data by station name or identifier, ZIP code, city, county, state, or country.

Search Tool »

MAPPING TOOL

Find and view past weather and climate data by station name or identifier, ZIP code, city, county, state, or country.

Mapping Tool »

DATA TOOLS

Access past weather and climate data using a collection of specialized tools.

Data Tools »

Figure 6.8
NOAA's Climate Data Online website.

■Climate Data Online Search

Start searching here to find past weather and climate data. Search within a date range and select specific type of search. All fields are required.

Select Weather Observation Type/Dataset ⊘

| Global Summary of the Month | ⬍ |

Select Date Range ⊘

| 1940-12-01 to 2019-12-01 | 🗓 |

Search For ⊘

| Stations | ⬍ |

Enter a Search Term ⊘

| Burlington, VT |

SEARCH

Figure 6.9
Input of data variables for downloaded file from NOAA's Climate Data Online website.

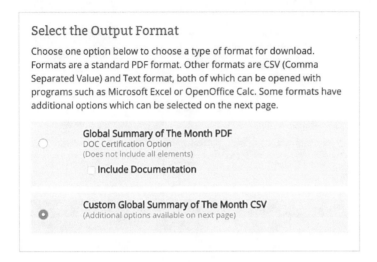

Figure 6.10
Selecting the format of a downloaded data file from NOAA's Climate Data Online website.

Select data types for custom output

The items below are data types that can be added to the output. Expand the data type category headers to view the categorized data type names and descriptions.

Show All / Hide All | Select All / Deselect All

☐ ⊞ Computed
☐ ⊞ Precipitation
☐ ⊞ Sunshine
☐ ⊟ Air Temperature
    ☑ Average Temperature. (TAVG)
    ☐ Cooling Degree Days Season to Date (CDSD)
    ☐ Extreme maximum temperature for the period. (EMXT)
    ☐ Extreme minimum temperature for the period. (EMNT)
    ☐ Heating Degree Days Season to Date (HDSD)
    ☐ Maximum temperature (TMAX)
    ☐ Minimum temperature (TMIN)
☐ ⊞ Wind

[BACK] [CONTINUE]

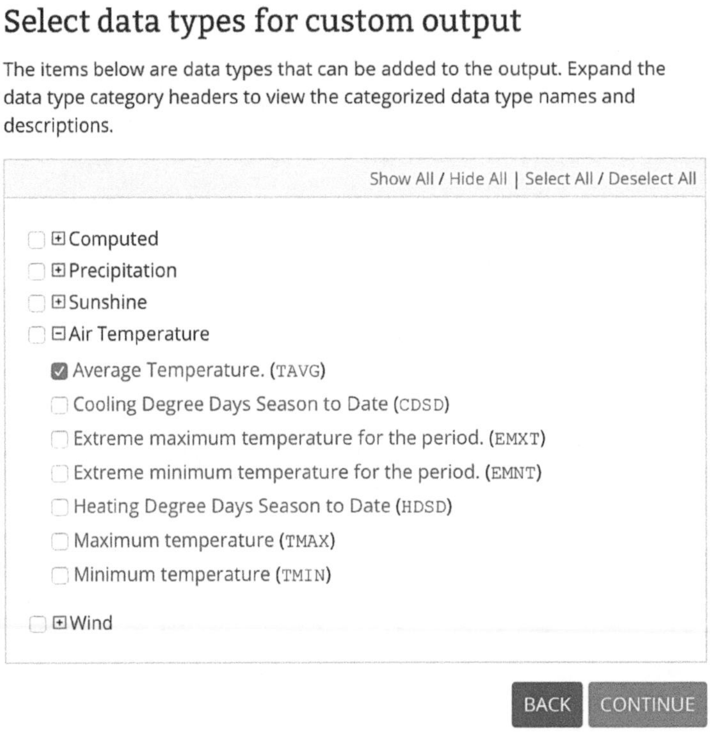

Figure 6.11
Selection of specific data variables from NOAA's Climate Data Online website.

REQUESTED DATA REVIEW	
Dataset	Global Summary of the Month
Order Start Date	1940-12-01 00:00
Order End Date	2019-12-01 23:59
Output Format	Custom Global Summary of The Month CSV
Data Types	TAVG
Custom Flag(s)	Station Name
Units	Standard
Stations/Locations	BURLINGTON INTERNATIONAL AIRPORT, VT US (Station ID: GHCND:USW00014742)

Figure 6.12
Verifying data to receive from NOAA's Climate Data Online website.

and submit the request. It sends a confirmation email right away and within minutes sends the link to download the data.[13] This is the primary source data that we analyzed for this example.

By looking at temperatures over a 78-year span at one weather station, we can analyze the temperature trends in that area over time rather than the short-term (daily or weekly) fluctuations. If we were to look at different weather stations around the world concurrently, we could begin to make inferences that were beyond Burlington, Vermont. If you add multiple weather stations to your dataset, be careful to look at the trends within one station and not across stations. The latitude and longitude of the location will influence the range of temperatures that appears. To keep the data sample consistent, analyze the data in each area separately and then determine the trends over time to see whether the temperatures are changing over the long term in the other areas, too.

To analyze the data that we have collected, we created an algorithm (algorithm 6.1) to process the data that applies to any program you are using.

```
Algorithm 6.1: Analyzing Temperature Data

Access the .csv data file
Isolate the data to specific rows of data that correspond to your
question
Find the specific columns of data that relate to your question
Perform calculations to answer your question
Graph the relevant data and calculations in a readable form
```

For our example, we used Google Sheets and the Python programming language to read the data from the file and then process and graph it.

To analyze the data, we will use

- **data usage** to collect and use raw data;
- **conditionals** to determine which rows and columns of information are relevant to the question;
- **abstraction** to visually present the numerical data to be analyzed; and
- **scalability** to understand what the larger data calculations are saying by looking at subsets of the data.

The algorithm to process the data begins with accessing the information in the .csv file. The file can contain a lot of data, so having a data investigation question helps

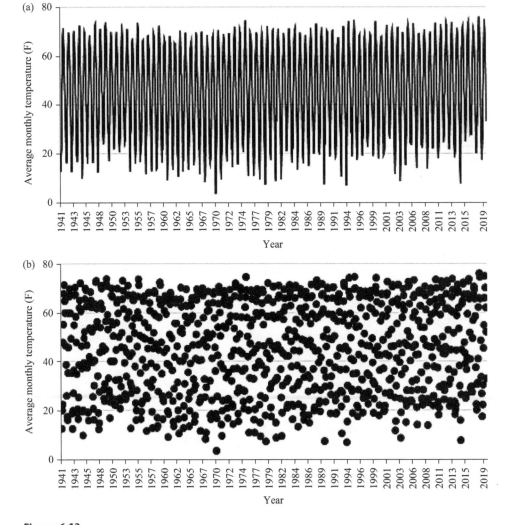

Figure 6.13
Line graph (a) and scatter plot (b) of the average monthly temperatures for Burlington, Vermont, from 1941 to 2019.

you narrow the focus of your data processing. The computer can process large amounts of data, but too much data in a graph or table can be overwhelming for the researcher and for the audience. Sometimes visual representations, rather than the numerical data alone, can better explain what is happening with the data, but not always.

Figure 6.13 shows a line graph (a) and a scatter plot (b) for data from December 1941 to December 2019. It is crowded and messy, which makes it very difficult to analyze with a graph alone. All we can tell is that there is a lot of variation in the data (which makes sense because average temperatures in Burlington, Vermont, can range from 3.6°F in the winter to 76°F in the summer). The computer can process large datasets with the different software programs available, but what do the calculations do and mean?

As an exercise to illustrate what is happening in the processing of the larger set of data, we chose to process and graph a *subset* of the data. We choose one month's (January's) average temperature as the subset to process, graph, and display with a trend line (or line of best fit) included. In exploring the subset data, we seek to answer the question: *Did the average January temperature in Burlington, Vermont, change over 78 years and, if so, by how much?* The line of best fit is the best approximating straight line through the data points that can illuminate trends in the data over time and will enable us to determine whether, on average, the temperature changes.

Once we understand how the data is processed on a smaller scale, we can go back to the complete larger set of data and process it on a larger scale, and make inferences appropriately. Later in this chapter, we come back to our original research question about average temperatures in Burlington, Vermont.

Using Spreadsheet Programs to Process the January Average Temperature Data Sample

Open the downloaded .csv file in Google Sheets. In our spreadsheet file, we see 78 years of weather data in rows for each month with the following column titles: STATION, NAME, DATE, and TAVG (as seen in figure 6.14).

Now that the data is in Google Sheets format, there are many ways to process and display it. We begin by describing a way to process the data such that any student with minimal spreadsheet knowledge could analyze and graph it. We also provide steps to process the data using more complicated Google Sheets commands.

One way to process the data is to group the rows so that only the January data for each year is showing (see figure 6.15); data for February through December are hidden within the grouping. To do this, highlight rows 3 through 13, go to the Data tab, and select Group rows 3–13. Then click the box with a "–" in it, and rows 3–13 will be hidden from view (see figure 6.15). Once only the January data is showing, graph the data by highlighting columns C and D and clicking the Insert Chart icon. Within the Chart Editor, you can select how you want your graph to look. We selected a line chart to show the yearly variation in temperature for the month of January. In the Custom section of the Chart Editor, on the Series tab we selected Trend Line (aka line of best fit or linear regression) and to have the trend line equation printed on the graph. A best-fit line (or trend line) is used to illuminate a data pattern over time. The best-fit line may pass through some points, no points, many points, or all points.

The best-fit line, or regression line, is a complicated equation that is best used with computer automation. The best-fit line uses the least-squares regression line formula to determine the best-fitting line that would minimize the distance between the data points and the regression line. It is found by calculating the sum of the squares of the vertical distances between the data points and the points on the line and makes it as small as possible.

	A	B	C	D
1	STATION	NAME	DATE	TAVG
2	USW00014742	BURLINGTON INTERNATIONAL AIRPORT, VT US	1940-12	22.9
3	USW00014742	BURLINGTON INTERNATIONAL AIRPORT, VT US	1941-01	12.7
4	USW00014742	BURLINGTON INTERNATIONAL AIRPORT, VT US	1941-02	20.1
5	USW00014742	BURLINGTON INTERNATIONAL AIRPORT, VT US	1941-03	22.5
6	USW00014742	BURLINGTON INTERNATIONAL AIRPORT, VT US	1941-04	47.9
7	USW00014742	BURLINGTON INTERNATIONAL AIRPORT, VT US	1941-05	55.2
8	USW00014742	BURLINGTON INTERNATIONAL AIRPORT, VT US	1941-06	67.8
9	USW00014742	BURLINGTON INTERNATIONAL AIRPORT, VT US	1941-07	71.4
10	USW00014742	BURLINGTON INTERNATIONAL AIRPORT, VT US	1941-08	64.9
11	USW00014742	BURLINGTON INTERNATIONAL AIRPORT, VT US	1941-09	60
12	USW00014742	BURLINGTON INTERNATIONAL AIRPORT, VT US	1941-10	46.5
13	USW00014742	BURLINGTON INTERNATIONAL AIRPORT, VT US	1941-11	38.8
14	USW00014742	BURLINGTON INTERNATIONAL AIRPORT, VT US	1941-12	26.1
15	USW00014742	BURLINGTON INTERNATIONAL AIRPORT, VT US	1942-01	17.5
16	USW00014742	BURLINGTON INTERNATIONAL AIRPORT, VT US	1942-02	16.2
17	USW00014742	BURLINGTON INTERNATIONAL AIRPORT, VT US	1942-03	35.5
18	USW00014742	BURLINGTON INTERNATIONAL AIRPORT, VT US	1942-04	45.8
19	USW00014742	BURLINGTON INTERNATIONAL AIRPORT, VT US	1942-05	59.9
20	USW00014742	BURLINGTON INTERNATIONAL AIRPORT, VT US	1942-06	66.6
21	USW00014742	BURLINGTON INTERNATIONAL AIRPORT, VT US	1942-07	69.8
22	USW00014742	BURLINGTON INTERNATIONAL AIRPORT, VT US	1942-08	67.4
23	USW00014742	BURLINGTON INTERNATIONAL AIRPORT, VT US	1942-09	59.8
24	USW00014742	BURLINGTON INTERNATIONAL AIRPORT, VT US	1942-10	49.4
25	USW00014742	BURLINGTON INTERNATIONAL AIRPORT, VT US	1942-11	35.4
26	USW00014742	BURLINGTON INTERNATIONAL AIRPORT, VT US	1942-12	18.8
27	USW00014742	BURLINGTON INTERNATIONAL AIRPORT, VT US	1943-01	12.6
28	USW00014742	BURLINGTON INTERNATIONAL AIRPORT, VT US	1943-02	20
29	USW00014742	BURLINGTON INTERNATIONAL AIRPORT, VT US	1943-03	27.2

Figure 6.14
Downloaded temperature data for Burlington, Vermont, in a spreadsheet.

The best-fit line or trend line is defined by $y = bx + a$, where a is the y intercept and b is the slope of the regression line. The slope of a trend line b indicates the predicted rate of change on the calculated best-fit line. The trend line for our January average temperatures from the 1941–2019 dataset is $y = 0.0574x + 15.8$, where y is the predicted average January temperature (°F) over the last 78 years and x is the number of months since the base year of 1941.

Based on the trend line, we can answer our question about whether the average January temperature in Burlington, Vermont, had increased over the last 78 years and, if so, by how much: yes, by about 4.5°F since 1941, as the following shows:

January 1941	January 2019
$y = 0.0574(1941-1941) + 15.8$	$y = 0.0574(2019-1941) + 15.8$
$y = 0.0574(0) + 15.8$	$y = 0.0574(78) + 15.8$
$y = 15.8°F$	$y = 20.3°F$

		A	B	C	D
	1	**STATION**	**NAME**	**DATE**	**TAVG**
⊞	2	USW00014742	BURLINGTON IN	1941-01	12.7
⊞	14	USW00014742	BURLINGTON IN	1942-01	17.5
−	26	USW00014742	BURLINGTON IN	1943-01	12.6
	27	USW00014742	BURLINGTON IN	1943-02	20
	28	USW00014742	BURLINGTON IN	1943-03	27.2
	29	USW00014742	BURLINGTON IN	1943-04	36.5
	30	USW00014742	BURLINGTON IN	1943-05	55
	31	USW00014742	BURLINGTON IN	1943-06	67.2
	32	USW00014742	BURLINGTON IN	1943-07	70.3
	33	USW00014742	BURLINGTON IN	1943-08	67.5
	34	USW00014742	BURLINGTON IN	1943-09	58.4
	35	USW00014742	BURLINGTON IN	1943-10	47.9
	36	USW00014742	BURLINGTON IN	1943-11	35
	37	USW00014742	BURLINGTON IN	1943-12	19
⊞	38	USW00014742	BURLINGTON IN	1944-01	20.6
⊞	50	USW00014742	BURLINGTON IN	1945-01	9.9
⊞	62	USW00014742	BURLINGTON IN	1946-01	19.2

Figure 6.15
Grouping temperature data for Burlington, Vermont, with only January's temperatures showing.

Based on this trend line, can we project what the average temperature in January will be for 2025? (Answer = 20.6°F.) Further statistical analysis calculations can tell you whether this average change in temperature as determined by the best-fit line is statistically significant.

Another way to process the data is to use the initial spreadsheet (see figure 6.16) and have the spreadsheet program grab the data that you are most interested in to help automatize the work. Figures 6.17 and 6.18 show in the command line how to grab the initial data and put it in a new sheet to process and perform statistical calculations. The **INDEX(reference, [row], [column])** command allows you to return the content of a cell, specified by row and column number. In this case, we are pulling out January's date and average temperature. For figure 6.17, the **INDEX** command is highlighted in cell A3, the **reference** is the sheet named 2009269, and C2:D948 is the array on sheet 2009269 from which you are pulling the data. The $ sign tells the spreadsheet program to keep array parameters constant as you copy and paste this command down the rows. The **[row]** variable 12*row(A1) + 1 allows you to go through the 2×947 array of data from C2:D948 and grab every twelfth row + one line of data for each subsequent cell as you copy and paste down the A column. The **[column]** is only selecting from the first column (Date) in our 2×947 array, so you put a 1 there.

The index command highlighted in figure 6.18 pulls data from cells C2:D948 of the sheet named 2009269, creating another 2×947 array. The **[row]** variable 12*row(B1) + 1 allows you to go through the 2×947 array and grab every twelfth row + one line of data for each subsequent cell as you copy and paste down the B column. The **[column]** is only selecting from the second column, Average Temperature, so you put a 2 there.

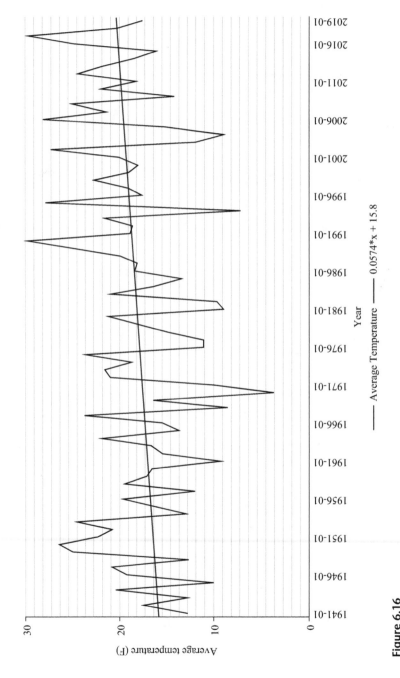

Figure 6.16
Graph of average January temperature for Burlington, Vermont, from a spreadsheet.

fx	=index('2009269'!$C$2:$D$948,12*row(A1)+1,1)		
	A	B	C
1	Year	Average Temperature	
2	1941-01	12.7	
3	1942-01	17.5	
4	1943-01	12.6	
5	1944-01	20.6	
6	1945-01	9.9	
7	1946-01	19.2	
8	1947-01	20.8	
9	1948-01	12.4	

Figure 6.17
Grabbing DATE information from the initial sheet to insert into column A of a new sheet.

Almost any spreadsheet app makes processing and graphing data doable with a couple of commands, but what do the graphs mean? How do you process the data so that you can accurately analyze it? Remember to avoid the ways of manipulating data outlined earlier in this chapter and that you (not the computer program) are ultimately in control of answering these questions.

Learning Activity 6.3: Using Primary Source Data to Ask and Answer Questions

Have your students pose a question (or multiple questions) that can be answered by analyzing data from a legitimate primary data source. Given the dataset, have them process the data and graph the results to help them answer their question(s). Then write or talk about the results. What did they learn about their topic of interest through this data analysis? Do their findings agree with publicly presented knowledge on the subject?

Using the Python Programming Language to Process the Data
Python is a popular programming language (and is the foundation of the Codesters platform used in the earlier chapters). It is used at many large and small companies and schools for anything from back-end web development, to scripting, to data processing. We are using it for the latter, as some of Python's strengths include reading in data from files and producing graphs.

We used Idle to run Python scripts, though there are many Python integrated developer environments available. We also used Python 3.7.4 when we ran our example code. For this program to work, you need to install some Python packages such as the following.

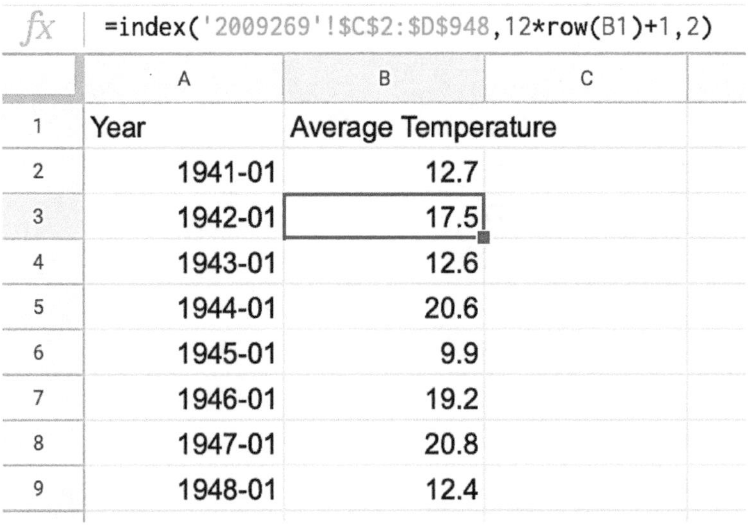

fx | =index('2009269'!$C$2:$D$948,12*row(B1)+1,2)

	A	B	C
1	Year	Average Temperature	
2	1941-01	12.7	
3	1942-01	17.5	
4	1943-01	12.6	
5	1944-01	20.6	
6	1945-01	9.9	
7	1946-01	19.2	
8	1947-01	20.8	
9	1948-01	12.4	

Figure 6.18
Grabbing TAVG data from the initial sheet to insert into column B of a new sheet.

- `Matplotlib` is a good library module for creating graphs in Python.
- `Numpy` is a library module for doing complex calculations. We used it to calculate the best fit to a line with our data and print the slope of the regression line.

Open a command line interface (typically CMD on Windows machines and Terminal on Linux and Mac machines) and run the commands `pip3 install matplotlib` and `pip3 install numpy`. To see whether it installed, you can create a new Python (.py) file with the lines `import matplotlib` and `import numpy` and try to run it. If it runs without error, you installed both packages successfully.

Based on algorithm 6.1, we need to map out the program (program 6.1). First, we want to read in the data from the file (program 6.2). The file contains a lot of data, so to narrow it down to our initial questions of *Has the average temperature in January for Burlington, Vermont, changed over the last 78 years and, if so, by how much?*, we need to choose one month and graph (program 6.3) the average temperature of that month for each year in our dataset. We use January in this example, but we created a variable called `month_string` in our code so that anyone can quickly change the month they want to look at and print out the graph.

```
Program 6.1: Python Setup

# import the .csv library so we can read in from a .csv file
import csv
# import matplotlib so we can graph the data
import matplotlib.pyplot as plt
# import numpy so we can fit a line to the data
from numpy.polynomial.polynomial import polyfit
# use January as the month to graph
month_string = '01'
```

The first three lines of code (not including the comment lines that start with #) import the library module we will need to get the data from the .csv file and graph it. Then we create a variable `month_string` for the month we want to graph and set its value to 01 for January. If instead you want to graph the average temperature for a different month (say June), then you would have to change this value (to 06 in this case) and update some of the graph labels later in the program.

Program 6.2: Read from Data File in Python

```
# open the filename.csv file
with open('BurlingtonVTData.csv') as csv_file:
    # use the reader from the csv library
    reader=csv.reader(csv_file, delimiter=',')
    # declare empty lists to hold what will be the x and y values to graph
    years=[]
    graph_temps=[]
    # skip the header line
    next(reader)
    # for each line of data in the file
    for row in reader:
        # if the month matches the month to graph
        if row[2][-2:] == month_string:
            # add the year and the average temperature to the lists to graph
            years.append(int(row[2][0:4]))
            graph_temps.append(float(row[3]))
```

Next, we open the .csv file. You will want to substitute `'BurlingtonVTData.csv'` with your file name with the .csv extension on it. Make sure it is in the same folder as this Python file on your machine because that is where Python looks for it when the program runs. If your .csv file is in another folder, you can either copy or move it to the folder with the Python file or change this line to have the absolute file path. Once the .csv file is open, we create a reader variable from the csv library. This line makes sure that it reads the data correctly by stating that commas separate each piece of data.

Now we declare two lists: one named `years`, to hold the years (which will be the x values of the graph), and one named `graph_temps`, to hold the average January temperatures (which will be the corresponding y values of the graph).

Then we skip the first line of the file (the one with the headers for all the columns) with a call to the `next` function. For each row of data in the .csv file, we check whether it is January data and, if so, store the year and temperature into the `years` and `graph_temps` lists. Each `row` in the file is a list of all data in that line. For example, the first line of data would be the list

```
['USW00014742', "BURLINGTON INTERNATIONAL AIRPORT, VT US", '1940-
12', '22.9']
```

We can access one value from this list by using square brackets and an integer index: `row[0]` would give us the first piece of data in the line (in this case, `'USW00014742'`), `row[1]` would give us the second piece of data in the list, and so on. Indexing in Python can also use negative values to get items from the back of the list: `row[-1]` would give us the last piece of data in the line (in this case, `'22.9'`), `row[-2]` would give us the second-to-last piece of data in the line, and so on. Everything in the list is represented as a string by default (which is why everything in the list is surrounded by quotation marks), even if it has numeric data. In our .csv file, it is the value at index 2 (or –2) that holds the year and month, formatted as YYYY-MM (e.g., 1940-12 for December 1940). We want to isolate the month part, so we use our square-bracket indexing again to grab the last two digits of the string: `[-2:]`. We compare `row[2][-2:]` to the `month_string` variable to tell whether this row contains January data. If it does, then we need to store two pieces of information from it: we add the year (`row[2][0:4]`) as an integer to the `years` list, and we add the average temperature from the column at index 3 (`row[3]`) as a floating-point number to the `graph_temps` list. We use the `append` function to add it to the end of the list.

Program 6.3: Graphing Data in Python

```
# use matplotlib to graph the data
ax=plt.subplot(111)
ax.plot(years, graph_temps)
# only print every tenth year on x-axis
ax.xaxis.set_major_locator(plt.MaxNLocator(10))
# make sure y-axis starts at 0
ax.set_ylim(bottom=0)
ax.hlines([5, 10, 15, 20, 25, 30], 1940, 2019)
# label graph and axes
plt.gcf().canvas.set_window_title('BVT January Temperatures')
plt.title('Average January Temperatures for Burlington, VT')
plt.xlabel('Year')
plt.ylabel('Average January Temperature (F)')
```

Once we are finished reading in from the file, we can construct our graph. Note that these lines of code are no longer indented, because they will be executed after the file-reading loop ends. The first thing we do is use the `matplotlib subplot` function to set up the graph. We give it the number 111 because we have one set of *x* values, one set of *y* values, and we are starting with the first data in the set. Next, we use the plot function and give our *x* values (the `years` list) and our *y* values (the `graph_temps` list) for it to graph.

Next, we change some settings. By default, it will print every *x* value. With 78 years, that would overflow the *x* axis. So, using the `xaxis.set_major_locator` function, we set it to print only every tenth year. Also, by default, it will calculate the *y* range based on the data. We always want the *y* axis to start at 0, so we set that manually with the `set_ylim` function. Note that if you have data that goes into negative values, you may be okay with the default behavior. We also want to have horizontal bars across the *y* axis every 5°, so we use the `hlines` function to specify the *y* values and *x* range of these lines (you will need to adjust these values for your dataset). These functions are available from the `matplotlib` library.

Next, we want to label our graph and axes. These four lines use different functions to set the window title (which shows up in the top bar of the window that pops up), the title of the graph (which prints above the graph), the *x*-axis label, and the *y*-axis label.

The last thing we want to do before we display the graph is to calculate the line that best fits the data (program 6.4). We let `numpy` do the calculation for us, giving its `polyfit` function the list of years, the list of average monthly temperature values, and a 1 to signify that we want a first-degree (linear) function. This function returns the slope and *y* intercept, which we store in `m_graph` and `b_graph` variables, respectively. We can use these to calculate the best-fit monthly temperatures for each year in our dataset (using the equation of a line $y = mx + b$), which we do in a `for` loop for the graph. Then we plot the graph line using another call to `matplotlib`'s `plot` function. For all data, we print the slope of the line and the first and last best-fit monthly temperature values from the range of our dataset.

Program 6.4: Best-Fit Line in Python

```
# use numpy to calculate the best fit line to graph
b_graph, m_graph=polyfit(years, graph_temps, 1)
# calculate coordinates from the line's y and b values
line_y_values = []
for value in years:
    line_y_values.append(value * m_graph+b_graph)
# plot the line on the graph
plt.plot(years, line_y_values, '-')
```

Finally, we display the graph (program 6.5) by using the `show` function. When you run the program, you will see the graph pop up on your screen.

Program 6.5: Display the Graph in Python

```
# display the graph in a new window
plt.show()
```

The graphs from the Google Sheets (see figure 6.16) and Python (see figure 6.19) programs are exactly the same, and the values for the best-fit lines are equal.

6.4 Revisiting the Large Dataset

Now that we have graphed the January data and gained a better understanding of what the best-fit line represents with our dataset, let's revisit the full dataset and compute the best-fit line for all the months. If you used the Google Sheets method, click on an empty cell in the spreadsheet of the initial dataset that you downloaded and use the LINEST command (short for line estimate): `=LINEST(D2:D949)`. This produces two cells of data, the first cell being the slope of the best-fit line $b = 0.00397$ and the second cell being the *y* intercept $a = 43.4$. This means the trend line for the dataset of monthly average temperatures from December 1940 to November 2019 in Burlington, Vermont, is $y = 0.00397x + 43.4$, where *y* is the predicted average monthly temperature (°F) over the last 78 years and *x* is the number of months after December 1940.

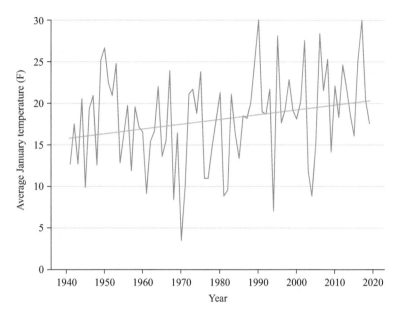

Figure 6.19
Graph of January average temperatures (F) for Burlington, Vermont, and best-fit line using
the Python programming language.

Based on the trend line, we can answer our question, *Has the average temperature for
Burlington, Vermont, changed over the last 78 years and, if so, by how much?* Yes, the average temperature has increased in Burlington, Vermont, because the slope of the best-fit
line is positive. How much has it increased? Let's plug our first and last months into the
equation to get the difference in temperature:

December 1940	November 2019
$y = 0.00397(0) + 43.4$	$y = 0.00397(947) + 43.4$
$y = 0 + 43.4$	$y = 3.76 + 43.4$
$y = 43.4°F$	$y = 47.2°F$

Note that for November 2019 we plugged in 947 for the number of months since
December 1940. This is because we have 948 rows of data, and the first row is December
1940, which is 0 months away from the start month, so the last row of November 2019
must be 947 months away from the start month. Now that we have the temperatures
of our best-fit line for the first and last months, we find that the difference in value is
$47.2 - 43.4 = 3.8°F$, so the temperature in Burlington, Vermont, increased by 3.8°F on
average over the last 78 years. The next interesting question is whether the change in
temperature is statistically significant.

Now let's perform the same computation in our Python program. You will need to
add the code in program 6.6.

Program 6.6: Best-Fit Line of All Data in Python

```
# declare an empty list to store all the temperature data
# add this line where you declare the years list
all_avg_month_temps = []
# add the average temperature to the list
# put this line in the "for row in reader" loop
all_avg_month_temps.append(float(row[3]))
# now add the rest to the end of the program
# use numpy to calculate the best fit line on all the data
b_all, m_all = polyfit(range(len(all_avg_month_temps)), all_avg_month_temps, 1)
# calculate the temperatures of the first and last month
print('First month temp (F):', b_all)
print('Last month temp(F):', (len(all_avg_month_temps)-1) * m_all+b_all)
print('Slope of best fit line:', format(m_all,'.5f'))
```

We add a list named `avg_month_temps` to store all the average temperature data from the file. Then, in the `for` loop, when we go through each row in our .csv file, we add the monthly average temperature to the `avg_month_temps` list. It is the fourth column of the dataset, so we index into our `row` list at index 3 (because indexing starts at 0).

Then, to find the best-fit line, we will use the `polyfit` function again. We give the function three inputs: the list of integers [0, 1, 2, . . . , 947] to keep track of the number of months since the beginning of the dataset, computed using the `len` and `range` functions to get the number of months and the list of integers in that range, respectively; the `avg_month_temps` list; and the value 1, because we still want a linear slope. We store the intercept and slope return values as `b_all` and `m_all` variables.

Next, we calculate and print the average temperature values of our best-fit line for our first and last months, as well as the slope of the best-fit line. We use the equation of a line ($y = mx + b$) with our variables ($y = $ `m_all`$*x + $ `b_all`), and the x values of the first (0) and last (947) months. The slope of the line (0.00397) and the first and last values (43.4°F and 47.2°F) that the Python program prints into the Shell window also exactly match the results from the Google Sheets program. The Python program has therefore helped us answer both our questions: yes, the temperature in Burlington, Vermont, has changed over the last 78 years, and it has increased by about 3.8°F.

With the answering of our research question and subquestion, several other questions started to pique our interest. How does the average temperature change affect the local ecosystem? How does this change in temperature affect the local economy? We also noticed a curious thing in the January average temperature dataset as we were processing it: there appeared to be a change in the upper and lower average temperatures after 1989. Why was that? What were the carbon dioxide levels during this time? How have the ocean temperatures changed during this time? Sometimes answering a question leads to more questions and opens more areas of interest.

6.5   Transferring Skills to Process Different Datasets

Now that we have experience processing data from .csv files, we can apply it to answer other research questions and other sets of data.

- What if we want to graph the amount of snowfall, amount of sunlight, maximum temperature, or minimum temperature instead of average temperature? We would go back to the NOAA NCDC website and from the Data Types for Custom Output webpage we would select the different data that we need (see figure 6.20) and perform the needed calculations and graphs.
- We could change the `row` index that we store in our `graph_temps` list (as well as the list name). Even better, we could create a variable for this index like the variable we created for the month and use the variable to index into the `row`. This is more readable and will be easier to change in the future.

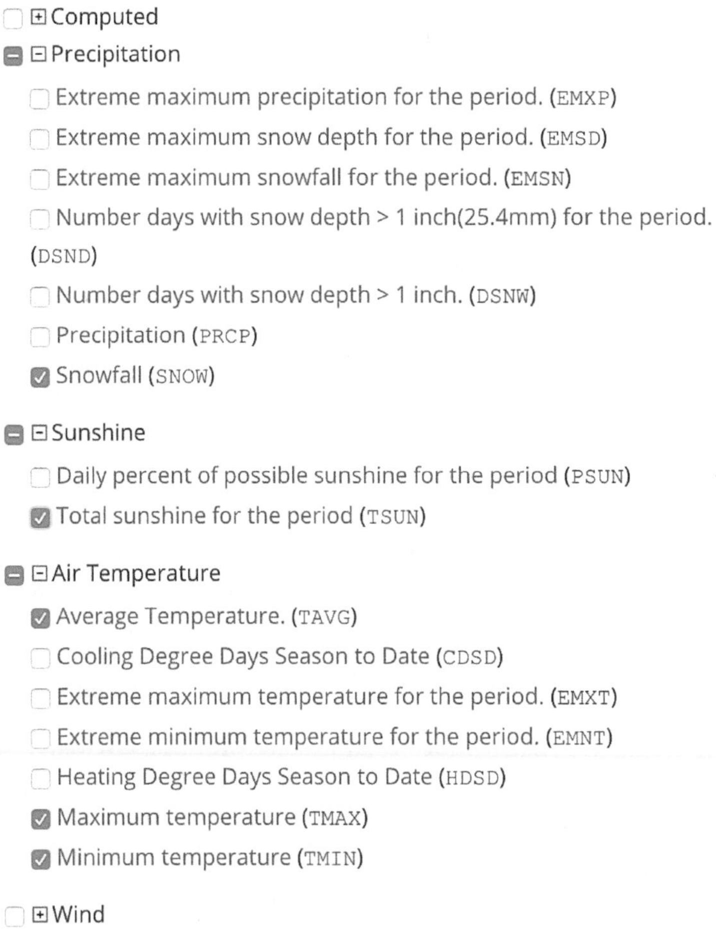

☐ ⊞ Computed

⊟ ⊟ Precipitation

   ☐ Extreme maximum precipitation for the period. (`EMXP`)

   ☐ Extreme maximum snow depth for the period. (`EMSD`)

   ☐ Extreme maximum snowfall for the period. (`EMSN`)

   ☐ Number days with snow depth > 1 inch(25.4mm) for the period.
   (`DSND`)

   ☐ Number days with snow depth > 1 inch. (`DSNW`)

   ☐ Precipitation (`PRCP`)

   ☑ Snowfall (`SNOW`)

⊟ ⊟ Sunshine

   ☐ Daily percent of possible sunshine for the period (`PSUN`)

   ☑ Total sunshine for the period (`TSUN`)

⊟ ⊟ Air Temperature

   ☑ Average Temperature. (`TAVG`)

   ☐ Cooling Degree Days Season to Date (`CDSD`)

   ☐ Extreme maximum temperature for the period. (`EMXT`)

   ☐ Extreme minimum temperature for the period. (`EMNT`)

   ☐ Heating Degree Days Season to Date (`HDSD`)

   ☑ Maximum temperature (`TMAX`)

   ☑ Minimum temperature (`TMIN`)

☐ ⊞ Wind

Figure 6.20
Other climate data types to be downloaded.

- What if the pattern of the scatter plot or line graph was more curved than straight? A best-fit line would not be the best solution. For this, we would need to change the `polyfit` function. Besides the coordinate values, the function also takes the degree (or number of coefficients in the equation) of the best-fit curve. We could change the `polyfit` function to be second degree (quadratic curve) by changing the last argument from a 1 to a 2 (or third degree by changing it to a 3 if the graphed data pattern more closely matched $y = x^3$, etc.). Then the function will return more variables to represent the coefficients of the quadratic equation.[14] For example, if you wanted to fit a cubic curve to your data, you would pass a 3 as the last argument to the `polyfit` function and would get four variables returned, representing a through d in the equation $y = ax^3 + bx^2 + cx + d$.

In our example, we asked the question, *Did the average temperature in Burlington, Vermont, change over 78 years and, if so, by how much?* What other questions can you answer with this data? What other questions do you have, and what data can you find to answer them?

It is also important to note what questions this information *doesn't* answer. We did not collect information from any other city on earth, so we cannot make any claims about global temperature change. We also did not explore the different factors affecting the rise in temperature and therefore could not conclude from our dataset whether humans are causing temperatures to rise more than they naturally would (as climate change would suggest). Be careful not to claim more results than your analysis of the data supports.

Learning Activity 6.4: Debating Data Results

Have students demonstrate how data can be used or manipulated to say different things or argue opposing facts with the same set of data.

1. Have your students determine, as a class, which topic they want to investigate or debate that has controversial and opposing sides. It could be a school, town or city, state, or national issue and could be related to issues they've heard about on the news, social media, or discussed among themselves.

2. Decide what questions or points of view exist for each side to investigate.

3. Create two teams in your classroom that will analyze and discuss the different sides of the question or argument.

4. Gather the same set of data information for the two teams to analyze, display, and discuss. This can be from

   - data the students collected on their own (e.g., surveys) or
   - data from a reputable database that they find on the internet. A reliable website satisfies the CRAAP test (see http://libguides.csuchico.edu/c.php?g=414315 &p=2822716).

5. Create manipulated data displays to support their side of the argument using only this one dataset, so they are using the same set of data to draw conclusions.

6. Present the arguments from the data displays. As team 1 presents their argument, have team 2 try to figure out the data manipulations that team 1 uses (and vice versa).

7. Report and debrief on the data manipulations that each team found and used. How did the manipulation of the data results and displays help each side of the argument? What did each team pay attention to in order to figure out the data manipulations?

6.6   Summary

By collecting, processing, and analyzing data downloaded from reputable internet sites, students can begin to ask questions and address issues that are pertinent to their real lives. They can help elevate issues and find solutions to pressing problems in our society today. Encourage your students to stay informed, identify biases and misinformation, and strive to solve the questions themselves by going directly to the primary source of the data.

In this chapter, we discuss how you can do this on your own with the content that you teach in order to integrate and embed computational thinking into your classroom content.

We know teachers worry, "How do I do all this on top of everything else I need to do?!" It is true that you have a lot to teach and students have a lot to learn. We advocate that you take small steps in the beginning, starting off small and taking on more as you are able. Change is a process that takes time and persistence. As you progress through a process to include computational thinking and/or programming in your instructional practices, you will need support in that process by gathering all the resources you can, collaborating with different people, persevering through roadblocks and obstacles, and learning from your mistakes.

In this chapter, we hear from teachers who used computational thinking in their classrooms. The first two stories come from teachers who incorporated computational thinking as part of a culminating unit project. The third story comes from a technology teacher whose goal was to teach loops and how to use random number generators, and who incorporated ideas from sections 2.1 (Kandinsky art) and 2.3 (Albers art) of chapter 2 to do it. In the fourth story, the teacher used embodied learning experiences to help her students overcome a misconception when drawing squares and equilateral triangles. The last episode is from an art teacher whose students designed and built an art installation over three months that included several aspects of computational thinking.

The practice of teaching is a complex enterprise. We understand the varied context every individual teacher is in, so we wrote the book with the belief that teachers are professionals who know their students' needs best. We believe that teachers are smart, industrious, and continuous learners who can take the information in this book and adapt it to fit their situations. We intended to give teachers flexibility and choice in how they present the material to their students rather than being too prescriptive regarding timing and organization. Different teachers we worked with confirmed this belief. One teacher commented, "I like how the book took it. It wasn't a lesson; it was outlining how to do this one problem and all the different parts of it. [It] made it easy to figure out a cool lesson plan. If a textbook has a lesson and I don't like parts of it, I discard it easily. I like that I could look at this and choose different pieces that I wanted to use." Another teacher commented that she could take the topology graph from chapter 3 and "use it for a unit on food chains . . . to examine what happens when a rabbit population tanks . . . to look at the different influencing factors. I won't use it for Harry Potter, it wouldn't make sense for my kids." For us, these comments verified that teachers are professionals who choose activities that work for them in their context.

7.1   Start Small: Have a Final Project That Contains Computational Thinking

Wiggins and McTighe (2005) argue that we should plan our lessons or units with a specific desired learning result in mind and then design the learning tasks such that students are able to demonstrate what they know and are able to do as a result of that learning at the end. Students can demonstrate what they know and are able to do through a performance task rather than a paper-and-pencil test. Wiggins and McTighe defined a performance task as an authentic task that uses a student's knowledge to effectively act or bring to fruition a complex product that "assesses the student's ability to efficiently and effectively use a repertoire of knowledge and skill to negotiate a complex and multistage task" (Wiggins and McTighe 2005, 154). These performance tasks incorporate computational thinking in that they require the breakdown of a complex and multistage task into its core components given the students' knowledge and understanding from the unit's big ideas, the transfer of learning to a new situation, and the creative displaying of that knowledge.

As the teacher, you decide how students demonstrate their knowledge to you, to their peers, and to the world. You could empower students to choose the means by which they demonstrate their mastery of the learning goals (e.g., do they want to present a slideshow or PowerPoint presentation, write a paper, create a video, write a song, or make a computer program).

For example, in a sixth-grade classroom, students had to discuss a significant event in a story and how it changed the trajectory of the characters' story arc from a book they were reading, drawing on specific details in the text. They were given the option, among many others, to create an animated program with the Scratch programming environment. A couple of boys took up their teacher's offer to use Scratch. They used the `think` and `say` commands to highlight important dialogue passages from the book. They created a different `backdrop` that reflected where some of the important scenes in the book took place. Students used the `move`, `glide`, and `turn` commands to highlight some key actions in the book. Creating an animated presentation of their knowledge about a book enabled the students to demonstrate their knowledge of the CCSS-ELA standards being assessed and incorporated computational thinking. The teacher created a rubric that outlined the key requirements for the assessment to ensure that the content was not lost in the creativity that the Scratch animation provided.

In another example, a sixth-grade social studies teacher gave the option of using *Minecraft* to create a digital diorama of Plimoth Plantation. The students had to satisfy the same NCSS standards as those who created a three-dimensional diorama. Just as the students had to gather information, plan their environment, solve problems, and persevere in making their three-dimensional models, students in the *Minecraft* environment had to apply those same computational thinking skills in the technology environment.

7.2   Scale Up: Create Lessons or Units of Learning That Include Computational Thinking Based on What Your Students Need to Know and Do

To create a lesson that includes rich tasks that integrate computational thinking with your content area, look at a standard you need to teach. What do the students need to know and do? What are the essential questions for your lesson or unit? After you have defined them, begin to think about the essential components of computational thinking that support learning the content standards or essential questions of your unit.

Are there ways that students can learn this content standard by including problem solving, collaboration, abstraction, and/or algorithmic processes? Then think about ways you can differentiate the learning with rich tasks that allow all students multiple entry points into the learning activity so that it is accessible to a wide range of learning abilities (low threshold); provides opportunities for extended learning and challenges advanced learners (high ceiling); incorporates a variety of approaches and allows diverse representations (wide walls); engenders interest in and engagement with the topic and is grounded in real-life experiences; encourages collaboration and discussion; sparks students' curiosity and promotes decision-making; and fosters creativity and individuality. As you think about including computational thinking in your lessons, always keep in mind the desired results and learning goals for your students.

One middle school technology teacher created a lesson based on sections 2.1 and 2.3 in chapter 2. She started the lesson by displaying a Kandinsky art image on the screen (similar to figure 2.2) with an opening prompt on the board that read, "What do you notice about this picture? Describe it. Describe how you could code it." She passed out paper and pencils and had students write for one minute. Using a think-pair-share pedagogical strategy, she had students turn and talk with a neighbor about their thinking. Afterward, she asked the class what they discussed and wrote down some of their ideas:

- "The circles change color when they overlap."
- "It looks like eyeballs floating in the ocean."
- "Some circles have a border."
- "You need a random circle generator."

She then prompted them for their coding ideas. They talked about the need for randomness for the colors and, after some prompting, mentioned loops to repeatedly draw the circles. Then the teacher had the students log into the computers and Google image search the artists Kandinsky and Albers, telling the students they could create a computer program in Scratch or Codesters that mimicked either artist's style or a combination of both. After about 40 minutes and walking around and working with different students, she displayed different students' projects on the screen.

- One student (working in Codesters) had static squares, circles, and triangles that were red, blue, yellow, orange, purple, and green (see figure 7.1).
- One student (working in Scratch) had squares of all different bright colors that were randomly moved and placed so the art looked like a whirlwind.
- One student (working in Codesters) took a picture of a Kandinsky picture and set it as the background image, then had different shapes appear on top of it.
- One student (in Scratch) created different squares and moved them so that they were concentric and in rainbow order.

After the lesson, the teacher reflected on her experience: "It was cool with how much range there was with what they could do. . . . I was worried that covering loops and hexadecimal and random at the same time would be too much, but it wasn't. They caught up with random quickly. There was a lot of stuff they could incorporate, [if they were done early] it was easy to think of other things they could do." She did learn that this was "easier on Codesters than Scratch, because in Scratch you have to have a lot of sprites . . . but it was good." The comment that made the teacher smile most was from a student

Figure 7.1
An example of the output from a student's simulation of Kandinsky's art style. Image: Courtesy of Codesters.

named Duncan, who told her, "I can't do art, but on the computer, I guess I'm not so bad." The teacher added that "it was cool for him to see that he can be an artist too. You say that the program is art, and now they know they can do art."

7.3   Learn All That You Can

Computational thinking is a way of thinking that is not new to a lot of people. Many people recognize the different components in the language of their content areas. However, integrating coding into your teaching is the newest piece of learning for many teachers. It takes time to learn new things. Cadieux Boulden et al. (2018) found that teachers' lack of time for learning how to code was the primary barrier to integrating computational thinking and coding into their teaching. Many teachers did not feel comfortable including coding in their lessons because they believed they lacked a background in computer programming. Structured time to learn new things may not be available at your school or in your school district, so you may need to start learning it on your own. There are a number of routes for overcoming this obstacle:

- Read some books about programming and its connection to teaching in the twenty-first century.
- Try out the different Hour of Code modules.
- Explore the Scratch, Codesters, or Python tutorials.
- Watch video tutorials on the internet about these coding languages. It does not have to be these languages specifically; there are a variety of programming languages out there you could learn.
- Have a tech-savvy friend or family member teach you about coding.

There are lots of resources available to learn how to code, and soon enough you can be a resource for other users.

For example, a sixth-grade mathematics teacher, after completing the Hour of Code Learning Course E, which included a lesson called "Drawing with Loops" (https://studio .code.org/s/coursee-2019), thought the lesson would be a good review for her students and would provide an opportunity for them to apply their understanding of different geometrical properties. As she watched her students in the computer lab one December day, she noticed them struggling to draw the different shapes with the `move forward 100 pixels` and `turn left` and `turn right` commands. In particular, she noticed them struggle with drawing the rocket's square window (https://studio.code.org/s/coursee -2019/stage/2/puzzle/5) and the equilateral triangle at the top of a rocket (https://studio .code.org/s/coursee-2019/stage/2/puzzle/6). She knew her students understood the properties of a square and an equilateral triangle, yet they struggled to draw the rocket's window or top with the `turn left` or `turn right` code commands. They coded the sprite to turn the incorrect number of degrees or to turn in the wrong direction.

The teacher did, however, love watching her students collaborate in trying to figure out how to draw the rocket top correctly. When a student found the solution to a problem, the solution ran through the classroom like wildfire. The teacher did question whether her students understood what they were copying from each other. Their time in the computer lab ended with only a couple of students having completed the "Drawing with Loops" lesson. The teacher decided that when they got back to the classroom, they were going to talk about the actions the sprite was taking on the screen based on the code the students wrote. Before the students shut down their computers, she asked them to screen capture their code and send her the pictures.

When her students came back to her the following day, she first had them share their understanding of the properties of a square and equilateral triangle, which she recorded on flip chart paper. Then she handed out a couple of examples from their screenshots from the day before that exemplified their struggles with why the code was not working as they wanted. In groups of three, she asked them to act out the action in the code—to be the sprite drawing the roof. From that experience, students realized that the direction the sprite was facing or where the sprite was located on the screen influenced how the next piece of code should be placed. The next time they went into the computer lab to work on their Hour of Code lesson, they had a deeper understanding of what they were doing when drawing the square and the triangle, and they applied that learning to draw the other shapes in the lesson.

7.4   Collaborate with Colleagues across Disciplines, Schools, and/or States

Sometimes you may be the only person in your school or district who is interested in integrating computational thinking and coding into your teaching, but you are not alone. There are other people who are interested in doing the same thing you are and are interested in working together. Send that cold email to find someone in your school, district, or community who is interested in transforming their practice to include more computational thinking in their teaching. Team up. Send out another email, asking to create a user group for teachers.

If you decide to include computer programming in your teaching, know that you do not have to be an expert coder to do this. There is an amazing online community that helps each other out. The Scratch, Codesters, and Python programming environments have an online help and share community that talks about problems with their programs. You can access that community for help and in the process teach your kids the skill of how to access help online safely.

For example, a middle school art teacher created with her seventh- and eighth-grade students an interactive, hands-on garden installation that incorporated major aspects of the Claude Monet garden in Giverny, France. She began her journey of incorporating computational thinking and coding into her teaching with one small flower that incorporated LED lights and sound. She made the flower as part of a course on creative maker spaces and using Arduinos. After she successfully crafted one small flower, she began to think about building a garden of flowers with lights and sound that worked independently of each other but wasn't sure where to begin.

Through her discussions and collaborations with a local technology education consultant and a technology specialist, the teacher learned of a garden created by MIT students that was used to teach coding. That information, in addition to the original flower prototype and her passion to integrate art with technological innovation, was enough to propel her. She proposed to her seventh-grade students that they make a garden of their own for their spring Fine Arts Festival. As part of this three-month unit, she introduced them to the artwork of French Impressionist Claude Monet and his garden in Giverny, France. Together, the teacher and her students identified three major areas of Monet's garden: the Japanese footbridge with pond, the willow tree, and the formal gardens. Through discussion and collaboration, the students also decided they wanted to create an arbor to welcome guests to their garden.

This teacher had never undertaken a project of this magnitude with her middle school students, yet the teacher and her students were invested in this art installation, and together they were determined to create their garden. The teacher assigned project managers (students whose primary role was to update their task lists and help others identify their next task to be completed) to help manage the time and the tasks.[1]

As the students began constructing their garden, the teacher realized she did not have all the answers to the many questions they asked. However, she saw this as an opportunity to teach her middle school students how to tackle unknown issues and devise solutions to their obstacles. She would say things like "I have no idea how we can make that. Let's do some research" or "Sounds like we need to build a prototype first." She was very transparent with her students regarding what she knew and didn't know. In order for the students to complete their project, they had to realize that their teacher did not have all the answers, nor could she do the project alone. As a collective unit, the students and teacher worked together collaboratively to complete their art installation.

Across multiple classes during their school day and various groups of students staying after school, they all pulled together to create their version of Monet's garden. In those three months, students learned to solder, create flowers with clay, and code. They painstakingly made over 80 LED flowers by hand and wired them to three bread-board Arduinos. There was even an interactive touch component to their garden, using Makey-Makey; guests of all ages were able to touch the art in order to hear different recorded sounds. This journey of teaching and learning resulted in an art installation that was a big success at the Fine Arts Festival. The teacher wrote, "I was proud of the final project, but what made me the happiest was the pride [the students] had in their artwork and their new skills. People from around the district were so impressed and my kids felt like rock stars. . . . It was an amazing experience, and I am so grateful for the support I received throughout the process but most importantly the hard work and investment of my students." After the Fine Arts Festival, the teacher and a small group of her students were invited to present their garden at Dynamic Landscapes, a technology education conference (personal communication, November 26, 2018).

This teacher's experience integrating computational thinking into her art class began with an initial idea, an interest, and a question, and it blossomed from there. The school year concluded with the students, the teacher, and the community seeing real-life learning take place in that classroom. Since then, it has led to a new idea, a new interest, and a new question—the cycle of inquiry built on this prior experience has become part of this teacher's teaching practice.

7.5   Keep Calm and Struggle On

Productive struggle is a good thing, not a bad thing, and not something you should shy away from. When you are trying out something new, you are going to struggle, and your students are going to struggle. It is totally normal. The part that can be destructive is when that struggle becomes frustration. If you are new to programming, let your students see how you troubleshoot and solve problems that arise.

As teachers, we can help equip our students with an awareness of the different phases and processes that occur in solving problems. Acknowledging and discussing students' emotional responses—both negative and positive—can help them realize that what they are experiencing is normal (Boaler 2015; Sousa 2016). We want students to experience productive struggle so that they can learn to persevere through problem-solving situations. One of the best ways for students to learn to overcome struggle productively is to watch their teachers learn from their own mistakes and get beyond their struggle points.

We have no doubt that a teacher's ability to incorporate computational thinking with unplugged activities is strong. Where we have witnessed teachers struggle is with the coding. When teachers experience struggle, it is often because the outcome of the code is not the outcome that they wanted, or a mistake was made. We want everyone to know that this is normal. When the code is not doing what you thought it was doing, go through the code line by line and figure out where the logic went awry. When you are debugging code, acting out the action in the code exactly as it is written often helps you find the errors. Also, don't be afraid to make mistakes when you are trying something new; use them as opportunities to learn and grow as an educator. Loucks-Horsley et al. (2009), Darling-Hammond et al. (2015), and Shulman (1986) argued that effective teaching requires a recursive process of planning, teaching, and reflecting on one's practice.

7.6   Summary

In making all of you aware of the ubiquity of computational thinking and computer science principles that drive twenty-first-century life, we hope that you see how it exists within every content domain and that it is accessible to all within the different content topics. By adapting the learning experiences in your classroom, you can inspire innovation in your students and help them rise to the challenge of being comfortable with facing and addressing challenging and complex problems. Computational thinking fosters skill development that is dynamic, creative, and applies critical thinking, productive struggle, perseverance, learning from mistakes, team building, and valuing the work of others. We hope that you will take the activities and rich tasks provided in these chapters and try some of them out with your students.

Appendix: Computer Programs

This chapter contains full versions of programs that appear throughout the text. Programs are presented in Processing (see www.processing.org), Codesters, and Python.

A.1 Drawing Cretan Labyrinths

The following Processing program draws a seven-circuit Cretan labyrinth on a computer screen, as shown in figure 4.7.

```
// file: labyrinth.pde
// Draws a seven-circuit Cretan labyrinth in two colors.
// Author: Robert R. Snapp

float t = 0;
float dt = 0.5;
Pvector last1;
Pvector last2;
Pvector pv1;
Pvector pv2;

void drawCross() {
    line(10, -80, 10, 0);
    line(-30,-40, 50, -40);
    arc(50,0,40,40, radians(180), radians(360));
    arc(-30,0,40,40, radians(180), radians(360));
    arc(-30,-80,40,40, radians(-90), radians(90));
    arc(50,-80,40,40, radians(90), radians(270));
}

void drawUpperArc(float r) {
    arc(0,0,r,r,0, radians(180));
}

void drawSWQuarter(float r) {
    arc(-30, 0, r, r, radians(180), radians(270));
}
```

```
void drawSEQuarter(float r){
    arc(50, 0, r, r, radians(270), radians(360));
}

void vbranch(float t, Pvector pv) {
    float rad=radians(t);
    if (t <= 0) {
        pv.x=50;
        pv.y=0;
    } else if (t <= 180) {
        pv.x=50*cos(rad);
        pv.y=50*sin(rad);
    } else if (t <= 360) {
        pv.x=20*cos(rad)-30;
        pv.y=20*sin(rad);
    } else if (t <= 540) {
        pv.x=-10*cos(rad);
        pv.y=10*sin(rad);
    } else if (t <= 630) {
        pv.x=10.0;
        pv.y=-40.0*(t-540)/90.;
    } else if (t <= 720) {
        pv.x=10.0;
        pv.y=-40*(t-630)/90.-40;
    } else if (t <= 810) {
        pv.x=-30+40*cos(rad);
        pv.y=-80-40*sin(rad);
    } else if (t <= 900) {
        pv.x=-30+120*cos(rad);
        pv.y=-120*sin(rad);
    } else if (t <= 1080) {
        pv.x=150*cos(rad);
        pv.y=-150*sin(rad);
    } else if (t <= 1170) {
        pv.x=50+100*cos(rad);
        pv.y=-100*sin(rad);
    } else if (t <= 1350) {
        pv.x=50+20*cos(rad);
        pv.y=-80-20*sin(rad);
    } else if (t <= 1440) {
        pv.x=50+60*cos(rad);
        pv.y=60*sin(rad);
    } else if (t <= 1620) {
        pv.x=110*cos(rad);
        pv.y=110*sin(rad);
    } else if (t <= 1710) {
        pv.x=-30+80*cos(rad);
        pv.y=80*sin(rad);
    } else {
```

```
            pv.x=-30;
            pv.y=-80;
        }
}

void hbranch(float t, Pvector pv) {
    float rad=radians(t);
    if (t <= 0) {
        pv.x=-30;
        pv.y=0;
    } else if (t <= 180) {
        pv.x=-30*cos(rad);
        pv.y=30*sin(rad);
    } else if (t <= 360) {
        pv.x=20*cos(rad)+50;
        pv.y=20*sin(rad);
    } else if (t <= 540) {
        pv.x=70*cos(rad);
        pv.y=70*sin(rad);
    } else if (t <= 630) {
        pv.x=40*cos(rad)-30;
        pv.y=40*sin(rad);
    } else if (t <= 720) {
        pv.x=40*(t-630)/90.-30;
        pv.y=-40;
    } else if (t <= 810) {
        pv.x=40*(t-720)/90.+10;
        pv.y=-40;
    } else if (t <= 900) {
        pv.x=50-40*cos(rad);
        pv.y =-40*sin(rad);
    } else if (t <= 1080) {
        pv.x=-90*cos(rad);
        pv.y=-90*sin(rad);
    } else if (t <= 1170) {
        pv.x=-30-60*cos(rad);
        pv.y=-60*sin(rad);
    } else if (t <= 1350) {
        pv.x=-30-20*cos(rad);
        pv.y=-80+20*sin(rad);
    } else if (t <= 1440) {
        pv.x=-30-100*cos(rad);
        pv.y=100*sin(rad);
    } else if (t <= 1620) {
        pv.x=-130*cos(rad);
        pv.y=130*sin(rad);
    } else if (t <= 1710) {
        pv.x=50-80*cos(rad);
        pv.y=80*sin(rad);
```

```
    } else {
        pv.x=50;
        pv.y=-80;
    }
}

void setup(){
    size(900,900);
    frameRate(480);
    smooth();
    background(240);

    last1=new PVector(0,0);
    last2=new PVector(0,0);
    pv1=new PVector(0,0);
    pv2=new PVector(0,0);
    vbranch(1710, last1);
    hbranch(1710, last2);
    vbranch(1710, pv1);
    hbranch(1710, pv2);
}

void draw() {
    translate(width/2, height/2);
    scale(2.5,-2.5);

    vbranch(1710-t, pv1);
    hbranch(1710-t, pv2);

    strokeWeight(3);
    stroke(200,0,0);
    line(pv1.x, pv1.y, last1.x, last1.y);
    last1=pv1;

    stroke(150, 150, 255);
    line(pv2.x, pv2.y, last2.x, last2.y);
    last2=pv2;

    t += dt;
}
```

A.2 Bumper Rocks

The following program is coded in Codesters to simulate elastic collision, as seen in figure 5.8.

```
# Author: Lisa Dion
# set the background image
stage.set_background("jupiter")
```

```
# create the rock with initial size and speed
rock=codesters.Sprite("rock")
rock.set_size(0.5)
rock.set_x_speed(2)
rock.set_y_speed(-3)

# create the asteroid with initial size, position, and speed
asteroid=codesters.Sprite("asteroid")
asteroid.set_size(0.5)
asteroid.go_to(-200, 0)
asteroid.set_x_speed(-1)
asteroid.set_y_speed(4)

# create a function for the "s" key to make the rock smaller
def s_key():
    # make the rock smaller
    rock.set_size(0.8)
# this line makes the code listen for the "s" key
stage.event_key("s", s_key)

# create a function for the "w" key to make the rock larger
def w_key():
    # make the rock bigger
    rock.set_size(1 / 0.8)
# this line makes the code listen for the "w" key
stage.event_key("w", w_key)

# create a function for collision of the objects
def collision(sprite, hit_sprite):
    # set variables
    size_sum=rock.get_size()+asteroid.get_size()
    x_vel_1=sprite.get_x_speed()
    x_vel_2=hit_sprite.get_x_speed()
    y_vel_1=sprite.get_y_speed()
    y_vel_2=hit_sprite.get_y_speed()
    rock_x=rock.get_x()
    rock_y=rock.get_y()
    asteroid_x=asteroid.get_x()
    asteroid_y=asteroid.get_y()
  # calculate the new velocities for 2-dimensional elastic collisions
    # the following 4 command lines are each on their own line
    sprite.set_x_speed(x_vel_1-((2*asteroid.get_size())/size_sum) *
((x_vel_1-x_vel_2)*(rock_x-asteroid_x)+(y_vel_1- y_vel_2)*(rock_y-
asteroid_y))  /  ((rock_x-asteroid_x)*(rock_x-asteroid_x)+(rock_y-
asteroid_y)*(rock_y-asteroid_y)) * (rock_x-asteroid_x))
    sprite.set_y_speed(y_vel_1-((2*asteroid.get_size())/size_sum) *
((x_vel_1-x_vel_2)*(rock_x-asteroid_x)+(y_vel_1- y_vel_2)*(rock_y-
asteroid_y))  /  ((rock_x-asteroid_x)*(rock_x-asteroid_x)+(rock_y-
asteroid_y)*(rock_y-asteroid_y)) * (rock_y- asteroid_y))
```

```
    hit_sprite.set_x_speed(x_vel_2-((2*rock.get_size())/size_sum) *
((x_vel_2-x_vel_1)*(asteroid_x-rock_x)+(y_vel_2- y_vel_1)*(asteroid
_y-rock_y))   /   ((rock_x-asteroid_x)*(rock_x-asteroid_x)+(rock_y-
asteroid_y)*(rock_y-asteroid_y)) * (asteroid_x-rock_x))
    hit_sprite.set_y_speed(y_vel_2-((2*rock.get_size())/size_sum)*((x
_vel_2-x_vel_1)*(asteroid_x-rock_x)+(y_vel_2- y_vel_1)*(asteroid_y-
rock_y))/((rock_x-asteroid_x)*(rock_x-asteroid_x)+(rock_y-asteroid
_y)*(rock_y-asteroid_y)) * (asteroid_y-rock_y))

# this line makes the program detect collision and
# call the function above
rock.event_collision(collision)

# create a function to move the objects and bounce off walls
def move(sprite):
    sprite.move_forward(1)
    if sprite.get_x() >= 250 or sprite.get_x() <= -250:
        sprite.set_x_speed(-sprite.get_x_speed())
    if sprite.get_y() >= 250 or sprite.get_y() <= -250:
        sprite.set_y_speed(-sprite.get_y_speed())

# have the program run forever
while True:
    move(rock)
    move(asteroid)
```

A.3 Basketball

The following program is coded in Codesters to simulate the physics involved in shooting a basketball, as seen in figure 5.9.

```
# Author: Lisa Dion
# set gravity's strength
stage.set_gravity(10)
stage.set_background("halfcourt")
net=codesters.Sprite("basketballnet", 200, 100)
# we do not want the net to fall
net.set_physics_off()
net.set_gravity_off()
player=codesters.Sprite("player3", -180, -130)
# we do not want the player to fall
player.set_physics_off()
player.set_gravity_off()
ball=codesters.Sprite("basketball", -150, -130)
# we do not want the ball to fall yet
ball.set_physics_off()
ball.set_gravity_off()
# create a rectangle along the floor
```

```
floor = codesters.Rectangle(0, -250, 500, 10, "red")
# create a function called shoot
def shoot(x_speed, y_speed):
    # set the ball's speed to make it move
    ball.set_x_speed(x_speed)
    ball.set_y_speed(y_speed)


# create a function for collisions
def collision(sprite, hit_sprite):
    # check for a score
    # the next two lines should be on one line of code
    if sprite.get_x() >= 165 and sprite.get_x() <= 215 and sprite.
get_y() >= 75 and sprite.get_y() <= 100 and sprite.get_y_speed() < 0:
        # stop the ball
        sprite.set_x_speed(0)
        sprite.set_y_speed(0)
        sprite.set_physics_off()
        sprite.set_gravity_off()
        # create a win message
        message = codesters.Text("You scored!", 0, 0, "white")
    # check if the ball hit the red floor
    elif hit_sprite.get_color() == "red":
        # stop the ball
        sprite.set_x_speed(0)
        sprite.set_y_speed(0)
        sprite.set_physics_off()
        sprite.set_gravity_off()
        # create a lose message
        message = codesters.Text("Try again!", 0, 0, "white")


ball.event_collision(collision)

# prompt the player for inputs
x_vel = int(player.ask("Enter an x-velocity:"))
y_vel = int(player.ask("Enter a y-velocity:"))
# now we want the ball to fall
ball.set_physics_on()
ball.set_gravity_on()
# this calls the function above
shoot(x_vel, y_vel)
```

A.4   Ping-pong

The following program is written in Codesters to demonstrate reflection, as discussed in section 5.3.

```
# Author: Lisa Dion
# import the random number generator library module
import random
```

```
# set a list of speeds that we will choose from
speeds = [-4, -3, 3, 4]
# create the ball and set initial values
ball = codesters.Circle(0, 0, 50, "green")
ball.set_size(0.5)
# set the ball velocity in x and y components
ball.set_x_speed(speeds[random.randint(0, len(speeds)-1)])
ball.set_y_speed(speeds[random.randint(0, len(speeds)-1)])
# create rectangles for the paddles
# sprite = codesters.Rectangle(x, y, width, height, "color")
player1 = codesters.Rectangle(-230, 0, 10, 50, "yellow")
player2 = codesters.Rectangle(230, 0, 10, 50, "gray")
# create rectangles against the left and right walls
left_wall = codesters.Rectangle(-250, 0, 10, 500, "red")
right_wall = codesters.Rectangle(250, 0, 10, 500, "red")


# create a function for when "w" is pressed
def w_key():
    # make sure there is room to move up
    if player1.get_y() < 220:
        player1.move_up(20)


# create a function for when "s" is pressed
def s_key():
    # make sure there is room to move down
    if player1.get_y() > -220:
        player1.move_down(20)


# create a function for when up is pressed
def up_key():
    # make sure there is room to move up
    if player2.get_y() < 220:
        player2.move_up(20)


# create a function for when down is pressed
def down_key():
    # make sure there is room to move down
    if player2.get_y() > -220:
        player2.move_down(20)


# make the program listen for the keys
stage.event_key("s", s_key)
stage.event_key("w", w_key)
stage.event_key("up", up_key)
stage.event_key("down", down_key)


# create a function to detect collision
def collision(sprite, hit_sprite):
    # make ball bounce off paddles by changing its x-direction
```

```
    ball.set_x_speed(-ball.get_x_speed())
    # check if the ball hit the left or right wall
    if hit_sprite.get_color() == "red":
        # stop the ball
        ball.set_x_speed(0)
        ball.set_y_speed(0)
        if hit_sprite.get_x() < 0:
            # ball hit left wall.
            msg=codesters.Text("Player 2 wins!", 0, 0, "red")
        else:
            # ball hit right wall.
            msg=codesters.Text("Player 1 wins!", 0, 0, "red")
# make the program listen for collisions
ball.event_collision(collision)
```

A.5 Reading Temperatures from a File

The following program is written in Python to read from a file and graph average January temperatures for Burlington, Vermont, as seen in figure 6.19.

```
# Author: Lisa Dion
# Import the csv library so we can read in from a csv file
import csv
# Import matplotlib so we can graph the data
import matplotlib.pyplot as plt
# Import numpy so we can fit a line to the data
from numpy.polynomial.polynomial import polyfit


# Use January as the month to graph
month_string='01'

# Open the csv file
with open('BurlingtonVTData.csv') as csv_file:
    # Use the reader from the csv library
    reader=csv.reader(csv_file, delimiter=',')
    # Declare an empty list for all the months' temps for
    # the best fit line
    all_avg_month_temps=[]
    # Declare empty lists to hold what will be the x and y
    # values to graph
    years=[]
    graph_temps=[]
    # Skip the header line
    next(reader)
    # For each line of data in the file
    for row in reader:
        # Add the average temperature to the list
        all_avg_month_temps.append(float(row[3]))
        # If the month matches the month to graph
```

```
        if row[2][-2:] == month_string:
        # Add the year and the average temperature to the
        # lists to graph
            years.append(int(row[2][0:4]))
            graph_temps.append(float(row[3]))

# Use matplotlib to graph the data
ax=plt.subplot(111)
ax.plot(years, graph_temps)
# Only print every tenth year on x-axis
ax.xaxis.set_major_locator(plt.MaxNLocator(10))
# Make sure y-axis starts at 0
ax.set_ylim(bottom=0)
ax.hlines([5, 10, 15, 20, 25, 30], 1940, 2019)
# Label graph and axes
plt.gcf().canvas.set_window_title('BVT January Temperatures')
plt.title('Average January Temperatures for Burlington, VT')
plt.xlabel('Year')
plt.ylabel('Average January Temperature (F)')

# Use numpy to calculate the best fit line to graph
b_graph, m_graph=polyfit(years, graph_temps, 1)
# Calculate coordinates from the line's y and b values
line_y_values=[]
for value in years:
    line_y_values.append(value * m_graph+b_graph)
# Plot the line on the graph
plt.plot(years, line_y_values, '-')

# Use numpy to calculate the best fit line on all the data
# The next command should be on one line
b_all, m_all=polyfit(range(len(all_avg_month_temps)),
all_avg_month_temps, 1)
# Calculate the temperatures of the first and last month
print('First month temp (F):', b_all)
# The next command should be on one line
print('Last month temp(F):', (len(all_avg_month_temps)-1)
* m_all+b_all)
print ('Slope of best fit line:', format(m_all,'.5f'))

# Display the graph in a new window
plt.show()
```

Notes

Chapter 2

1. At the time of this writing, Codesters is free for teachers but requires payment to create a "classroom" for students to access.

Chapter 3

1. The information about Conway's Game of Life is from http://www.conwaylife.com /wiki/Conway's_Game_of_Life.

Chapter 4

1. These myths are recounted in Plutarch's *Theseus* and Ovid's *Metamorphoses*.

2. It has twelve roofed courts, with doors facing one another, six to the north and six to the south and in a continuous line. One wall on the outside encompasses them all. There are double sets of chambers in it, some underground and some above, and their number is three thousand; there are fifteen hundred of each. We ourselves saw the aboveground chambers, for we went through them and so can talk of them, but the underground chambers we can speak of only from hearsay. For the officials of the Egyptians entirely refused to show us these, saying that there were, in them, the coffins of the kings who had built the labyrinth at the beginning and also those of the holy crocodiles. So we speak from hearsay of these underground places; but what we saw above ground was certainly greater than all human works. The passages through the rooms and the winding goings-in and out through the courts, in their extreme complication, caused us countless marvelings as we went through, from the court into the rooms, and from the rooms into the pillared corridors, and then from these corridors into other rooms again, and from the rooms into other courts afterwards.

—Herodotus (1987, book II, §148)

3. Matthews (1922) is available online via Project Gutenberg: http://www.gutenberg.org /ebooks/46238.

4. A related exercise is the "telephone challenge," in which two students are connected by telephone or alternatively seated back-to-back. One student, let's call her Alice, looks at a simple design, perhaps figure 4.1; the other student, let's call him Bob, holds a pencil and a sheet of unruled paper. Using only verbal cues, Alice must get Bob to draw a faithful replica of the design she is viewing.

5. The medial axis is an upwardly directed ray that emanates from the center of the cross.

6. This is essentially the definition of what is known as *algorithmic complexity*.

7. Doob (1990, chap. 8) suggests that the *entire* work is designed as a literary labyrinth on many levels; for example, the "circuitous wanderings" of Aeneas and his party through the Mediterranean Sea mirror the twists and turns of a labyrinth.

8. Computer scientists usually include 0 in the natural numbers, which mathematicians sometimes exclude.

9. Interestingly, decimal numbers can also be thought of as lists; for example, 123 represents the value $3 + 20 + 100$, which can be associated with the list (3, 2, 1).

Chapter 5

1. This equation is from http://www.sciencecalculators.org/mechanics/collisions/.

Chapter 6

1. On global warming, see US National Oceanic and Atmospheric Administration (NOAA), National Climatic Data Center (NCDC), http://www.ncdc.noaa.gov/cdo-web/, last accessed February 1, 2020.

2. On species extinction, see IUCN, *The IUCN Red List of Threatened Species*, https://www.iucnredlist.org, last accessed February 1, 2020.

3. On immigration trends, see Department of Homeland Security, *Immigration Data and Statistics*, http://www.dhs.gov/immigration-statistics, last accessed February 1, 2020.

4. On school funding, see US Census Bureau, *Public Education Funding: 2017 Public Elementary–Secondary Education Finance Data*, https://census.gov/data/tables.html, last accessed February 1, 2020. You can go to https://www.census.gov and https://www.census.gov/data.html to gather data on various topics related to census questions.

5. On gun violence in the United States, see Centers for Disease Control and Prevention, Web-Based Injury Statistics Query and Reporting System (WISQARS), *Fatal and Nonfatal Injury Data*, https://www.cdc.gov/injury/wisqars, last accessed February 1, 2020.

6. On food insecurity, see US Department of Agriculture, USDA Economic Research Service, Food Security in the US, https://www.ers.usda.gov/topics/food-nutrition-assistance/food-security-in-the-us/, last accessed February 1, 2020.

7. On the spread of infectious diseases and other health-related issues, see Centers for Disease Control, Data and Statistics, https://www.cdc.gov/DataStatistics/, last accessed February 1, 2020.

8. On wealth distribution, see US Census Bureau, *Small Area Income and Poverty Estimates*, https://www.census.gov/programs-surveys/saipe/data/datasets.html, last accessed February 1, 2020.

9. See Mapping Police Violence, database download, https://mappingpoliceviolence.org/s/MPVDatasetDownload.xlsx, last accessed February 1, 2020.

10. US Census Bureau, American Fact Finder, https://factfinder.census.gov/faces/tableservices/jsf/pages/productview.xhtml?src=bkmk, last accessed February 1, 2020.

11. FBI, Uniform Crime Reporting, *Table 1: Crime in the United States by Volume and Rate per 100,000 Inhabitants, 1999–2018*, https://ucr.fbi.gov/crime-in-the-u.s/2018/crime-in-the-u.s.-2018/topic-pages/tables/table-1, last accessed February 1, 2020.

12. We have 78 years because the data from the weather station we chose in Burlington, Vermont, is not available before December 1940. You may want to include a different time frame if more data is available from your location.

13. If you are using Safari as a web browser, it may not let you download it as a .csv file, so you may need to use another web browser, such as Google Chrome or Firefox, when you click the link that NCDC sends you.

14. One note about this (for our dataset) is that the years start at 1940, so that can influence the curvature. We recommend changing the `years` argument in this line to `range(len(years))` to have it start counting at 0 instead of 1940. This change is also needed when the y values are calculated inside the `for` loop, so that the data remains consistent.

Chapter 7

1. To read more about this installation, see https://www.facebook.com/GeneratorVT/videos /monets-garden-created-and-coded-by-mt-abraham-union-middle-school-with-generator /805713946294145/.

References

ABET (Accreditation Board for Engineering and Technology). 2018. *Criteria for Accrediting Engineering Programs 2018–2019, General Criterion 3: Student Outcomes*. https://www.abet .org/accreditation/accreditation-criteria/criteria-for-accrediting-engineering-programs-2018 -2019/.

Aguirre, Julia, Karen Mayfield-Ingram, and Danny Martin. 2013. *The Impact of Identity in K–8 Mathematics: Rethinking Equity-Based Practices*. Reston, VA: National Council of Teachers of Mathematics.

Ahmed, Afzal. 1987. *Better Mathematics: A Curriculum Development Study Based on the Low Attainers in Mathematics Project*. London: Her Majesty's Stationery Office.

Aho, Alfred V. 2012. "Computation and Computational Thinking." *Computer Journal* 55 (7): 832–835.

Alcuin of York. 1992. "Problems to Sharpen the Young." Translated by John Hadley and David Singmaster. *The Mathematical Gazette* 76 (475): 102–106.

Angeli, Charoula, Joke Voogt, Andrew Fluck, Mary Webb, Margaret Cox, Joyce Malyn-Smith, and Jason Zagami. 2016. "A K–6 Computational Thinking Curriculum Framework: Implications for Teacher Knowledge." *Journal of Educational Technology and Society* 19 (3): 47–57.

Averbach, Bonnie, and Orin Chein. 2000. *Problem Solving through Recreational Mathematics*. Mineola, NY: Dover.

Barr, Valerie, and Chris Stephenson. 2011. "Bringing Computational Thinking to K–12: What Is Involved and What Is the Role of the Computer Science Education Community?" *ACM Inroads* 2 (1): 48–54.

Barrios, Tina, J. Ambler, A. Anderson, P. Barton, S. Burnette, C. Feyten, and C. Yahn. 2004. *Laptops for Learning: Final Report and Recommendations of the Laptops for Learning Task Force*. University of South Florida. http://etc.usf.edu/l4l/report.pdf.

Belenky, Mary Field, Blythe M. Clinchy, Nancy Rule Goldberger, and Jill Mattuck Tarule. 1996. *Women's Ways of Knowing: The Development of Self, Voice, and Mind*. New York: Basic Books.

Bell, Tim, Jason Alexander, Isaac Freeman, and Mick Grimley. 2009. "Computer Science Unplugged: School Students Doing Real Computing without Computers." *New Zealand Journal of Applied Computing and Information Technology* 13 (1): 20–29.

Bellman, Richard. 1958. "On a Routing Problem." *Quarterly of Applied Mathematics* 16:87–90.

Blakeslee, Sarah. 2004. "The CRAAP Test." *LOEX Quarterly* 31:6–7.

Blakeslee, Sarah. 2010. *Evaluating Information: Applying the CRAAP Test*. Chico: Meriam Library, California State University. https://library.csuchico.edu/help/source-or-information-good.

Blickenstaff, Jacob Clark. 2005. "Women and Science Careers: Leaky Pipeline or Gender Filter?" *Gender and Education* 17 (4): 369–386.

Boaler, Jo. 2000. "Exploring Situated Insights into Research and Learning." *Journal for Research in Mathematics Education* 31 (1): 113–119.

Boaler, Jo. 2011. "Changing Students' Lives through the De-tracking of Urban Mathematics Classrooms." *Journal of Urban Mathematics Education* 4 (1): 7–14.

Boaler, Jo. 2015. *What's Math Got to Do with It? How Teachers and Parents Can Transform Mathematics Learning and Inspire Success*. 2nd ed. New York: Penguin Books.

Boaler, Jo. 2016. *Mathematical Mindsets: Unleashing Students' Potential through Creative Math, Inspiring Messages and Innovative Teaching*. San Francisco: Jossey-Bass.

Boaler, Jo, and Megan Staples. 2008. "Creating Mathematical Futures through an Equitable Teaching Approach: The Case of Railside School." *Teachers College Record* 110 (3): 608–645.

Boulden, Danielle Cadieux, Eric Wiebe, Bita Akram, Osman Aksit, Philip Sheridan Buffum, Bradford Mott, Kristy Elizabeth Boyer, and James Lester. 2018. "Computational Thinking Integration into Middle Grades Science Classrooms: Strategies for Meeting the Challenges." *Middle Grades Review* 4 (3). https://scholarworks.uvm.edu/mgreview/vol4/iss3/5.

Bransford, John D., Ann L. Brown, and Rodney R. Cocking, eds. 2000. *How People Learn: Brain, Mind, Experience, and School*. Expanded ed. Washington, DC: National Academy Press.

Bray, Wendy S. 2013. "How to Leverage the Potential of Mathematical Errors." *Teaching Children Mathematics* 19 (7): 424–431.

Brennan, Karen, and Mitchel Resnick. 2012. "New Frameworks for Studying and Assessing the Development of Computational Thinking." Presented at the annual meeting of the American Educational Research Association, Vancouver, Canada, April 13–17, 2012.

Brooks, Martin G., and Jacqueline Grennon Brooks. 1999. "The Courage to Be Constructivist." *Educational Leadership* 7 (3): 18–24.

Bundy, Alan. 2007. "Computational Thinking Is Pervasive." *Journal of Scientific and Practical Computing* 1 (2): 67–69.

Cairo, Alberto. 2019. *How Charts Lie: Getting Smarter about Visual Information*. New York: Norton.

Cathart, W. George, Yvonne M. Pothier, James H. Vance, and Nadine S. Besuk. 2016. *Learning Mathematics in Elementary and Middle Schools: A Learner Centered Approach*. Boston: Pearson Education.

CCSSI (Common Core State Standards Initiative). 2010. *Common Core State Standards for Mathematics*. Washington, DC: National Governors Association Center for Best Practices and the Council of Chief State School Officers. http://www.corestandards.org/assts/CCSSI_Math%20Standards.pdf.

Cohen, Elizabeth G. 1994. *Designing Groupwork: Strategies for the Heterogeneous Classroom*. New York: Teachers College Press.

Cohen, Elizabeth G., and Rachel A. Lotan. 1995. "Producing Equal-Status Interaction in the Heterogeneous Classroom." *American Educational Research Journal* 32 (1): 99–120.

Cohen, Elizabeth, and Rachel Lotan, eds. 1997. *Working for Equity in Heterogeneous Classrooms: Sociological Theory in Practice*. New York: Teachers College Press.

College Board. 2017. *AP Computer Science Principles: Including the Curricular Framework*. New York: College Board.

Creswell, John W. 2012. *Educational Research: Planning, Conducting, and Evaluating Quantitative and Qualitative Research*. Boston: Pearson Education.

Cuny, Jan. 2011. "Transforming Computer Science Education in High Schools." *Computer* 44 (6): 107–109.

Darling-Hammond, Linda, Brigid Barron, P. David Pearson, Alan H. Schoenfeld, Elizabeth K. Stage, Timothy D. Zimmerman, Gina N. Cervetti, and Jennifer L. Tilson. 2015. *Powerful Learning: What We Know about Teaching for Understanding*. San Francisco: Wiley.

Dede, Chris. 2010. "Comparing Frameworks for 21st Century Skills." In *21st Century Skills: Rethinking How Students Learn*, edited by James Bellanca and Ron Brandt, 51–76. Bloomington, IN: Solution Tree.

Delpit, Lisa. 2006. *Other People's Children: Cultural Conflict in the Classroom*. New York: The New Press.

Denning, Peter J. 2017a. "Remaining Trouble Spots with Computational Thinking." *Communications of the ACM* 60 (6): 33–39.

Denning, Peter J. 2017b. "Computational Thinking in Science." *American Scientist* 105 (1): 13–17. https://doi.org/10.1511/2017.124.13.

Dewey, John. 1916. *Democracy and Education*. New York: Macmillan.

Dewey, John. 1938. *Experience and Education*. New York: Simon and Schuster.

Dewey, John. 1964 [1899]. "The School and Society." In *John Dewey on Education: Selected Writings*, edited by R. Archambault, 295–310. Chicago: University of Chicago Press.

Dodge, Yadolah. 2003. *The Oxford Dictionary of Statistical Terms*. Oxford: Oxford University Press.

Doob, Penelope Reed. 1990. *The Idea of the Labyrinth: From Classical Antiquity through the Middle Ages*. Ithaca, NY: Cornell University Press.

Drake, Susan M., and Rebecca C. Burns. 2004. *Meeting Standards through Integrated Curriculum*. Alexandria, VA: ASCD.

Dweck, Carol. 2006. *Mindset: The New Psychology of Success*. New York: Random House.

Even, Shimon. 1979. *Graph Algorithms*. Rockville, MD: Computer Science Press.

Florida Center for Instructional Technology, University of South Florida, College of Education. 2017. *The Technology Integration Matrix*. https://fcit.usf.edu/matrix/matrix/.

Ford, Lester R., Jr. 1956. *Network Flow Theory*. Publication no. P-923. Santa Monica, CA: RAND Corporation.

Fosnot, Catherine Twomey, and Randall Stewart Perry. 1996. "Constructivism: A Psychological Theory of Learning." *Constructivism: Theory, Perspectives, and Practice* 2:8–33.

Fox, Mary Frank, Gerhard Sonnert, and Irina Nikiforova. 2009. "Successful Programs for Undergraduate Women in Science and Engineering: Adapting versus Adopting the Institutional Environment." *Research in Higher Education* 50 (4): 333–353.

Fraenkel, Jack R., Norman E. Wallen, and Helen H. Hyun. 2015. *How to Design and Evaluate Research in Education*. 9th ed. New York: McGraw Hill Education.

Fuchs, Lynn S., Douglas Fuchs, Robin Finelli, Susan J. Courey, and Carol L. Hamlett. 2004. "Expanding Schema-Based Transfer Instruction to Help Third Graders Solve Real-Life Mathematical Problems." *American Educational Research Journal* 41 (2): 419–445.

Giancoli, Douglas C. 2005. *Physics: Principles with Applications*. 6th ed. Upper Saddle River, NJ: Pearson Education.

Gibson, J. Paul. 2012. "Teaching Graph Algorithms to Children of All Ages." In *Proceedings of the 17th ACM Annual Conference on Innovation and Technology in Computer Science Education, ITiCSE '12, Haifa, Israel*, 34–39. New York: ACM. https://doi.org/10.1145/2325296 .2325308.

Greenwald, Anthony G., Mahzarin R. Banaji, Laurie A. Rudman, Shelly D. Farnham, Brian A. Nosek, and Deborah S. Mellott. 2002. "A Unified Theory of Implicit Attitudes, Stereotypes, Self-Esteem, and Self-Concept." *Psychological Review* 109 (1): 3–25.

Grover, Shuchi, and Roy Pea. 2013. "Computational Thinking in K–12: A Review of the State of the Field." *Educational Researcher* 42 (1): 38–43.

Gutstein, Eric, and Bob Peterson. 2013. *Rethinking Mathematics: Teaching Social Justice by the Numbers*. 2nd ed. Milwaukee: Rethinking Schools.

Hadley, John, and David Singmaster. 1992. "Problems to Sharpen the Young." *The Mathematical Gazette* 76 (475): 102–126. https://doi.org/10.2307/3620384.

Harlow, Danielle Boyd, Hilary Dwyer, Alexandria K. Hansen, Charlotte Hill, Ashley Iveland, Anne E. Leak, and Diana M. Franklin. 2016. "Computer Programming in Elementary and Middle School: Connections across Content." In *Improving K–12 STEM Education Outcomes through Technological Integration*, edited by Michael J. Urban and David A. Falvo, 337–361. Hershey, PA: IGI Global.

Hattie, John. 2009. *Visible Learning: A Synthesis of over 800 Meta-analyses Relating to Achievement*. New York: Routledge.

Hattie, John. 2017. *Visible Learning plus 250+ Influences on Student Achievement*. Visible Learning. https://visible-learning.org/wp-content/uploads/2018/03/VLPLUS-252-Influences -Hattie-ranking-DEC-2017.pdf.

Henderson, Peter B., Thomas J. Cortina, Orit Hazzan, and Jeannette M. Wing. 2007. "Computational Thinking." In *Proceedings of the 38th ACM SIGCSE Technical Symposium on Computer Science Education*, 195–196. New York: Association for Computing Machinery Press.

Herodotus. 1987. *The History*. Translated by David Grene. Chicago: University of Chicago Press.

Hilgard, Ernest R., Robert P. Irvine, and James E. Whipple. 1953. "Rote Memorization, Understanding, and Transfer: An Extension of Katona's Card-Trick Experiments." *Journal of Experimental Psychology* 46 (4): 288–292.

Hill, Catherine, Christianne Corbett, and Andresse St. Rose. 2010. *Why So Few? Women in Science, Technology, Engineering, and Mathematics*. Washington, DC: American Association of University Women.

Hogan, Maureen P. 2008. "The Tale of Two Noras: How a Yup'ik Middle Schooler Was Differently Constructed as a Math Learner." *Diaspora, Indigenous, and Minority Education* 2 (2): 1–25.

ISTE (International Society for Technology in Education). 2016. *Standards for Students.* https://www.iste.org/standards/for-students.

Jacobs, Heidi Hayes. 2010. *Curriculum 21: Essential Education for a Changing World.* Alexandria, VA: ASCD.

Jacobs, Heidi Hayes, and Marie Hubley Alcock. 2017. *Bold Moves for Schools: How We Create Remarkable Learning Environments.* Alexandria, VA: ASCD.

Jacobs, Victoria R., and Rebecca C. Ambrose. 2008. "Making the Most of Story Problems." *Teaching Children Mathematics* 15 (5): 260–266.

Jansen, Amanda, and James Middleton. 2011. *Motivation Matters and Interest Counts: Fostering Engagement in Mathematics.* Reston, VA: National Council of Teachers of Mathematics.

Johnson, David W., and Roger T. Johnson. 1992. "Positive Interdependence: Key to Effective Cooperation." In *Interaction in Cooperative Groups: The Theoretical Anatomy of Group Learning*, edited by R. Hertz-Lazarowitz and N. Miller, 174–202. New York: Cambridge University Press.

Johnson, David W., and Roger T. Johnson. 2010. "Cooperative Learning and Conflict Resolution: Essential 21st Century Skills." In *21st Century Skills: Rethinking How Students Learn*, edited by James Bellanca and Ron Brandt, 201–220. Bloomington, IN: Solution Tree Press.

Kafai, Yasmin B., and Quinn Burke. 2014. *Connected Code: Why Children Need to Learn Programming.* Cambridge, MA: MIT Press.

Katona, George. 1940. *Organizing and Memorizing.* New York: Columbia University Press.

Kay, Ken. 2010. "21st Century Skills: Why They Matter, What They Are, and How We Get There." In *21st Century Skills: Rethinking How Students Learn*, edited by James Bellanca and Ron Brandt, xiii–xxxi. Bloomington, IN: Solution Tree Press.

Kern, Hermann. 2000. *Through the Labyrinth: Designs and Meanings over 5000 Years.* Munich: Prestal.

Klawe, Maria, Telle Whitney, and Caroline Simard. 2009. "Women in Computing—Take 2." *Communications of the ACM* 52 (2): 68–76.

Labaree, David F. 1997. "Public Goods, Private Goods: The American Struggle over Educational Goals." *American Educational Research Journal* 34 (1): 39–81.

Lee, Irene, Fred Martin, Jill Denner, Bob Coulter, Walter Allan, Jeri Erickson, Joyce Malyn-Smith, and Linda Werner. 2011. "Computational Thinking for Youth in Practice." *ACM Inroads* 2 (1): 32–37.

Lemke, Cheryl. 2010. "Innovation through Technology." In *21st Century Skills: Rethinking How Students Learn*, edited by James Bellanca and Ron Brandt, 243–274. Bloomington, IN: Solution Tree Press.

Levitin, Anany, and Maria Levitin. 2011. *Algorithmic Puzzles.* Oxford: Oxford University Press.

Lingard, Robert W. 2010. "Teaching and Assessing Teamwork Skills in Engineering and Computer Science." *Journal of Systemics, Cybernetics and Informatics* 18 (1): 34–37.

Logan, Keri, and Barbara Crump. 2007. "The Value of Mentoring in Facilitating the Retention and Upward Mobility of Women in ICT." *Australasian Journal of Information Systems* 15 (1): 41–57.

Lotan, Rachel. 2006. "Teaching Teachers to Build Equitable Classrooms." *Theory into Practice* 45 (1): 32–39.

Loucks-Horsley, Susan, Katherine E. Stiles, Susan Mundry, Nancy Love, and Peter W. Hewson. 2009. *Designing Professional Development for Teachers of Science and Mathematics.* 3rd ed. Thousand Oaks, CA: Corwin Press.

Lu, James J., and George H. L. Fletcher. 2009. "Thinking about Computational Thinking." *ACM SIGCSE Bulletin* 41 (1): 260–264.

Lucas, Édouard. 1891. *Récréations Mathématiques.* Vol. 1. 2nd ed. Paris: Gauthier Villars.

Manchester, Bette, Mike Muir, and Jim Moulton. 2004. "'Maine Learns': The Four Keys to Success of the First Statewide Learning with Laptop Initiative." *THE (Technological Horizons in Education) Journal* 31 (12): 14–16.

Margolis, J., R. Estrella, J. Goode, J. J. Holme, and K. Nao. 2008. *Stuck in the Shallow End: Education, Race and Computing.* Cambridge, MA: MIT Press.

Margolis, Jane, and Allan Fisher. 2002. *Unlocking the Clubhouse: Women in Computing.* Cambridge, MA: MIT Press.

Matthews, William Henry. 1922. *Mazes and Labyrinths: A General Account of Their History and Developments.* New York: Longmans, Green and Co.

Mayer, Richard E. 2004. "Should There Be a Three-Strikes Rule against Pure Discovery Learning?" *American Psychologist* 59 (1): 14–19.

Moore, Edward F. 1959. "The Shortest Path through a Maze." In *Proceedings of the International Symposium on the Theory of Switching, Part II,* 285–292. Cambridge, MA: Harvard University Press.

Moretti, Franco. 2011. "Network Theory, Plot Analysis." *New Left Review* 68:80–102.

Muir, Mike. 2006. *Technology to Improve Learning: Strategies for Middle Level Leaders.* Westerville, OH: National Middle School Association.

Nager, Adams, and Robert D. Atkinson. 2016. "The Case for Improving U.S. Computer Science Education." http://dx.doi.org/10.2139/ssrn.3066335.

Nardelli, Enrico. 2019. "Do We Really Need Computational Thinking?" *Communications of the ACM* 62 (2): 32–35.

Nardi, Peter M. 2006. *Doing Survey Research: A Guide to Quantitative Methods.* 2nd ed. Boston: Pearson Education.

National Center for Education Statistics. 2016. *Bachelor's Degrees Conferred to Females by Postsecondary Institutions, by Race/Ethnicity and Field of Study: 2013–14 and 2014–15.* https://nces.ed.gov/programs/digest/d16/tables/dt16_322.50.asp?current=yes.

NCSS (National Council for the Social Studies). 2017. *College, Career, and Civic Life (C3) Framework for Social Studies State Standards: Guidance for Enhancing the Rigor of K–12 Civics, Economics, Geography, and History.* Silver Spring, MD: National Council for the Social Studies.

NCTM (National Council of Teachers of Mathematics). 2001. *Principles and Standards for School Mathematics.* Reston, VA: National Council of Teachers of Mathematics.

NCTM (National Council of Teachers of Mathematics). 2014. *Principles to Actions: Ensuring Mathematical Success for All.* Reston, VA: National Council of Teachers of Mathematics.

NGSS Lead States. 2013. *Next Generation Science Standards: For States, by States.* Washington, DC: National Academies Press.

NRC (National Research Council). 2012. *A Framework for K–12 Science Education: Practices, Crosscutting Concepts, and Core Ideas.* Washington, DC: National Academies Press. https://doi.org/10.17226/13165.

Ovid. 1916. *Metamorphoses*, Vol. 1: Books 1–8. Translated by Frank Justus Miller. Cambridge, MA: Harvard University Press.

Papert, Seymour. 1980. *Mindstorms: Children, Computers, and Powerful Ideas.* New York: Basic Books.

Peterson, Roger Tory. 2008. *Peterson Field Guide to Birds of North America.* New York: Houghton Mifflin Harcourt.

Piaget, Jean. 1954. *The Construction of Reality in the Child.* New York: Routledge.

Piaget, Jean. 1973. *To Understand Is to Invent: The Future of Education.* New York: Grossman.

Piaget, Jean. 1977. "Problems of Equilibration." In *Topics in Cognitive Development*, edited by M. H. Appel and L. S. Goldberg, 3–13. Boston: Springer.

Pierre-Louis, Kendra. 2019. "Why Is the Cold Weather So Extreme If the Earth Is Warming?" *New York Times.* January 31, 2019. https://www.nytimes.com/interactive/2019/climate/winter-cold-weather.html.

Piggott, Jennifer. 2011. "Rich Tasks and Contexts." NRICH. http://nrich.maths.org/5662.

Plutarch. 1914. *Lives,* Vol. 1, *Theseus and Romulus. Lycurgus and Numa. Solon and Publicola.* Translated by Bernadotte Perrin. Cambridge, MA: Harvard University Press.

Puentedura, Ruben R. 2009. *As We May Teach: Educational Technology, from Theory into Practice.* http://www.hippasus.com/rrpweblog/archives/000025.html.

Puentedura, Ruben R. 2014. *Building Transformation: An Introduction to the SAMR Model.* http://www.hippasus.com/rrpweblog/archives/2014/08/22/BuildingTransformation_AnIntroductionToSAMR.pdf.

Repenning, Alexander, David Webb, and Andri Ioannidou. 2010. "Scalable Game Design and the Development of a Checklist for Getting Computational Thinking into Public Schools." In *Proceedings of the 41st ACM Technical Symposium on Computer Science Education*, 265–269. New York: ACM.

Resnick, Mitchel. 2016. "Designing for Wide Walls." https://medium.com/@mres/designing-for-wide-walls-323bdb4e7277.

Responsive Classroom. 2013. "Spider Web." *Keeping Morning Meeting Greetings Fresh and Fun.* https://www.responsiveclassroom.org/keeping-morning-meeting-greetings-fresh-and-fun/.

Rideout, Victoria J., Ulla G. Foehr, and Donald F. Roberts. 2010. *Generation M 2: Media in the Lives of 8- to 18-Year-Olds.* Menlo Park, CA: Henry J. Kaiser Family Foundation.

Riegle-Crumb, Catherine, Barbara King, Eric Grodsky, and Chandra Muller. 2012. "The More Things Change, the More They Stay the Same? Prior Achievement Fails to Explain Gender Inequality in Entry into STEM College Majors over Time." *American Educational Research Journal* 49 (6): 1048–1073.

Rowling, J. K. 1998. *Harry Potter and the Sorcerer's Stone.* New York: Arthur A. Levine Books.

Saavedra, Anna Rosefsky, and V. Darleen Opfer. 2012. "Learning 21st-Century Skills Requires 21st-Century Teaching." *Phi Delta Kappan* 94 (2): 8–13.

Sax, Linda J., Kathleen J. Lehman, Jerry A. Jacobs, M. Allison Kanny, Gloria Lim, Laura Monje-Paulson, and Hilary B. Zimmerman. 2017. "Anatomy of an Enduring Gender Gap: The Evolution of Women's Participation in Computer Science." *Journal of Higher Education* 88 (2): 258–293.

Schuster, Carl, and Edmund Carpenter. 1996. *Patterns That Connect*. New York: Abrams.

Sherin, Miriam G., Edith Prentice Mendez, and David A. Louis. 2000. "Talking about Math Talk." In *Learning Mathematics for a New Century: NCTM 2000 Yearbook*, edited by M. J. Burke and F. R. Curcio, 188–196. Reston, VA: National Council of Teachers of Mathematics.

Shulman, Lee S. 1986. "Those Who Understand: Knowledge Growth in Teaching." *Educational Researcher* 15 (2): 4–14. https://doi.org/10.3102/0013189X015002004.

Simon, Herbert A., and Allen Newell. 1971. "Human Problem Solving: The State of the Theory in 1970." *American Psychologist* 26 (2): 145–159.

Simpson, Elizabeth, and Frances A. Clem. 2008. "Video Games in the Middle School Classroom." *Middle School Journal* 39 (4): 4–11.

Snapp, Robert R., and Maureen D. Neumann. 2015. "An Amazing Algorithm." *Mathematics Teaching in the Middle School* 20 (9): 540–547.

Solomon, Gwen, and Lynne Shrum. 2007. *Web 2.0: New Tools, New Schools*. Washington, DC: ISTE.

Sousa, David A. 2016. *How the Brain Learns*. 5th ed. Thousand Oaks, CA: Corwin Press.

Tarry, Gaston. 1895. "Le problème des Labyrinthes." *Nouvelles Annales de Mathématiques* 3 (14): 187–190.

Tomlinson, Carol Ann. 2017. *How to Differentiate Instruction in Academically Diverse Classrooms*. 3rd ed. Alexandria, VA: ASCD.

Turchi, Tommaso, and Alessio Malizia. 2016. "A Human-Centred Tangible Approach to Learning Computational Thinking." *EAI Endorsed Transactions on Ambient Systems* 3 (9): e6. https://doi.org/10.4108/eai.23-8-2016.151641.

Tyack, David B., and Larry Cuban. 1995. *Tinkering toward Utopia*. Cambridge, MA: Harvard University Press.

Tyson, Neil deGrasse. 2012. Twitter post. May 19, 2012, 3:08 pm. https://twitter.com /neiltyson.

Vee, Annette. 2013. "Understanding Computer Programming as a Literacy." *Literacy in Composition Studies* 1 (2): 42–64.

Virgil. 2006. *The Aeneid*. Translated by Robert Fagles. New York: Viking.

von Glasersfeld, Ernst. 1990. "An Exposition of Constructivism: Why Some Like It Radical." In *Constructivist Views on the Teaching and Learning of Mathematics*, edited by R. B. Davis, C. A. Maher, and N. Noddings, 19–29. Reston, VA: National Council of Teachers of Mathematics.

Voogt, Jake, Petra Fisser, Jon Good, Punya Mishra, and Aman Yadav. 2015. "Computational Thinking in Compulsory Education: Towards an Agenda for Research and Practice." *Education and Information Technologies* 20 (4): 715–728.

Vygotsky, Lev S. 1997 [1978]. "Mind in Society: The Development of Higher Psychological Processes." In *Readings on the Development of Children*, 2nd ed., edited by Mary Gauvain and Michael Cole, 29–36. New York: W. H. Freeman.

Walser, Nancy. 2008. "Teaching 21st Century Skills." *Harvard Education Letter* 24 (5): 1–3.

Warshauer, Hiroko Kawaguchi. 2015. "Productive Struggle in Middle School Mathematics Classrooms." *Journal of Mathematics Teacher Education* 18 (4): 375–400.

Weintrop, David, Elham Beheshti, Michael Horn, Kai Orton, Kemi Jona, Laura Trouille, and Uri Wilensky. 2016. "Defining Computational Thinking for Mathematics and Science Classrooms." *Journal of Science Education and Technology* 25 (1): 127–147.

Wells, David. 1992. *The Penguin Book of Curious and Interesting Puzzles*. London: Penguin Books.

Whitney, Telle, and Valerie Taylor. 2018. "Increasing Women and Underrepresented Minorities in Computing: The Landscape and What You Can Do." *Computer* 51 (10): 24–31.

Wiggins, Grant, and Jay McTighe. 2005. *Understanding by Design*. Expanded 2nd ed. Alexandria, VA: ASCD.

Wilson, Cameron, Leigh Ann Sudol, Chris Stephenson, and Mark Stehlik. 2010. *Running on Empty: The Failure to Teach K–12 Computer Science in the Digital Age*. ACM. http://www.csta.acm.org/Runningonempty/.

Wing, Jeannette M. 2006. "Computational Thinking." *Communications of the ACM* 49 (3): 33–35.

Wing, Jeannette M. 2008. "Computational Thinking and Thinking about Computing." *Philosophical Transactions of the Royal Society A: Mathematical, Physical and Engineering Sciences* 366 (1881): 3717–3725.

Wing, Jeannette M. 2016. "Progress in Computational Thinking, and Expanding the HPC Community." *Communications of the ACM* 59 (7). https://doi.org/10.1145/2933410.

Wolf, Nancy B. 2015. *Modeling with Mathematics: Authentic Problem Solving in the Middle School*. Portsmouth, NH: Heinemann.

Wright, Craig. 2001. *The Maze and the Warrior*. Cambridge, MA: Harvard University Press.

Yadav, Aman, Hai Hong, and Chris Stephenson. 2016. "Computational Thinking for All: Pedagogical Approaches to Embedding 21st Century Problem Solving in K–12 Classrooms." *TechTrends* 60 (6): 565–568.

Young, Hugh D., and Roger A. Freedman. 2000. *Sears and Zemansky's University Physics*. Vol. 1. 10th ed. San Francisco, CA: Addison-Wesley.

YPAR (Youth-Led Participatory Action Research). 2015. *YPAR-Hub: Young People Empowered to Change the World*. http://yparhub.berkeley.edu.

Index

Note: Page numbers in italics indicate figures.